A Guidebook for Teaching
COMPOSITION

808.042
St24g

A Guidebook for Teaching
COMPOSITION

Second Edition

GENE STANFORD

MARIE SMITH

Allyn and Bacon, Inc.   Boston • London • Sydney • Toronto

This book is part of A GUIDEBOOK FOR TEACHING Series

Copyright 1982, 1977 by Allyn and Bacon, Inc., 470 Atlantic Avenue, Boston, Massachusetts 02210.

All rights reserved. No part of the material protected by this copyright notice, except the Reproduction Pages contained within, may be reproduced or utilized in any form or by any means, electronic or mechanical, including photocopying, recording, or by any information storage and retrieval system, without written permission from the copyright owner.

The Reproduction Pages may be reproduced for use with this text, provided such reproductions bear copyright notice, but may not be reproduced in any other form for any other purpose without permission from the copyright owner.

Acknowledgments: Material on pp. 13, 14, 205-207, and 247 is reprinted from Gene Stanford, *Steps to Better Writing,* © 1972 by Holt, Rinehart and Winston, Publishers.

Library of Congress Cataloging in Publication Data

Stanford, Gene.
  A guidebook for teaching composition

  (A Guidebook for teaching series)
  Bibliography: p.
  1. English language—Study and teaching (Secondary)
2. English language—Composition and exercises.
I. Smith, Marie N. II. Title. III. Series: Guidebook for teaching series.
LB1631.S683 1982   808'.042'0712   81-7908
ISBN 0-205-07370-0 (pbk.)   AACR2

Managing Editor: Robert Roen
Printed in the United States of America

Printing number and year (last digits):
10 9 8 7 6 5 4 3 2 1   86 85 84 83 82 81

About the Authors

GENE STANFORD earned a bachelor's degree at Washington University and master's and doctor's degrees at the University of Colorado. He taught English at Horton Watkins High School in Ladue, Missouri, and served as Director of Teacher Education Programs at Utica College of Syracuse University. He is active in the National Council of Teachers of English and conducts workshops for teachers throughout the country. Dr. Stanford is author or coauthor of *A Guidebook for Teaching Creative Writing*, *Steps to Better Writing*, and *Better Writing: From Paragraph to Essay*. He is Consulting Editor for Allyn and Bacon's *Guidebook for Teaching* series and presently holds the position of Director of the Child Life Department, Children's Hospital, Buffalo, New York.

MARIE SMITH earned a bachelor's degree at Grinnell College and a master's degree at Washington University. She teaches creative writing and composition courses at Horton Watkins High School in Ladue, Missouri, and has taught writing courses at Washington University. She is coauthor of *A Guidebook for Teaching Creative Writing* and *Better Writing: From Paragraph to Essay*.

Contents

Preface ix

Chapter 1 DESIGNING THE COMPOSITION PROGRAM 1
Approaches to Teaching Writing 2
Organizing for Instruction in Composition 5
Marking Students' Compositions 7
Resources for Designing a Composition Program 20
Resources for Marking and Evaluating Compositions 22

Chapter 2 TEACHING STUDENTS THE SKILLS NEEDED FOR PREWRITING 25
Objectives 26
Learning Experiences 26
   Topic I: Understanding Prewriting 26
   Topic II: Loosening Up 27
   Topic III: Finding Ideas to Write About 29
   Topic IV: Developing Strategies for Prewriting 30
Assessing Achievement of Objectives 31
Resources for Teaching the Skills of Prewriting 32

Chapter 3 TEACHING STUDENTS TO WRITE PARAGRAPHS 33
Objectives 34
Learning Experiences 34
   Topic I: Topic Sentences 34
   Topic II: Developing a Topic Sentence into a Complete, Unified Paragraph 36
   Topic III: Putting Developmental Details in the Best Order 40
   Topic IV: Making the Paragraph Flow Smoothly 42
Assessing Achievement of Objectives 47

Resources for Teaching Paragraph Writing 47
    Audio-Visual Materials 47
    Print Materials 48

Chapter 4   **TEACHING STUDENTS TO WRITE EXPOSITORY ESSAYS 51**
Objectives 51
Learning Experiences 52
    Topic I: Choosing a Subject 52
    Topic II: Restricting the Subject 53
    Topic III: Turning a Subject into a Thesis 54
    Topic IV: Organizing the Paper 60
    Topic V: Providing Transitions 64
    Topic VI: Constructing Introductions and Conclusions 65
    Topic VII: Writing the Complete Essay 67
Assessing Achievement of Objectives 68
Resources for Teaching the Expository Essay 69
    Audio-Visual Materials 69
    Print Materials 69

Chapter 5   **TEACHING THE RESEARCH PAPER 73**
Objectives 73
Learning Experiences 74
    Topic I: Locating Information in the Library 74
    Topic II: Preparing for Research 80
    Topic III: Gathering Information 82
    Topic IV: Organizing and Writing the Paper 86
Assessing Achievement of Objectives 87
Resources for Teaching the Research Paper 88
    Audio-Visual Materials 88
    Print Materials 88

Chapter 6   **TEACHING STUDENTS TO REVISE 91**
Objectives 91
Learning Experiences 92
    Topic I: Using a Guide to Revision 92
    Topic II: Correcting Errors in Mechanics 94
    Topic III: Language That Gets in the Way 97
    Topic IV: Becoming Sensitive to Style 101
Assessing Achievement of Objectives 102
Resources for Teaching Proofreading and Revision 102
    Audio-Visual Materials 102
    Print Materials 103

Appendix A   Addresses of Producers of Resources 107
Appendix B   Sample Answers 111
Appendix C   Reproduction Pages 127
Appendix D   Feedback Form 281

Preface

This is not, we hope, just another book about teaching expository writing. From the planning of the first edition through the revisions for this second edition, we have tried to make this a book that will serve a unique purpose: providing the classroom teacher with so many specific ideas and resources for teaching students to write that he or she could never use them all. There are already too many books that outline in a general way the "best" way to teach composition, that urge the teacher to adopt one approach or another. But most of these, although they contain many excellent, thought-provoking ideas, do not go very far beyond describing a general theory of teaching writing and suggesting a few exercises to implement it.

In contrast, we have attempted to produce a comprehensive handbook with an emphasis on practicality. We began by resolving to cover all forms of writing that most classroom teachers teach, from expository paragraphs to more "creative" forms such as poetry and fiction. However, since so many different types of writing needed to be addressed and since some teachers give one kind more of their energy than another, we decided to limit this book to expository writing, including the wealth of practical material we believe teachers have been looking for.

This volume, then, deals with how to organize a composition program, how to mark student papers, how to teach expository paragraphs, essays, and research papers, and how to teach skills of revision. In its companion volume, *A Guidebook for Teaching Creative Writing*, we have provided students with experiences that stimulate them to write, teaching them to create images of people and events and to write about literature. Taken together, the two books cover the entire range of high school writing activities. For convenience, the teacher can choose whichever book deals with the kind of writing he or she stresses.

For each type of writing that it deals with, *A Guidebook for Teaching Composition* provides instructional objectives, notes for brief presentations by the teacher to explain new concepts to the class, classroom activities, discussion questions, small group activities, projects, individual assignments, annotated lists of useful resources, and even sample evaluation items. Perhaps the most valuable feature of the book is the section of Reproduction Pages, which can be used to make masters for spirit duplication or transparencies for the overhead projector—saving the teacher hours of preparation time.

Although the book often suggests a sequence of activities that might be useful in teaching a particular skill, the teacher can choose those materials and strategies that he or she wants to use, without being locked into prescribed lesson plans. In general, for each topic the book provides:

1. An introduction to the concepts that the section or chapter deals with.

2. A list of objectives that the methods and materials in the chapter help the student achieve, saving teachers the tedium of writing behavioral objectives for lesson plans.

3. Teaching strategies, including total class activities, explanations by the teacher, independent projects, small group tasks, and worksheets.

4. Sample evaluation devices for determining whether the student has achieved the objectives of the unit.

5. Annotated lists of resources, including both audio-visual and print materials.

This edition of the book contains new material and changes that were suggested by readers' feedback. A completely new chapter on prewriting has been included, and a new section on style has been added to the chapter on revision. Throughout the book, modifications of more difficult activities have been given for slower students, answers for exercises have been added, and content has been updated. A new format should make this edition of the book even easier to use.

Rather than promote a single approach to teaching writing, we have suggested activities and materials that teachers with a wide variety of teaching styles and philosophies will find useful. Thus, for example, although we describe numerous activities that put students to work in small groups, we have also included explanations of how the same activities can be used with students working on their own. The reader is encouraged to understand the rationale for each of the approaches and to choose those that are most consistent with his or her own goals and students' needs.

We do, however, have our own viewpoint, our own biases, based on our own philosophy of education developed from a number of years of teaching writing in many different settings. This viewpoint is evident throughout the book. We believe, for example, that students learn more when they are actively involved in the process than when they are sitting passively listening to the teacher. In addition, we believe that learning is enhanced when students are interacting with other persons and that students can learn from one another as well as from the teacher. We believe, also, that developing a skill such as writing is generally most successful when that skill is broken down into small steps or subskills and approached sequentially rather than randomly. Finally, because writing almost always involves self-disclosure, we are convinced it must take place in a climate that is free from threat.

Most activities and approaches included in this book were developed for, and used successfully, with our own classes. As a result of the feedback received on the first edition, we know that many of our readers also found them successful. We invite you to send us your comments about this new edition, using the Feedback Form that appears in Appendix D. It can be torn out and mailed with a minimum of inconvenience. We would sincerely appreciate your suggestions and promise a personal reply. Your comments will help us decide what kinds of changes to make in future editions of *A Guidebook for Teaching Composition*.

Although most of the material in this book is derived from our own experience, we acknowledge the contributions made by a number of other persons. Paul Janeczko, Jerome Megna, Roger C. Schustereit, and Robert Evans gave us permission to include teaching materials that they developed. Our students John Richardson and Joe Finkelstein contributed samples of their writing. The National Council of Teachers of English and Holt, Rinehart and Winston allowed us to use excerpts from material that they had published. Finally, our special thanks go to Deborah Perry, who helped prepare the resource lists.

Gene Stanford
Marie Smith

1

Designing the Composition Program

On the walls of caves, on buffalo hides, on tablets of clay and monuments of stone, our ancestors struggled with pictures, then symbols representing objects, and finally symbols representing sounds, to create a form of communication more permanent than the wind that carried their voices. The needs for writing were much the same two thousand years ago as they are today. Archaeologists have found the laws of Hammurabi, explanations of the universe in the mystical poetry of Lao Tzu, the laundry list of a man named Theophanes, and letters from a little schoolboy named Theon to his father. Civilized people everywhere kept records of daily activities, set down philosophical insights, and communicated with friends and family at a distance.

Writing is even more essential now, and anyone who cannot write is deprived of participation in many important activities of our culture. There is a wide range of kinds of writing in our society, and the methods of teaching writing must vary according to the purposes of the person who is learning to write.

The most basic need for writing is in everyday business transactions and personal communications. Grocery lists, job applications, notes to the repairman, records for taxes or business, and telephone messages all require, minimally, legible handwriting, decipherable spelling, and understandable syntax. In addition, for those concerned about a reputation as an educated person, these communications require the use of standard English. For most students, the basic writing skills gained in the first six years of schooling are sufficient for these simple writing tasks. However, for students who arrive in high school without the rudiments of spelling, punctuation and syntax, remedial tutoring may be necessary. And even advanced students may need help in preparing for the more complex writing tasks demanded in our computerized society. Some states, for example, are beginning to require that all students who graduate from high school possess certain minimal "survival skills." While some may argue that teaching students to fill out income tax forms is not an appropriate goal for the English teacher, if no one else in the school is teaching this survival skill, the English teacher may have to accept the responsibility.

Informal interpersonal communication is the second type of writing that most people in our society engage in—some very rarely and others for hours every day. Love letters, thank you notes, letters to parents, letters to friends, sympathy notes, and persuasive letters all require skills different from those used in practical communication. Use of standard English is not essential; but skills in style, description and characterization can be useful for such writing, as is a sense of the appropriate approach for the audience and the occasion. Many skills of good essay writing can transfer easily to letter writing, but they are not likely to do so unless the teacher points out the possibility. Special instruction in more effective interpersonal communication can probably be justified for all students.

In addition, many people use writing as a way of exploring ideas and of understanding themselves and others better. At one time or another in their lives, they may use their diary or journal entries, poetry, or even letters to friends to explore their own thoughts and philosophical ideas or their relationships to things, people, or events. Recognizing that putting a feeling on paper often makes it easier to cope with, some use writing to help handle such emotions as anger, fear, loss, and hurt.

A final use of writing is the sharing, exploration, and evaluation of ideas. In high school and college, students use writing to demonstrate their understanding of other people's ideas. Journalists, both student and professional, and other nonfiction writers disseminate thoughts and information.

A writing program should consider all these possible uses of writing as well as the needs of the individual students. Everyone in our culture needs to be able to use writing for the first and second purposes—for nuts-and-bolts business writing and friendly communication. However, only part of the population uses writing to express feelings or to share ideas. It is therefore probably not productive to expect every student to do extensive reflective writing or to develop finesse in the use of the essay.

However, as adult education and re-education become increasingly possible and popular, it is impossible to decide that a student is not "college prep" and therefore does not need to learn to write essays. It is probably appropriate, therefore, not only to require all students to demonstrate competence in utilitarian writing and letter writing, but to require, as well, at least minimal competence with the essay and reflective writing from most students, and to provide, for those students who choose to take them, courses aimed at developing a high level of proficiency in these latter modes.

APPROACHES TO TEACHING WRITING

There are a number of possible ways to teach writing. All have some use, but all also have limitations. The major approaches that most teachers find useful are (1) imitation, (2) following rules and patterns, (3) trial and error with criticism, (4) extensive writing, and (5) instruction in grammar.

Imitation is one of the most basic human methods of learning, and, deliberately or not, almost all writers have employed imitation to some extent in their learning to write. Early research in the teaching of composition indicated that exposure to good literature could have as powerful an effect on improvement in writing as actual writing practice could have. Certainly, a student who has never read a good essay is unlikely to write one. Thus, many teachers find it useful to expose composition students to many examples of good writing in hopes that they will adopt some of the techniques. Other teachers are more deliberate in their use of imitation. They give students a passage by a good writer and ask them to produce a piece of writing on a different topic in the same form and style as the model.

Imitation is usually fairly effective in teaching style and patterns of organization. Most people's minds work in such a way that they are better able to produce what the teacher wants if they have a model to show them what is expected. Of course, learning by imitation does limit one's creativity. The risk of suppressing creativity, however, is not a problem for most high school English teachers, who are rarely faced with students who can be termed "artists," and certainly it is simple enough to devise individualized assignments for students who find imitation confining.

For students who are so deficient in writing skills that even imitation is not possible, dictation can be an effective teaching method. This approach is rarely used in modern American schools but is described in detail in *How the French Boy Learns to Write* by Rollo Walter Brown. (See the resources list at the end of this chapter.) Students who are quite deficient in basic writing skills can practice spelling and punctuation and gain some sense of fluent composition by writing dictations.

A second method of teaching writing, *following rules and patterns*, is particularly effective when combined with the use of models as described above. In this approach, teachers precede writing assignments with direct instruction in how to write. For example, the teacher may explain that a paragraph is a general statement (topic sentence) followed by specific statements that explain or support the general statement. The teacher may give students several paragraphs, have them locate the general statement and the specific statements, and then ask them to write their own paragraph in this form. If the students do not understand the difference between a general statement and a specific statement, the teacher will have to give more explanations and examples, perhaps having them identify which is general and which is specific in a number of pairs of sentences. This approach assumes that there are certain principles and formulas that good writers generally follow and that students can benefit from learning them before starting to write.

However, if taken to extremes this approach can have harmful effects. Janet Emig, in her analysis of the writing processes of twelfth graders (see *The Composing Processes of Twelfth Graders* in the resource list at the end of this chapter), points out that most of the principles and formulas taught in English classes, such as the five-paragraph theme and the need for every paragraph to have a topic sentence, are not practiced by the best professional writers. The five-paragraph theme, she points out, exists nowhere in literature except in the American high school classroom. This rather artificial pattern of writing (an introduction, a thesis statement with three divisions, and a conclusion that recapitulates the thesis statement and its divisions) can be useful for producing a coherent piece of writing in a limited time, as when writing an essay test, but it is hardly conducive to creative thought and imaginative exploration of ideas. As Emig reminds us, it is not the way good writers compose, and to proclaim it as such to students is dishonest. Many of the formulas drilled into generation after generation of students cannot be found in articles in better magazines and books. One need only examine a few articles in *Harper's, Saturday Review*, the *New Yorker* or other high-quality magazines to discover these formulas and rules do not fare very well.

A third method of teaching writing, *trial and error with criticism*, involves having students write and then having the teacher critique the results. While this method is extremely frustrating and unnecessarily punitive for most students, highly creative and advanced students who feel cramped and constricted by models and formulas and who are highly motivated to write well may thrive on it. For students who object to formulas or models, the teacher may find an effective alternative to be an individual contract, with students free to write in any style they like and the teacher critiquing the work.

For average students, though, teachers should give some preliminary instruction before making the assignment and then inform the students after they have completed the assignment how well they put the principles into practice. Most students will feel less frustration about having their work criticized if they have been taught *how* to approach an assignment before they begin to write. Almost all students, though, can benefit from receiving feedback from the teacher in the form of criticism (used in its positive sense). Suggestions for marking and evaluating student writing are given in the second part of this chapter.

Still another approach to teaching writing is what might be termed *extensive writing* or *free writing.* Daniel Fader and Elton McNeil in their *Hooked on Books* and Ken Macrorie in *Writing to Be Read* and his other books advocate that teachers do less teaching of *how* to write and simply encourage students to write as much as possible. They see the teaching of principles and the criticizing of students' work as inhibiting students' impulses to express themselves. Their approach focuses instead on freeing students to write about the things that matter to them, in a manner that each student chooses, without the fear of a poor grade for not meeting the teacher's expectations. The emphasis is on *quantity* and *student choice:* students improve their skills by extensive practice, and since they write about things that really matter to them, the results are more likely to be good because they are real.

The approach often utilizes journals, in which students write regularly (sometimes at home each day, sometimes in class one day a week) and which are not graded—often not even read—by the teacher. For many teachers, the journal can produce very exciting results:

> In my experience student response to the journal has been almost universally positive, making it the closest thing yet to a sure-fire teaching device. The so-called nonwriters like to write in journals, while "writers" go berserk writing in them. Teachers enjoy reading journals. In short, all of the problems traditionally associated with writing seem to be almost magically solved when people try the journal.[1]

For others, the journal is less a panacea. For one thing, it does not take into account the two most basic ways humans learn: by precept and by example; it depends only on practice. To assume that regular, profuse writing in a journal will make one a better writer is a little like assuming that practicing the piano is sufficient to make one graduate from playing "Leap Frog Leap" to *Moonlight Sonata.* Most of us also need lessons to show us *how* to play better and a sympathetic teacher to point out our mistakes.

Nevertheless, when used in conjunction with other methods, the journal and other "free" writing activities can be valuable. They tend to counteract the restricting influence of teaching principles and patterns. Students are encouraged to deal with ideas and issues that have significance for them. If the journal is not graded, they are more likely to feel free to express themselves honestly. Having been liberated to explore ideas that really matter, students may find themselves thinking about things they want to communicate to others. These ideas can then be expanded in more structured writing assignments.

Instruction in grammar is the final approach to teaching that we will examine. Once considered absolutely essential in the preparation of a good writer, a technical knowledge of grammar is no longer viewed by most teachers as adding much to the student's ability to write. Knowing the names of the parts of speech or being able to diagram a sentence, for example, does virtually nothing to improve writing skill, as countless research studies have confirmed.[2] Even excessive concern for teaching mechanics, such as usage, punctuation and spelling—which some teachers often confuse with grammar—has little effect on students' compositions. An ability to proofread, spot errors and correct them, is useful in preparing a

---

1. Stephen N. Judy, *Explorations in the Teaching of Secondary English* (New York: Dodd Mead & Company, 1974), p. 87.
2. J. Stephen Sherwin, *Four Problems in the Teaching of English: A Critique of Research* (Scranton, Pa.: Intext, 1969).

composition for the audience—particularly for publication—but this skill is editing, not composing. And proficiency in the former is not necessary for proficiency in the latter.

If there is a possible exception to the principle that instruction in grammar does not improve writing ability, it is in the case of transformational/generative grammar. Two studies published by the National Council of Teachers of English[3] conclude that students' fluency improves and the complexity of their sentences increases when they are taught transformational grammar. However, a later NCTE publication[4] claims that such results can be achieved through practice exercises without formal instruction in grammar. Of course, "syntactic maturity" is only one aspect of good writing, and other skills most certainly have to be developed as well. Therefore, concerning the value of grammar instruction, we agree with most leaders in the profession that, as Theodore Hipple states, "perhaps most pernicious of all the reasons for the failures in the secondary school efforts to produce abler writers is the insistence of many teachers that inordinate amounts of time spent on the study of formal grammar will produce, as if by magic, students who write well."[5]

ORGANIZING FOR INSTRUCTION IN COMPOSITION

Having surveyed the five most frequently utilized approaches to the teaching of composition and assessed their strengths and weaknesses, what can we say about choosing the right approach and implementing it in the classroom?

First of all, it is essential to know your purpose in teaching writing to a particular class at a particular time. What is the class's present level of writing skill? What are the students' future writing needs likely to be? What does your school's or your state's curriculum guide require you to teach? What composition skills do you judge to be most important for these students to master? What do the students want to learn about writing? Are these students who talk and write freely about their own ideas and feelings but who could use help in organizing and developing their ideas? Or are they students who are so concerned about meeting standards of correctness that they are afraid to relax and say what they really mean? Are the majority of the class gifted students who may have talents for creative writing they want to develop? Or are they relatively nonverbal students who are unlikely to attend college and who want and need to master more practical forms of communication? Are almost all bound for college and thus sure to be faced with research papers and writing about literature? Are they seventh graders for whom a complete, well-developed paragraph is an appropriate goal, or are they high school seniors who have been writing multiparagraph essays for several years? These are not simple questions to answer, and no response will always apply to every student in the class. Nonetheless, before embarking on a composition program, it is important to think carefully about what students in the class *really* need to learn about writing. Only then can you begin planning how to teach them.

In a year-long English course, composition is only one of many skills that need attention. After deciding what composition skills students need to master, you should work out a sequential plan for teaching these skills, beginning with the more basic and moving toward the more advanced. In most of the following chapters—particularly Chapters 2 and 3—we have organized the suggested learning experiences in a rough sequence of this type.

---

3. Donald Bateman and Frank Zidonis, *The Effect of a Study of Transformational Grammar on the Writing of Ninth and Tenth Graders* (Urbana, Ill.: National Council of Teachers of English, 1966) and John C. Mellon, *Transformational Sentence-Combining* (Urbana, Ill.: National Council of Teachers of English, 1969).
4. Frank O'Hare, *Sentence Combining* (Urbana, Ill.: National Council of Teachers of English, 1973).
5. Theodore W. Hipple, *Teaching English in Secondary Schools* (New York: Macmillan Company, 1973), p. 149.

Once you have outlined the sequence of skills or skill-building activities you plan to follow, you face the decision of whether to teach all these skills in a single composition unit of, say, four to ten weeks' duration or to intersperse them with other activities such as reading, language study, and oral communication. The single unit on composition has its attractive features: (1) students can perceive the orderly progression of skill development, (2) assignments come soon enough after each other that students do not forget what they have learned from one before beginning the next, (3) you do not have to juggle many different kinds of materials and activities but can concentrate on the development of one set of skills, and (4) students are more likely to realize that improvements are taking place in their writing ability.

There are serious drawbacks to a single unit on composition, however. First, the work load for students (writing papers) and for you (responding to papers) is likely to be very heavy. Second, students—and you—are likely to tire of working on one set of skills for such a long time, and boredom and resistance are almost inevitable. On the other hand, spacing the composition work assures that you will not be flooded with hundreds of papers to respond to, and provides the variety that can help prevent boredom. Thus it would seem that interspersing the composition activites with other aspects of the course is the best approach.

You must also guard against several potential problems. If you have not carefully planned the sequence of activities before the term begins, you will probably lose sight of the skills you are building; instead of an orderly progression of ideas, you are likely to end up giving students a random, unrelated, disjointed set of experiences. You must also guard against letting too much time elapse between composition activities, and you may often need to review skills briefly before introducing new material.

With elective programs gaining popularity, the planning of a composition program has become a serious problem in many schools. Faced with the prospect of a student changing teachers every nine weeks (or more or less often) over three or four years, the teacher concerned about the serious business of developing skill in composition is tempted to throw in the towel, decide that composition is not important after all, and settle back and enjoy teaching "Sports in Literature" or "Literature of the Occult." Real creativity is required to plan an effective composition program that is consistent with the freedom of choice and flexibility so important to elective programs.

Many schools with elective programs require some sort of basic composition course of all students before freeing them to select other electives. The rationale is that in this one nine- to twenty-week course, the student will learn basic principles that will be reinforced in other courses by writing assignments related to the course content. In some cases the plan works well; in others, not so well.

Another approach is to design an individualized composition program that a student completes totally independent of the regular elective program. Students work in a writing lab one or two days a week on assignments tailored to their particular needs. The writing lab is supervised by teachers who are specialists in composition and do not teach in the regular elective program.

Still another approach is for the English faculty to agree on a sequence of skill-building assignments that cover the entire range of composition skills considered minimally essential. All students must complete the sequence over the span of two or three years, regardless of what electives they choose. The specific topic for each assignment is suggested by the teacher of the elective, but the type of writing assignment (paragraph developed with examples, persuasive essay of at least five paragraphs, etc.) depends on where the student stands in terms of the sequence. Thus, in "Sports in Literature," the teacher may make a writing assignment—say, a composition on the role of women in athletics—for which one student would submit a single paragraph and another student a research paper.

MARKING STUDENTS' COMPOSITIONS

In the preceding sections we have been concerned about the decisions the teacher must make *before* students write. But even after you settle on a writing program, make the assignment, and finally collect the papers, the problems have not ended. Now you are faced with the question of how to respond to what the students write.

This dilemma is examined somewhat humorously in an "educational drama" by Roger C. Schustereit which summarizes many of the current issues related to marking of compositions:

The Big C—A Melodrama[6]

Characters:

Cynthia, a student

Harold, a student

James Landry, English coordinator, must have horn rimmed glasses

Louise Hathaway, a new teacher, must have innocent look

Clifford Plater, Alice Stein, and Richard McGowen, all seasoned veteran teachers with looks to match

> SCENE I: *The hall just before lunch.* Mr. Landry *is on the way to* Louise Hathaway's *classroom when he overhears a conversation between two students,* Harold *and* Cynthia, *in front of their lockers.*

Cynthia: How's it going, Harold?

Harold: Hi, Cyn. I guess O.K.

Cynthia: Did you get your paper back from Mrs. Hathaway yet?

Harold: Yah. (Harold *hands the paper to* Cynthia)

Cynthia: (*after a quick glance, handing* Harold *his paper*) Wow, it looks like she bled all over it.

Harold: (*amused, as he walks toward the lunchroom*) Yah, ya' just got the scenic tour of the red C.

> (Mr. Landry, *stifling a grin, enters* Louise Hathaway's *room. Louise is seated at her desk laboriously considering a pile of compositions, red pencil in hand.*)

---

6. Roger C. Schustereit, "The Big C—A Melodrama" (unpublished manuscript). Used with permission of the author. The bibliography from Mr. Schustereit's article has been incorporated into the resource list at the end of this chapter.

Landry:	Hi, Louise. Ready for lunch?
Louise:	*(slightly startled)* No, Jim. I've got too much grading to do. I turned two sections back, but I still have three to go.
Landry:	Yah, I heard Harold talking about his paper in the hall.
Louise:	That Harold. He makes so many grammatical mistakes. I just don't know.
Landry:	*(amused, yet condescending)* Yes, he was commenting on the predominant color of his paper.
Louise:	*(defensively)* Well, I try to give them feedback. I know a teacher needs to comment on written work; I try to say what I feel's appropriate.[7]
Landry:	*(gently)* O.K., but filling a page with corrections in red may do more harm than good.[8]
Louise:	*(sarcastically)* Well, what am I supposed to do? Use green ink?
Landry:	No, you're supposed to quit grading and come on down to the office for lunch.

(The two leave together)

SCENE II: *The English Office during lunch.* Mr. Landry *and* Louise *enter. They find* Clifford Plater, Alice Stein *and* Richard McGowen *seated and, in various stages, eating lunch.*

Cliff:	*(with good humor)* Alas, the perpetrator of the composition unit arrives.
Landry:	Very funny, Cliff.
Cliff:	*(walking to coffee pot)* Ah yes, group, he has a supply of Murine for the eyes and liniment to keep the fingers nimble.
Alice:	*(very serious)* Come on. Grading isn't all that painful.
Cliff:	*(mock surprise)* Oh, really?
Louise:	Jim and I were just getting into that subject, but his hungry stomach cut off the discussion.
Alice:	*(emphatically)* No, really. Composition correction has changed from some kind of pursuit in red ink by a bleary-eyed monster.[9]
Cliff:	*(resuming his seat)* Wow, I didn't know we had a resident poet.
Alice:	Ah, come on. You can cramp your fingers and ruin your eyes all you want to, marking every comma splice and misspelling, but that kind of correction is no better than moderate evaluation by the teacher when it comes to really improving the quality of writing.[10]

---

7. E. B. Page, "Teacher Comments and Student Performance: A Seventy-four Classroom Experiment in School Motivation," *The Journal of Educational Psychology* 49, no. 4 (August 1958): 173-81.
8. Ray C. Maize, "A Theme a Day," *NEA Journal* 42, no. 6 (September 1953): 335-36.
9. Joseph Mersand, "What Has Happened to Written Composition?" *English Journal* 50, no. 4 (April 1961): 231-37.
10. Lois V. Arnold, "Writer's Cramp and Eyestrain—Are They Paying Off?" *English Journal* 53, no. 1 (January 1964): 10-15.

Louise:	Well, what do *you* propose?
Alice:	Let the kids do their own correcting.
Cliff:	Oh, sure. I've tried something like that, but I still wonder if it's not just a way for us to get out of the work.
Landry:	I read an article in *English Journal* about a study that showed that students' correcting their own papers wasn't really any better or worse than when the teachers did it.
Cliff:	*(interrupting)* See what I mean?
Landry:	But, the teacher method required eight times as many after school hours as the peer method did.[11]
Louise:	Is that for real?
Alice:	*(rising to throw a paper sack away)* Sure it is. I don't read or grade a single paper outside of class.
Cliff:	How do you manage that—give study periods?
Alice:	*(grinning)* We have a resident cynic too. *(pause)* The kids do most of the correcting. I divide them into groups, and they do most of the tedious work. Then, they select the best papers, and we take a look at them as a class.
Louise:	How do you do that?
Alice:	*(resuming seat)* I use the opaque projector or have my student aide ditto them.[12]
Louise:	Do the students do a good job?
Alice:	Other than being a bit too critical at times, after they get a general idea about evaluation they do a pretty darn good job.[13]
McGowen:	*(upon completion of that last sandwich)* But what about the student who never has a paper selected as best?
Alice:	Well, it usually works out. But I like to think that while a student thinks about and criticizes somebody else's paper, his paper and its weaknesses are on his mind.[14]
McGowen:	I had this prof in Oregon who did something like that. We met as a class only once a week. We got our assignment and then wrote the paper. Then we met in groups of three or four and went over each other's papers. But what really helped was when the groups got together with the prof for fifteen minutes or so with all the comments of all the students summarized.

---

11. Robert V. Denby, "NCTE/ERIC Report-Composition Evaluation," *English Journal* 57, no. 8 (November 1968): 1215-21.
12. Maize, "A Theme a Day," pp. 335-36.
13. Loren V. Grisson, "Student Leadership in Evaluating Compositions," *English Journal* 48, no. 6 (September 1959): 338-39.
14. Ken Macrorie, *Uptaught* (New York: Hayden Book Co., Inc., 1970), p. 95.

Landry:	How did your professor get ready for the conference?
McGowen:	After the groups got together, we turned in the papers. He really looked more at the criticisms than the papers themselves. He claimed it really cut down on his grading time.[15]
Cliff:	What did he do with all that free time away from class and grading?
McGowen:	Played golf, he said.
Cliff:	Now that sounds like a good idea. *(pause)* You know, I like student involvement and all, but I still like to do the grading.
Louise:	I *do* know what you mean.
Cliff:	When I start a composition unit, I have the students determine norms for mechanics, and then I do the rest of the evaluation.
McGowen:	I don't follow you, Cliff.
Cliff:	Well, they decide on certain criteria for spelling, run-ons, and so on. If a paper meets the criteria, I grade it. If it doesn't, I put "not acceptable" at the top, and they try again.
Alice:	But you're still marking their errors.
Cliff:	No, I don't mark specific mistakes. I just put "N/A" at the top.
Louise:	Isn't that a bit rough?
Cliff:	Well, we have writing lab sessions in class to work on common problems where they work in groups, and I set up rotating student-teacher conferences to work on individual papers.[16]
Alice:	But you're still spending a lot of time cramping your fingers.
Cliff:	*(with mock sarcasm)* "Into each life a little rain must fall!"
Alice:	*(dully)* Ho. Ho. Ho.
Cliff:	What we need to is get Jim to hit up the school board for a computer to do the grading.
Landry:	Thanks a bunch, Cliff.
Alice:	Seriously, there is a computer they use for grading themes. It even puts out personalized feedback.[17]
Cliff:	Just go have a little rap with friendly ol' HAL.
McGowen:	God, I wonder how much that would cost?
Landry:	Too much.
Cliff:	Well, we could hire lay readers.

---

15. Charlton Laird, "Freshman English during the Flood," *College English* 18, no. 3 (December 1956): 131-38.
16. Sister Miriam Bernadette, "Evaluation of Writing: A Three-Part Program," *English Journal* 54, no. 1 (January, 1965): 23-27.
17. Arthur Daigon, "Computer Grading of English Composition," *English Journal* 55, no. 1 (January 1966): 46-52.

Landry:	I proposed that last year.
Louise:	Wait a minute. What are lay readers?
Cliff:	Housewives—qualified, of course—who grade papers on a part-time basis. They supposedly do a good job though.[18]
Louise:	Why did the board say no?
	(Laughter)
Landry:	Well, other than money, they said they were afraid part-timers would be too distant from students' individual needs and problems.[19]
Louise:	Well, why not hire a regular teacher to do nothing else?[20]
Landry:	Money again.
Cliff:	Yah, and who would want that job? You'd spend all your salary on Murine and liniment.
McGowen:	Well, I don't need the liniment, but sometimes I need throat lozenges to go along with the Murine.
Alice:	Throat lozenges?
McGowen:	Yah, I use a tape recorder for corrections.
Louise:	Are you kidding?
McGowen:	No, I can give clearer, fuller corrections with a tape than I can with a red pencil.[21]
Louise:	*(interested)* How do you do it?
McGowen:	Well, the kids number each line of their papers so I can refer to their specific weaknesses. It lets me talk personally with each student.
Louise:	Is it faster?
McGowen:	When I first started using tapes, I got carried away. But after a while you get the hang of it, and it gets better.[22]
	(Bell rings)
Cliff:	Well, an end to another episode of the English Faculty's sandwich and potato chip symposium.
	SCENE III: *The hall two weeks later, just before lunch. Mr. Landry rounds the corner and overhears another conversation between* Harold *and* Cynthia.
Cynthia:	Hey, Harold, I heard Mrs. Hathaway was doing something different on grading your themes.

---

18. Paul M. Ford, "Lay Readers in High School Composition Programs: Some Statistics," *English Journal* 50, no. 8 (November 1961): 522-28.
19. Paul H. Kreuger, "Some Questions on the Lay Reader Program," *English Journal* 50, no. 8 (November 1961): 529-33.
20. Marcia Mahnke, "Aide-to-Order for the Composition Teacher," *English Journal* 53, no. 1 (January 1964): 40-41.
21. Nachman Cohen, "Correcting Compositions without a Pencil," *English Journal* 39, no. 10 (December 1950): 579-580.
22. Lee Frank Lowe, "Theme Correcting via Tape Recorder," *English Journal* 52, no. 3 (March 1963): 212-14.

Harold: Yah, she's telling us where we messed up on those cassettes we had to buy.

Cynthia: Hey, that's the way McGowen does it. How do you like it?

Harold: *(amused)* It's O.K., I guess. Now I get to hear the red C in her own voice!

As Schustereit's melodrama illustrates, views on what constitutes good marking of papers vary considerably. But one point is clear: evaluating students' compositions for the purpose of grading is quite a different process from marking students' compositions to help them improve their writing. If a teacher is interested only in evaluation, there is no need to put any marks on the paper except for a letter or number at the top or bottom. Simply grading is a real temptation to the overworked teacher, but it does nothing to teach the student about writing—and most teachers realize they are hired to teach, not just grade.

Therefore, we must search for an effective way to respond to students' writing so that it helps them improve their skills. Specifically we need a method that does not require an inordinate amount of the teacher's time.

To be most helpful, the teacher's response to a composition should provide the student with feedback—that is, accurate information about his or her performance. Good feedback is focused, specific, and constructive. Instead of providing focused feedback, however, many teachers—such as Louise Hathaway in "The Big C"—flood students with more information than they can possibly assimilate by marking every conceivable error. These teachers confuse commenting on a composition with proofreading, although the two processes are quite different. Proofreading is correcting the mechanical errors in a piece of writing. This is a very useful skill, and is needed for almost any piece of writing that is going to be judged by its reader. A proofreader does a great service for his or her friends by correcting their errors in letters of application or school reports or even friendly letters. However, the proofreader rarely teaches the writer how to improve writing skill. Example I is a student's paper that has been proofread rather than responded to. The student receiving this paper back from the teacher is likely to be so overwhelmed with all the corrections that he or she will not even bother to read them all, let alone figure out what is the matter with each "error." Were this piece of writing headed for publication, such editing/proofreading would probably be welcomed, but we assume it is not being published. Therefore, the teacher is hardly justified in such heavy editing, which will probably only discourage the student.

Since good feedback is focused, the teacher should limit comments to one or two types of errors and should provide explanations and suggestions for correcting them. Understanding why two errors were made is about all we can expect the average student to learn from feedback on an assignment such as this. Thus, in Example II (see p. 14), we will see how the teacher focuses on the feedback on two of the students' major recurring errors, and explains them in enough detail that the student can understand why they are errors.

Also, it is even more likely that a student will remember a suggestion made by the teacher if he or she is required to practice the skill immediately. The "assignment sheet" following Example II (see p. 15) has been used by one of the authors to give students individualized practice related to the errors made in their own compositions. The error is marked on the composition with the number corresponding to the assignment on this sheet. The sheet is attached to the composition, and the teacher fills in the blanks indicating what practice exercises the student should complete. In some cases, as for error #2, the teacher gives the student specific instructions for practice exercises tailored to a particular problem not covered in the text. Thus, the student cannot simply look at the comments on a paper and disregard them, but must understand the nature of the problem and practice writing sentences that are error free.

EXAMPLE I RESPONDING BY PROOFREADING

CARS I WOULD NOT WANT TO OWN

~~There are~~ Over a quarter of a million automobiles ∧one sold in the United States each year. Many types are available; foreign cars and American cars, convertAbles and sedans, big cars and little cars. This variety is the result of the wide range of tastes of don't the driving population. There is three kinds of cars which ~~doesn't~~ ap suit my taste at all, and which I would never own. One type is impractical, another is little and ugly, and a third is poorly made.

An example of an impractical car is the Excalibur SS, perhaps you have never seen one of these cars. It bears a strong resemblance to the Dusenberg of years ago or to an old MG, early 1951 or 1952. One of the things I don't like about it are that it only comes in a convertAble model. That's fine in the summer or on a sunny day, but when it rains or when winter comes, it's rather impractical. Winter is perhaps the roughest though, mainly because the car is not even equipped with a heater. And the softtop has plastic side windows and a plastic rear window that leaks and yellows in the sun and becomes brittle with age. This car is fitted with a 327 But it cubic inch engine from the Corvette Stingray ~~the car~~ does not weigh more than 2000 pounds, compared to the Corvette, which weighs approximately 3200 pounds this year. With over 350 horsepower and so little weight, the Excalibur is very dangerous. You can't come near controlling it on acceleration around curves or on a panic stop. Combining these shortcomings with a $10,000 price tag, you have a very impractical car.

Another
A car that I wouldn't want is one of those ugly little foreign "bugs" you see everywhere. The Volkswagen is a good example. This simply isn't my idea of a car with good looks. In addition, it's too small for safety. If you were hit in the side by a large car or by a truck, you'd be finished. You also can't ride for great distances in comfort, because the engine is too noisy and the interior is cramped. Another shortcoming is that Volkswagen's are too common. I don't want a car that every mother's son has, and if you look around any large parking lot in this city, you are bound to see at least ten Volkswagen's. Besides being so common, this car is too underpowered for freeway driving. It's almost impossible to pass a car on the expressway at sixty miles per and hour, if there is a stiff crosswind blowing, you would think you were on a roller coaster. This is both unpleasant and unsafe.

The third type of car that I wouldn't like to own is one that is cheaply made. Ford Mustangs fall into this class. My family owned one once, and before we got rid of it the muffler fell off at least five times. By the time we sold it six months later, there were rattles in every corner. Meanwhile, the paint had started peeling off, to say nothing of the first layer of chrome on the bumpers. To top it off, whenever the driver made a hard left turn, the door on the passenger's side would fly open. [My uncle owns a Cougar, and it doesn't have these problems.]

Add Conclusion summarizing

EXAMPLE II FOCUSED FEEDBACK

Ann—you're having trouble with several grammar rules: 1) "to" is a preposition meaning toward; "too" meand [sic] excessively and is an adverb. You 4 placed in your third paragraph where you used the wrong one of these words. 2) a verb agrees with (matches) the subject, even when it does not follow it. Note CARS I WOULD NOT WANT TO OWN the sentences I have marked.

There are over a quarter of a million automobiles sold in the United States each year. Many types are available; foreign cars and American cars, convertables and sedans, big cars and little cars. This variety is the result of the wide range of tastes of the driving population. There is three kinds of cars which doesn't
                                    ~~are~~ (subject)   ~~don't~~
suit my taste at all, and which I would never own. One type is
            one
impractical, another is little and ugly, and a third is poorely made.

An example of an impractical car is the Excalibur SS, perhaps you have never seen one of these cars. It bears a strong resemblance to the Dusenberg of years ago or to an old MG, early 1951 or 1952. One of the things I don't like about it ~~are~~ that it only comes
        (subject)   is
in a convertable model. That's fine in the summer or on a sunny day, but when it rains or when winter comes. Mainly because the car is Winter is perhaps the roughest though. And the softtop has plastic side windows and a plastic rear window that leaks and yellows in the not even equipped with a heater. This car is fitted with a 327 sun and becomes briddle with age. This car is fitted with a 327 cubic inch engine from the Corvette Stingray. The car does not weigh more than 2000 pounds, compared to the Corvette, which weighs approximately 3200 pounds this year. With over 350 horsepower and so little weight, the Excalibur is very dangerous, you can't come near controlling it on accelleration around curves or on a panic stop. Combining these shortcommings with a $10,000 price tag, you have a very impractical car.

A car that I wouldn't want is one of those ugly little foreign "bugs" you see everywhere. The Volkswagen is a good example, this simply isn't my idea of a car with good looks. In addition, its to small for safety. If you were hit in the side by a large car or by a truck, you'd be finished. You also can't ride for great distances in comfort, because the engine is to noisy and the interior is cramped. Another shortcomming is that Volkswagen's are to common. I don't want a car that every mothers son has, and if you look around any large parking lot in this city, you are bound to see at least ten Volkswagen's. Besides being so common, this car is to underpowered for freeway driving. Its almost impossible to pass a car on the expressway at sixty miles per hour, if there is a stiff crosswind blowing, you would think you were on a roller coaster. This is both unpleasant and unsafe.

The third type of car that I wouldn't like to own is one that is cheaply made. Ford Mustangs fall into this class my family owned one once, and before we got rid of it the muffler fell off at least five times. By the time we sold it six months later, there
    went (subject)
~~was~~ rattles in every corner. Meanwhile, the paint had started peeling off, to say nothing of the first layer of chrome on the bumpers. To top it off, whenever the driver made a hard left turn, the door on the passenger's side would fly open. My uncle owns a Cougar, and it doesn't have these problems.

Group_____ Period _____

ERROR NO.   ASSIGNMENT

1. Study carefully the explanation on pages __128-132__ in your grammar textbook, paying particular attention to rule number __6g__ on page __128__. Determine how this applies to the error you made in your composition. On a separate sheet of paper work exercise __14__, page __130__ and turn it in with the revision of your composition.

2. Study carefully the explanation on pages __226__ in your grammar textbook, paying particular attention to rule number_____ on page_____. Determine how this applies to the error you made in your composition. On a separate sheet of paper work exercise_____, page_____ and turn it in with the revision of your composition.

Write ten sentences, each containing two complete thoughts, the second of which begins with he, she, or it.

3. *Example: My mother is a good cook; she makes good cake.*

    Study carefully the explanation on pages __454__ in your grammar textbook, paying particular attention to rule number __21K__ on page_____. Determine how this applies to the error you made in your composition. On a separate sheet of paper work exercise_____, page_____ and turn it in with the revision of your composition.

4. Study carefully the explanation on pages __146__ in your grammar textbook, paying particular attention to rule number __7C__ on page __146__. Determine how this applies to the error you made in your composition. On a separate sheet of paper work exercise __15__, page __148-149__ and turn it in with the revision of your composition.

5. Study carefully the explanation on pages_____ in your grammar textbook, paying particular attention to rule number_____ on page_____. Determine how this applies to the error you made in your composition. On a separate sheet of paper work exercise_____, page_____ and turn it in with the revision of your composition.

6. Study carefully the explanation on pages_____ in your grammar textbook, paying particular attention to rule number_____ on page_____. Determine how this applies to the error you made in your composition. On a separate sheet of paper work exercise_____, page_____ and turn it in with the revision of your composition.

7. Study carefully the explanation on pages_____ in your grammar textbook, paying particular attention to rule number_____ on page_____. Determine how this applies to the error you made in your composition. On a separate sheet of paper work exercise_____, page_____ and turn it in with the revision of your composition.

8. Study carefully the explanation on pages_____ in your grammar textbook, paying particular attention to rule number_____ on page_____. Determine how this applies to the error you made in your composition. On a separate sheet of paper work exercise_____, page_____ and turn it in with the revision of your composition.

Good feedback is also specific. In order to improve their writing, students must know exactly what the teacher likes or dislikes about the paper. Instead of writing "good organization" at the end of the paper, the teacher should note "good transition" and "effective topic sentence" at the points where they occur.

Feedback should also be constructive and should include both positive and negative elements. Students need to be told when they are doing well. In the atmosphere of our schools, most students do not trust their own judgment—or it never occurs to them to make any judgment of their own work. Thus, the teacher's response is extremely important. A student who has spent hours constructing a creative introduction to an essay but is given no recognition for it by the teacher may assume that the writing was no good or conclude that it was certainly not worth the trouble it took. Learning theorists tell us that rewarded behavior will persist. Because we want the good things students do in their writing to persist, we should praise the things that students are doing right as well as point out the things they are doing wrong. When we feel we must point out errors, comments should be phrased as suggestions for improvement, not punishment. Note in Example III (see p. 17) how the teacher praises or recognizes several aspects of what is in many ways a lackluster essay and points out problems as gently as possible. Note too how the teacher includes a personal reaction or two to let the student know that the content as well as the form is being responded to.

To summarize, compositions should not simply be graded. They should be marked to help students improve their writing skills. The teacher should focus on a reasonable number of errors rather than attempt to proofread and correct every single error. Instead of revising the paper for the student, the teacher should point out ways the paper could be improved and have the student make the changes. Furthermore, good features of the composition should be praised, even if they are not particularly outstanding, and the teacher should react in a personal way to ideas in the composition.

Of course, this kind of thorough commenting on students' papers is quite time-consuming, and most teachers do not have time to make such extensive comments on as many papers as students need to write. Therefore, the teacher may need to discover approaches to marking papers that save time yet give students the help they need. Several of these were mentioned briefly in the short play that introduced this section. One of those suggestions, having students correct each other's themes, merits examination in greater detail here.

If organized properly, having students mark each other's papers has benefits far beyond merely saving the teacher time. One approach, which also improves students' skill in working together, is to divide the class into small groups of three or four students and tell them that they are to help each other improve their papers. Explain that each student will be given not only the grade for his or her own paper but also the average grade for the papers in the group. With advanced students, little more in the way of instructions is required. For most students, though, it is helpful to focus their attention on only one or two specific aspects of writing. For example, after you have taught students how to write paragraphs with a clear topic sentence, let the group help each other review their paragraphs, making sure that each paper has a good topic sentence. Thus, students don't get bogged down or totally confused over what to look for in suggesting improvements. With slightly more capable students, you might require each small group to designate one member to check spelling, one to check punctuation, one to check organization, and one to check content, and so on.

Students particularly skillful in one aspect of writing could be designated as tutors and either assigned to help those students with problems or made available when needed. For

EXAMPLE III POSITIVE REINFORCEMENT

CARS I WOULD NOT WANT TO OWN

There are over a quarter of a million automobiles sold in the United States each year. Many types are available: foreign cars and American cars, convertables and sedans, big cars and little cars. This variety is the result of the wide range of tastes of the driving population. There is three kinds of cars which doesn't suit my taste at all, and which I would never own. One type is impractical, another is little and ugly, and a third is poorly made.

An example of an impractical car is the Excalibur SS, perhaps. It bears a strong resemblance you have never seen one of these cars. It bears a strong resemblance to the Dusenberg of years ago or to an old MG, early 1951 or 1952. One of the things I don't like about it are that it only comes in a convertable model. That's fine in the summer or on a sunny day, but when it rains or when winter comes, its rather impractical. Winter is perhaps the roughest though. Mainly because the car is not even equipped with a heater. And the softtop has plastic side windows and a plastic rear window that leaks and yellows in the sun and becomes briddle with age. This car is fitted with a 327 cubic inch engine from the Corvette Stingray. The car does not weigh more than 2000 pounds, compared to the Corvette, which weighs approximately 3200 pounds this year. With over 350 horsepower and so little weight, the Excalibur is very dangerous, you can't come near controlling it on acceleration around curves or on a panic stop. Combining these shortcomings with a $10,000 price tag, you have a very impractical car.

A car that I wouldn't want is one of these ugly little foreign "bugs" you see everywhere. The Volkswagen is a good example, this simply isn't my idea of a car with good looks. In addition, its to small for safety. If you were hit in the side by a large car or by a truck, you'd be finished. You also can't ride for great distances in comfort, because the engine is to noisy and the interior is cramped. Another shortcomming is that Volkswagen's are to common. I don't want a car that every mothers son has, and if you look around any large parking lot in this city, you are bound to see at least ten Volkswagen's. Besides being so common, this car is to underpowered for freeway driving. Its almost impossible to pass a car on the expressway at sixty miles per hour, if there is a stiff crosswind blowing, you would think you were on a roller coaster. This is both unpleasant and unsafe.

The third type of car that I wouldn't like to own is one that is cheaply made. Ford Mustangs fall into this class my family owned one once, and before we got rid of it the muffler fell off at least five times. By the time we sold it six months later, there was rattles in every corner. Meanwhile, the paint had started peeling off, to say nothing of the first layer of chrome on the bumpers. To top it off, whenever the driver made a hard left turn, the door on the passenger's side would fly open. My uncle owns a Cougar, and it doesn't have these problems.

example, Doreen may be an excellent speller, but she may write very dull papers. She could be appointed a tutor for spelling but could also be encouraged to seek help from someone who writes interesting papers. If students are used as tutors, the teacher should spend time discussing ways that they can be helpful. Classes could brainstorm ideas, and the teacher could list on the board behaviors that students find valuable in someone who is assisting them. They will probably list such things as clear explanations, friendliness, and encouraging persons to do things themselves. Then they could list behaviors that are not helpful, such as ridiculing others or implying that a person is hopeless and can never learn.

The possibilities and advantages of student tutors, if the approach is well organized and the students are instructed properly, cannot be overemphasized. The tutor as well as the tutee can learn a tremendous amount about the subject matter and also about human relations. Most students develop their own informal tutoring networks naturally. Unfortunately, some teachers see students helping students as cheating, because the teacher views his or her primary role as evaluating rather than teaching. It is important to encourage students' natural concern and willingness to help each other. To counteract any tendency of students to do the work for others rather than help them learn, you should discuss with students the ways that they can be most helpful to each other. For example, writing papers for others actually hurts students in the long run because they do not learn from it; however, it is helpful for students to sit down with friends and give them suggestions—reminding them of the rules they learned in class, giving them tips about ways to think up topic sentences or support for topic sentences. Point out that simply correcting a friend's errors is generally not the most helpful thing to do, but that explaining how to avoid those errors can be very helpful.

A carefully organized plan for involving students in the grading and marking of papers has been suggested by Jerome Megna.[23] In our view his S.E.G. program (Sensitivity, Exposure, Grading), gives too much emphasis to grading and not enough to making suggestions that will help writers improve their skills. Nevertheless, the structure he suggests can be utilized with whatever emphasis the teacher desires.

> In the first phase of the program, "Sensitivity," the teacher's role is to make the students sensitive to one another. They must be made willing to express their personal feelings and willing to accept the feelings of the others. Techniques for the achievement of this goal will vary, depending upon class size, existing conditions of class intimacy, and general level of maturity. I have found it helpful to have the class form a huge circle and to ask each student in rotation to tell the rest of the class about himself or herself. Although I encourage everyone to ask questions of the individual who is speaking, the person must always be made to feel comfortable declining to answer.
>
> At first, the teacher may have to be the "asker of questions," but as the others begin to feel more at ease, they will gradually assume the role. The teacher should tell about him or herself too when his or her turn comes up. It is important that no one feel embarrassed or threatened by what is said. This phase of the program may last as long as three or four complete sessions.
>
> The second phase, "Exposure," can usually be completed in four sessions, but this, too, may vary from class to class. This phase entails exposing the students to the process of how themes are corrected and evaluated. Here, the teacher has the opportunity of "thinking out loud" while correcting individual themes. The entire class is asked to write in pencil or type a paragraph or two on any subject of their choosing. After making transparencies of fifteen or twenty of the compositions, the teacher begins the evaluation process on an overhead projector, keeping in mind to preserve the anonymity of each writing. A magic marker is useful for corrections and marginalia. Students are asked to memorize correction symbols and are encouraged to comment on the evaluation process as they are watching it.

---

23. Jerome F. Megna, "The S.E.G. Method of Teaching Composition" (unpublished manuscript). Used with permission of the author.

The purpose of this phase is to establish criteria in grading. As the sessions progress and more students express themselves on the grading process, the class as a whole will begin to evolve its own philosophy of evaluation through establishing guidelines for the writing of themes. This phase is both dialectic and democratic. The students are told that they will eventually assume the responsibility of applying these criteria to one another's themes. When all the students understand and agree to the method of evaluation, the second phase of the program is completed.

"Grading" is the final and most complex phase of the program. Before initiating this phase, the students must be grouped in clusters of no more than six but no fewer than four. Students are usually willing to group themselves, but sometimes a teacher's intervention may be necessary. After the grouping has been done, it is useful to have each group spend an entire session with one another in order to come to know each other better. Although no special goals need to be set at the beginning of this session, if there is still strong reserve among members of the group, the teacher may wish to provide an agenda for each group in order that they might achieve greater rapport.

Toward the end of this session, each group elects a secretary who is responsible for facilitating the procedure for the grading sessions. After the election of secretaries, the teacher assigns to the entire class their first theme. It is suggested that the first theme be from three- to four-hundred words in length, typewritten (if possible), and stapled in the upper left-hand corner. The front page of each theme should be the title page, and this should contain only the following information: (1) the last four digits of the social security number of the student (or some other identifying number); (2) the title and date of the theme; and (3) the chronological number of the theme which the student is writing.

The grading session begins by having the secretaries of each group collect the themes in their respective groups. After they check to see that the themes are nameless and numbered, they give their batch to the secretary of a designated group. If there are four groups, the first theme grading session can be arranged as follows:

Group 1 will give their themes to Group 2

Group 2 will give their themes to Group 3

Group 3 will give their themes to Group 4

Group 4 will give their themes to Group 1

In order not to penalize any group by having their papers rigorously graded by the same group consecutively, the numerical pattern should be shifted during the following session.

Group 1 will give their themes to Group 3

Group 2 will give their themes to Group 4

Group 3 will give their themes to Group 2

Group 4 will give their themes to Group 1

During the third grading session, Group 1 will give their papers to Group 4, etc. The teacher should record the shifting patterns of exchange so that no group receives the same people's papers for two consecutive sessions.

Besides theme collection and distribution, the secretary of each group has three specific responsibilities: (1) to make sure each person in the group has the opportunity to read, comment upon, and grade each theme; (2) to inscribe in Roman numerals in the upper left-hand corner of each title page the "rank" the group has collectively assigned to it; and (3) to staple "q-sheets" to the top middle portion of the title page of each theme.

The Roman numeral "rank" is based upon the group's decision as to which theme is best, second best, and so forth. It may be decided by a secret vote or by the grades which the group has assigned to each theme. The criteria for the "best" are creativity, originality, interest, and anything else that the group collectively decides an outstanding theme should possess. Mechanical flawlessness is not necessarily a hallmark of the "best" theme. The "best" themes of each group should be reproduced and distributed to the entire class for discussion before the next theme grading session.

"Q-sheets" are quarter sheets of paper. Before beginning to grade the themes, each person in a group should have as many q-sheets as there are themes for the group to grade. Each q-sheet should contain the following information: (1) the last four digits of the social security number of the theme which was graded; (2) the personal comments which the the grader wishes to make; (3) a grade; and (4) the full signature of the grader. Graders may assign grades with a plus or a minus, but "split" grades should be discouraged. The grades may range from A to F, and some groups may decide that any theme which has more than a certain number of mechanical errors merits the grade of F despite its content.

Mechanical errors should be corrected on the theme itself, using the symbols memorized in phase two of the program. These mistakes are usually in spelling, diction, punctuation, grammar, organization and logic. If a grader is unsure of the mechanical correctness of a theme, he or she is encouraged to ask fellow members of the group or the teacher for assistance. More personal, subjective comments should be written on the q-sheets. These may include what he or she considered the level of interest of the theme, the continuity of ideas, the transitions between paragraphs, etc. After grading a theme and writing a q-sheet for it, the grader should pass the theme along to the next person in the group but hold on to the q-sheet. In this way graders are not prejudiced by the marks assigned to the theme by previous graders. By and large, students view the assigning of grades very seriously and come to realize the complexity of the evaluation process.

When all the students of one group have read and graded the themes assigned to them, they assist the secretary in stapling all the q-sheets to the top middle portion of each of the respective title pages. It is at this point that the secretary attempts to elicit from the group members which theme they consider best, second best, etc. The secretary then inscribes this "rank" in Roman numerals in the upper left-hand corner of the title page. When the "best" from each group is reproduced, distributed, and discussed, the teacher should prod the class into refining its criteria for future evaluation. The distribution of the "best" themes also provides an incentive for the individual student to write an especially good theme.

When themes are returned to the authors, they reread their papers with the corrections, comments, and grades, and self-evaluate their own papers at the end of the theme. The grades they received on the q-sheets may not always correlate. It may even happen that the writer of the theme feels that the comments are unfair or irrelevant. He or she is encouraged to discuss with the individual graders why they assigned the grades they did. Beneath the author's own reactions to the comments and evaluation of the respective merit of the corrections, the student then assigns him or herself a grade. Usually this grade corresponds to the mean or median grade assigned by the group who corrected the theme, but this is left up to the individual student. At the very end of the session, the teacher collects the themes. By reading the comments and grades of the group who evaluated each paper, their corrections and marginalia on the theme, and the reaction, defense (if any), and self-evaluation of the student who wrote the theme, the teacher can diagnose the difficulties of the writer in a fraction of the time it would otherwise have taken.

By the third session, the elaborate procedures of the S.E.G. method are carried out effortlessly by the students. Significant improvement in writing techniques and style will be apparent to anyone who reads themes from the first grading session and from the fourth or fifth session. Because of the high level of participation, students, given their choice, prefer the active, self-evaluation S.E.G. method to more traditional methods of learning composition.

RESOURCES FOR DESIGNING A COMPOSITION PROGRAM

The following is a selected list of print materials useful in planning a composition program. Addresses of publishers can be found in Appendix A.

The Composing Process of Twelfth Graders by Janet Emig. National Council of Teachers of English. Report of a research study in which twelfth graders gave autobiographies of their writing experience and composed orally in the presence of an investigator. Findings confirm that school-sponsored composing is "extensive" (reportorial, cognitive) and self-sponsored writing is more reflective (affective, spontaneous, investigative).

The author suggests new ways of teaching composition, based on her findings. She discusses prewriting, planning, oral composition, and behavioral patterns of students while engaged in the composition process.

Emphasis: Composition edited by Richard Knudson. New York State English Council. A special issue of *English Record*. Fourteen articles including "A Sequence of Writing Tasks for a Twenty-Week Composition Elective for Juniors and Seniors." Interesting and informative.

Explorations in the Teaching of Secondary English by Stephen N. Judy. Dodd, Mead and Company. A general language arts methods text. Includes discussions of numerous aspects of teaching composition.

Group Inquiry Techniques for Teaching Writing by Thom Hawkins. National Council of Teachers of English. A handbook on how to use small-group techniques for teaching composition. The author tells how to set up groups and discusses some typical problems teachers may encounter. A number of classroom-tested tasks that relate closely to teaching composition are described.

The Holt Guide to English: A Contemporary Handbook of Rhetoric, Language and Literature, 2d ed., by William F. Irmscher. Holt, Rinehart & Winston. A thorough reference book on rhetoric, language, literature, criticism, and composition. Includes explanations of contemporary knowledge in each of these areas.

How the French Boy Learns to Write by Rollo Walter Brown. National Council of Teachers of English. This classic report on teaching composition in French schools has been used as a model in U.S. schools. Includes complete course outlines concerning composition, grammar, literature, and classroom practices while providing a rationale for learning a foreign language in order to improve skills in one's native language.

"Reflections on Writing" edited by Stephen N. Judy. *English Journal* 64, no. 4 (April 1975):60-72. National Council of Teachers of English. A special issue of *English Journal* containing numerous articles on teaching writing, including "How to Get Kids to Write," "How to Completely Individualize a Writing Program," and "Evaluating Creative Writing." Contains helpful ideas, tips, and suggested teaching techniques.

Research in Written Composition by Richard Braddock, Richard Lloyd-Jones, and Lowell Schoer. National Council of Teachers of English. Summarizes existing information about composition. Provides a detailed review and summary of several excellent studies. Bibliography included.

Rhetoric and Composition: A Sourcebook for Teachers by Richard L. Groves. Hayden Book Co., Inc. A collection of published articles offering a wealth of practical ideas and information for teaching writing. Topics include: "Motivating Student Writing," "A Reluctant Medium: The Sentence," "The Paragraph and Beyond," "The Pedagogy of Composition" and "The Uses of Classical Rhetoric."

On Righting Writing edited by Ouida H. Clapp. National Council of Teachers of English. This 1975 report of the Committee on Classroom Practices in Teaching English contains a thorough collection of teaching ideas on several aspects of writing.

Strategies for Teaching the Composition Process by Carl Koch and James M. Brazil. National Council of Teachers of English. A resource book of practical student-centered group activities for teaching the composition process. The first section, "The Comfort Zone," includes ways of helping students overcome fears of writing. "Prewriting" helps generate topics and "The Writing State" gives suggestions for forming and structuring ideas. "The Postwriting Stage" focuses on editing and proofreading.

Teaching Composition in the Senior High School by Samuel J. Rogal. Littlefield, Adams and Co. Designed for intern and in-service teachers in order to help them structure the composition program. Discusses the program's purpose, organization, format, requirements, scope, flexibility, limitations, and restrictions. Also provides instruction in teaching formal aspects of composition—the teacher's responsibilities, legitimate writing assignments, and the importance of good student-teacher relations.

Teaching English in Secondary Schools by Theodore W. Hipple. Macmillan Inc. Deals with various aspects of teaching English, including "Classroom Approaches to Written Composition," "Selected Issues in the Teaching of Composition," and "Composition Evaluation." A good general resource for teachers.

Teaching English Today by Dwight L. Burton, Kenneth L. Donnelson, Bryant Fillon, and Beverly Haley. Houghton Mifflin Co. A general language arts methods text. Includes sections on teaching written composition, teacher accountability, evaluation of student performance, and evaluating as a monologue or a dialogue. Helps teachers to set standards, plan for effective instruction, and evaluate in a fair and consistent manner.

Teaching High School Composition edited by Gary Tate and Edward P. J. Corbett. Oxford University Press. A collection of writings on composition, including a special section on evaluation.

"Teaching/Writing" edited by Ben F. Nelms. *English Education* 6 no. 2 (December 1974/January 1975). National Council of Teachers of English. A special issue of *English Education*. Articles include "Freeing Teachers to Write," "Five Half-Truths about the Teaching of Composition," and "Teaching Writing" by English teachers with a special interest in composition.

Teaching Written English Today by W. K. Jones and A. J. Francis. J. Weston Walch, Publisher. Discusses learning to write, steps in finding ideas, and advanced writing and style. Contains a foreword to teachers and a section of criticism and evaluation with sample student papers and teacher comments.

They Really Taught Us How to Write edited by Patricia Geuder, Linda Harvey, Dennis Loyd, and Jack Wages. National Council of Teachers of English. A number of high school teachers who are recognized as outstanding writing instructors describe a variety of methods for teaching composition. Examines pre-writing activities, the writing process itself, evaluation practices, and various types of writing—journalistic, creative, analytical, and expository. Contains excellent ideas and suggestions.

Uptaught by Ken Macrorie. Hayden Book Co., Inc. Presents more emphasis on simply letting students write freely than on teacher giving feedback, but recommends peer evaluation of writing through discussion. The author considers computerized grading to be an imposition on students' creativity.

Writing Aids through the Grades: One Hundred Eighty-Six Developmental Writing Activities by Ruth Kearney Carlson. Teachers College Press. Presents numerous activities designed to promote and encourage composition. Offers outstanding suggestions for involving even the most reluctant writer in composition and communication.

Writing for the Fun of It by Robert C. Hawley and Isabel L. Hawley. Education Research Associates. Discusses the overall writing program—teaching writing, motivating, organizing, practicing and learning rules of mechanics, and coordinating literature with writing. Offers numerous suggestions for activities and instruction related to evaluation. Clear and direct.

RESOURCES FOR MARKING AND EVALUATING COMPOSITIONS

The following is a selected list of print materials on marking and grading papers. Addresses of publishers can be found in Appendix A.

"Aide-to-Order for the Composition Teacher" by Marcia Mahnke. *English Journal* 53, no. 1 (January 1964): 40-41. National Council of Teachers of English. Article on hiring full time staff members to grade compositions and assist in teaching writing.

"Assessing Compositions: A Discussion Pamphlet by a Subcommittee of the London Association for the Teaching of English." London Association for the Teaching of English. Presents thirty student compositions with in-depth teacher's comments and grades. Very helpful reference. Clear and easy-to-understand evaluative framework.

"An AV Aid to Teaching Writing" by Virginia Fitzpatrick. *English Journal* 57, no. 3 (March 1968): 372-74. National Council of Teachers of English. Describes techniques for tape recording teachers' comments on compositions.

"Can We Evaluate Compositions?" by T. A. Koclanes. *English Journal* 50, no. 4 (April 1961): 252ff. National Council of Teachers of English. Urges that when teachers correct themes, they look for writing improvement, not just give a grade.

"Computer Grading of English Composition" by Arthur Daigon. *English Journal* 55, no. 1 (January 1966): 46-52. National Council of Teachers of English. Discusses mechanization in the classroom via machine-graded compositions. The machine's grades correlate significantly with the grade assigned by teachers.

Emphasis: Use and Misuse of Standardized Testing edited by Richard L. Knudson. *English Record* 26, no. 2 (Spring 1975). New York State English Council. This special issue of *English Record* contains eleven articles dealing with evaluation and testing. "The Limitations of Standardized Tests as They Apply to Measuring Growth in English Curriculum Areas," "Grades and Growth in a Writing Program," and "A Proposal for a Test in English for Students in Grades 11 and 12" comprise some of the articles.

End-of-Year Examinations in English for College-Bound Students, Grades 9-12. National Council of Teachers of English. Presents sample essay examinations in language, literature, and composition that college-bound students should be able to pass at the end of each year of secondary school. Includes ten student responses for each question and an evaluation of each.

Evaluating Writing by Charles R. Cooper and Lee Odell. National Council of Teachers of English. A collection of essays on six approaches to describing, measuring, and judging writing skill. Approaches range from "Individualized goal setting, self-evaluation and peer evaluation" to "Computer-aided description of mature word choices in writing."

"Evaluating a Theme: Twenty-five High School and College Teachers Analyze and Grade a High School Theme" edited by A. K. Steven. *Newsletter of the Michigan Council of Teachers of English*, vol. 5, no. 6 (Spring 1958): 1-16. National Council of Teachers of English. The same student essay is evaluated, graded, and commented upon by twenty-five different English teachers. The diversity of opinion is interesting, the comments are enlightening and the grading is often surprising. A thought-provoking article.

"Evaluation of Writing: A Three-Part Program" by Sister Miriam Bernadette. *English Journal* 54, no. 1 (January 1865): 23-27. National Council of Teachers of English. Suggests criteria for mechanics be set by students; recommends lab writing and student-teacher conferences for feedback.

"Freshman English during the Flood" by Charlton Laird. *College English* 18, no. 3 (December 1956): 131-138. National Council of Teachers of English. Previews the Oregon Plan for composition feedback based on peer evaluation and student-teacher conferences.

A Guide for Evaluating Student Composition: A Collection of Readings edited by Sister M. Judine. National Council of Teachers of English. Seven separate articles examine the evaluator and cover standards, marking, and guiding and praising the student. Specific discussion of evaluating the theme, expository writing, and junior and senior high school papers. Includes articles on types of grading and essay and composition rating scales.

How to Handle the Paper Load edited by Gene Stanford and the Classroom Practices in Teaching English Committee. National Council of Teachers of English. Articles on classroom techniques for evaluating papers or the writing process. Articles focus on the topic of ungraded writing and include "Teacher Involvement—Not Evaluation," "Student Self-Editing," "Practice with Parts," "Focused Feedback," and "Alternative Audiences." Practical articles on various creative techniques.

"Lay Readers in High School Composition Program: Some Statistics" by Paul M. Ford. *English Journal* 50, no. 8 (November 1961): 522-28. National Council of Teachers of English. Presents positive statistics on a lay reader program that is based on the theory that students need to write more to improve compositions and that lay readers can make this possible.

Measure for Measure edited by Allen Berger and Blanche Hope Smith. National Council of Teachers of English. Forty-three articles dealing with measurement, testing, and evaluation, plus a section on grading compositions. An excellent presentation of teachers' ideas and experiences.

Measuring Growth in English by Paul B. Diederich. National Council of Teachers of English. A collection of articles by a senior research associate at Educational Testing Service on different testing approaches. Testing and measurement concepts and terms relevant to evaluating writing are explained.

"Myth and Method" by Carolyn Logan. *English Journal* 59, no. 4 (April 1970): 548-50. National Council of Teachers of English. Emphasizes that teachers should write positive comments on papers so students will not be inhibited in writing.

"NCTE/ERIC Report—Composition Evaluation" by Robert V. Denby. *English Journal* 57, no. 8 (November 1968): 1215-21. National Council of Teachers of English. Reports that peer group evaluation of composition is not significantly more helpful to students than teacher evaluation, but it is much less time consuming for the teacher.

"Redpencilitis: Cause and Cure" by Joe W. Andrews. *English Journal* 42, no. 1 (January 1953): 20-24. National Council of Teachers of English. Discusses techniques for improving students' attitudes toward the correction of compositions.

A Scale for Evaluation of High School Student Essays. National Council of Teachers of English. Brief outline of standards for evaluating essays, giving specific consideration to key areas—content, organization, syle, and mechanics. Presents several sample essays with critical comments.

"Some Questions on the Lay Reader Program" by Paul H. Krueger. *English Journal* 50, no. 8 (November 1961): 529-33. National Council of Teachers of English. Negative opinion on lay readers because they do not know the people whose papers they are evaluating.

"Student Leadership in Evaluating Compositions" by Loren Grissom. *English Journal* 48, no. 6 (September 1969): 338-39. National Council of Teachers of English. Advocates that students become involved in correcting themes before they submit their papers to the teacher.

"Students Like Corrections" by Katherine Keene. *English Journal* 45, no. 4 (April 1956): 212-15. National Council of Teachers of English. Points out the value of marking errors and mentions giving themes two grades—one for mechanics and one for interest value.

Suggestions for Evaluating Junior High School Writing edited by Lois M. Grose, Dorothy Miller, and Erwin R. Steinberg. National Council of Teachers of English. Discusses procedures, principles, and methods for evaluating junior high school papers. Presents three sets of graded themes for grades seven, eight, and nine. Provides helpful information and instructive remarks directed to both the student and the teacher. Clear and direct.

Suggestions for Evaluating Senior High School Writing by the Association of English Teachers of Western Pennsylvania. National Council of Teachers of English. Illustrates effective methods of evaluating student work with numerous examples, models, and explanations. Answers pertinent questions: how do teachers develop fair and consistent evaluative standards, what is the ideal relationship between content and mechanics, and how extensive should the teacher's comments be? Presents a lucid rationale, provides examples of student papers that have been effectively evaluated, and provides definite instruction to the teacher.

"Teacher Comments and Student Performance: A Seventy-four Classroom Experiment in School Motivation" by E. B. Page. *The Journal of Educational Psychology* 49, no. 4 (August 1958): 173-81. Study shows that written comments have a positive effect on "effort, or attention, or attitude, or whatever it is that causes learning to improve."

Wad-Ja-Get? by Howard Kirschenbaum, Sidney B. Simon, and Rodney W. Napier. Hart Publishing Company. An excellent discussion of grading fallacies and alternative grading systems, plus a consideration of grading creative writing.

"What Criteria Do You Use in Grading Compositions?" by Paul F. Schumann. *English Journal* 57, no. 8 (November 1968): 1163ff. National Council of Teachers of English. Calls for increased objectivity in grading compositions by developing and using explicit criteria for evaluation.

"What Has Happened to Written Composition?" by Joseph Mersand. *English Journal* 50, no. 4 (April 1961): 231-37. National Council of Teachers of English. "Composition correction has changed from a pursuit in red ink by a bleary-eyed teacher-detective to a constructive evaluation which is shared in by the student-writer and the class."

"Writers Cramp and Eyestrain—Are They Paying Off?" by Lois V. Arnold. *English Journal* 53, no. 1 (January 1964): 10-15. National Council of Teachers of English. Study shows that intensive evaluation is no more effective in improving the quality of writing than moderate evaluation.

2

Teaching Students the Skills Needed for Prewriting

Good writing requires two kinds of work: the creative, intuitive generation and synthesis of ideas and the careful, craftsmanlike shaping of those ideas into a form. Recent research on the brain suggests that these two functions may be so separate that they are actually performed by different sides of the brain—that is, the right side of the brain senses ideas and "sees" the total picture, and the left side logically and analytically goes through the steps of constructing the piece of writing.

The intuitive generation of ideas usually comes first in the writing process, and this period of thinking that precedes writing is called prewriting. Prewriting is the time in which the writer's mind starts with a vague hunch and develops it into a fairly clear picture of the ideas to be presented in the writing.

This thinking it through period is difficult for teachers to work with. First, it is very easy to confuse creative thinking with daydreaming. The process also varies widely, sometimes happening in an intuitive flash, sometimes requiring long periods of reading or discussing ideas, and sometimes requiring several fresh starts. Some people do all of their prewriting work in their heads; others fill page after page with doodles, lists, sketchy notes, or formal outlines. There is no right or wrong way to plan an essay, though each individual can find ways that work and ways that do not work. Even the most skilled writers find that intuitive thinking is not totally under conscious control, not totally predictable. Therefore, it is quite difficult to teach.

The Greeks considered intuitive thinking so mystical and so important that they personified it as The Muse. Many unsuccessful writers still think of inspiration as a capricious god that will visit them or not as it pleases. Skilled writers, however, know that the muse rarely comes uninvited and develop skills in using their intuitive faculties.

This chapter will help the teacher explain the prewriting process to students and provide them with useful exercises for stimulating and developing their creative thinking skills. Additional activities serving the same function can be found in Chapter 1 in *A Guidebook for Teaching Creative Writing*, the companion volume to this book.

While the activities relating to the intuitive aspects of the writing process have all been collected into this chapter, it is important to remember that the writing process must integrate the skills taught in this chapter with those taught in later chapters. It might be useful to begin the writing course with some of the activities from this chapter and to use others to stimulate creative thinking at the beginning of each major composition project during the year.

OBJECTIVES

As a result of the learning experiences in this chapter, students should be able to:

1. Explain the concept of prewriting.
2. Relax and write freely.
3. Collect ideas for future writing assignments.
4. Maintain a journal in preparation for more formal writing projects.
5. Employ several strategies for developing ideas for essays.
6. Use a problem-solving strategy to work through the ideas for an essay.

LEARNING EXPERIENCES

Topic I: Understanding Prewriting

1. *Teacher Presentation.* Explain to students that most people are not able simply to sit down and write on a topic. Before they begin writing, most people do a certain amount of thinking about the topic. The process of thinking through a piece of writing before actual writing is called prewriting.

    Point out that it is important to distinguish between prewriting and procrastination. Procrastination is putting off working on an idea. Prewriting is the incubation of an idea. The easiest way to tell the difference between procrastination and prewriting is that procrastination usually comes before you begin working on a project. You put off thinking about it. Prewriting comes after you have defined a problem or idea and includes deliberate work on it. Note that prewriting includes some deliberate, conscious efforts to choose an idea and develop it. Making lists, reading, jotting down ideas, discussing ideas with friends, and making outlines are all parts of prewriting.

    In addition, prewriting often includes periods when you are not consciously thinking about the topic; nevertheless, a part of your mind is still working on it. Often if you put a difficult problem aside for a day or two and relax, you will either get a sudden insight about it or will find that it is much easier to work on when you return to it. Part of your mind has been working all along. This process is similar to the incubation period of a chicken in an egg. The idea matures in a part of your brain though you are not conscious of its growth. The need for incubation is the main reason that you should begin work on a composition early. Even if you do no actual writing, you should think about the composition so that your ideas can incubate before you have to put something down on paper.

2. *Activity.* Read the following situations to students and ask them to decide which students are involved in prewriting and which are procrastinating. Answers are given in parentheses.

   a. May was frustrated because she had to write a composition on happiness and she couldn't think of anything to say. "Maybe if I sleep on it, an idea will come to me," she thought. (procrastination)

   b. George was working on his essay. He started his outline but soon stopped working on it because the ideas just didn't fit together. He knew where the difficulty lay but he just could not find a solution. He decided to go to bed and try again the next day. (prewriting)

   c. Paula was working on her history essay about the main effects of the Civil War. She jotted down all of the ideas she could think of, then decided to take some time out to play tennis before writing the essay in hopes that some more ideas would come to her. (prewriting)

   d. Sal was working on his English composition while he watched television. He wrote a little between each of the innings of the baseball game and wrote some more when the action was slow in a detective show. (Not exactly either. Watching television is not an activity that promotes incubation and working during commercials is not enough time to focus on a problem.)

3. *Activity.* As students work on compositions, have them keep a journal describing the process they used to prepare for writing—both the conscious activities, such as writing an outline, and the subconscious ideas that seemed to be developing when they were not deliberately thinking about the project.

Topic II: Loosening Up

1. *Activity.* Divide students into groups of three or four. Give each group a stimulating action picture and ask the students to brainstorm, listing everything that they can see in the picture. If a group seems to be having trouble, give some hints. Encourage students to try to find twenty-five or more details.

   After the groups have listed all the details they can think of, ask each individual student to write a general statement identifying what he or she considers to be the most important idea from the picture. Each student can then write a paragraph, selecting the details from the list that support his or her topic sentence.

2. *Activity.* It is easier to think up ideas to write about if one follows a pattern or strategy. In writing description, unskilled students often describe a few major details, then stop. However, if they adhere to the following pattern, students can often write effortlessly a much longer description than they might have thought possible.

   First, choose a place for students to describe. It might add to the class's interest if you take them outside or to a special place in the school. Tell students to decide which part of the area they will begin with and then to determine the direction they are going to follow, making sure that they cover all parts of the area. Ask them to draw a little diagram or note directions for themselves. For example: "I will start in the upper front left corner, go around the ceiling clockwise, then the walls clockwise and then the floor clockwise." Have students then write a description of the entire area, including every detail they have on their list.

After students have finished (or when a few students finish), ask them to exchange papers and see if their partners discovered anything that they did not see.

3. *Activity.* Using the same procedure as in Activity 2, have students describe an interesting object that you bring to class. This time require them to focus on all the senses, not just sight, in their description. Have them first note a strategy for describing the object and then have them write their description.

4. *Activity.* Assign students to describe an event, something that has happened to them today. The event need not be especially interesting or unusual. Tell students not to worry about the mechanics of writing but to concentrate on describing the event in complete detail.

5. *Activity.* Follow up on Activity 4 by assigning students to observe and write about a specific event such as eating in the cafeteria, a fire drill, a school program, or a football game. Ask students first to prepare a strategy for observing the event and then to write in detail what they experienced.

6. *Activity.* Another writing project that will usually enable even the most reluctant writer to produce an acceptable piece of writing is an explanation of a simple task one does daily. Ask students to choose one of the following topics and write about it. treat these topics humorously.

   a. How to make sure that you get up and get to school on time.

   b. How to choose clothes for school.

   c. How to fix breakfast.

   d. How to get from your house to school.

   e. How to entertain yourself in this neighborhood after school.

   f. How to do my job (either outside employment or jobs at home).

7. *Activity.* Assign students to keep a diary and to write in it for ten minutes every day. You may want to give them time in class or assign the work to be done at home. Suggest that students each day record the events that happened to them, describe a person whom they met, or tell in detail about something that they did.

8. *Activity.* Assign students to write character sketches. Suggest that they first describe the person head to toe, then tell about the person's personality, and finally tell about some of the things the person has done.

9. *Activity.* Suggest that the class write a novel. With the students, select names for the main character and the main character's closest friends and describe the characteristics of the main character. Then encourage each student to write adventures for the main character. After a number of adventures have been written, allow class members to share them, either by passing them around the room, having the best read aloud, or making copies of some of the most interesting. If students have become involved in the project, you may want to let them continue by putting the episodes

in order, selecting a major problem to serve as the climax, and generally unifying the novel.

Topic III: Finding Ideas to Write About

1. *Teacher presentation.* Ask the class to share how often they have trouble getting ideas for a composition. Then ask students where they think professional writers get the ideas for their writing. Point out that getting ideas is not the primary problem. Everyone's mind is full of ideas all day long. Most people probably have five or ten ideas that would make good composition topics every day. The mind is like a jungle, full of ideas running wild. The trouble is that when you need them, they all seem to disappear. The problem is not to create new ideas but to capture the ideas that you have.

2. *Activity.* Point out that the first step in capturing ideas is to recognize them. Suggest that just as someone who knows nothing about nature can walk all day through the forest without seeing any signs of the abundant animal life, so an untrained writer can spend all day without recognizing any ideas. Ask students to look at the narrative on Reproduction Page 1. You may reproduce this page with a photocopy machine or make a spirit master or a transparency for the overhead projector with a copy machine. Ask students to list all the ideas that Katie has during the day. After students have made their individual lists, let them compare the ideas.

3. *Activity.* Either encourage or require students to keep a journal in which they jot down ideas for use in future compositions.

    Let students select their own approach to keeping a journal, but you might give them some suggestions. Students may want simply to jot down a sentence or two about each idea as it happens, or they may want to write longer entries at times when they are alone. Activities 4 through 8 could be done in a journal form or as separate activities.

4. *Activity.* Assign students to collect poems, quotations, magazine articles, or newspaper clippings that give them ideas for compositions. They may want to save these by pasting them in their journal or by putting them in a folder.

5. *Activity.* Ask students to choose one of the following topics or to make up similar topics of their own and to note in their journals for a week all the examples they find that fit the topics.

    a. Ways people waste time.

    b. People who are treated well.

    c. Embarrassing situations.

    d. Ways people try to improve themselves.

    e. Tasks people are willing to work hard doing.

    f. Things that are really done well.

    g. Ways people make fools of themselves.

6. *Activity.* If students do well with Activity 5, suggest the following more advanced observation topics. Ask students to choose one of the topics and make systematic observations about it for one week.

a. What makes a person popular in your school? Watch several popular people and notice the things they do differently from other people.

b. What makes an outstanding athlete? Watch the best athletes on a team at practice. What specific skills or abilities do they have that make them stand out? Are there some things that all outstanding players have in common, or does each person have different skills?

c. How does the weather affect you and other people? Is there a difference in the behavior of teachers and students when the weather is different?

7. *Activity.* Undertake an extended observation project with your class, possibly in conjunction with a social studies teacher. Topics that you might ask the class as a whole to gather information on include the following.

a. Ethnic influences in our community.

b. Connections between people in our community and the world beyond the United States.

c. People who have unique skills or talents.

d. Ways our community is deteriorating and ways it is improving.

8. *Activity.* After completing Activity 7, suggest that students interview people in the community who would add more information on the topic. The following articles describe projects of this type and their results.

Hector Lee, "American Folklore in the Schools," *English Journal* (October 1970): 994-99.

Patricia Peterson, "The Foxfire Concept," *Media and Methods* (November 1973): 16-25.

Eliot Wigginton, "The Foxfire Approach: It Can Work for You," *Media and Methods* (November 1977): 48-52.

Deborah Insell, "Foxfire in the City," *English Journal* (September 1975): 36-38.

David Laubach, "Beyond Foxfire," *English Journal* (May 1979): 52-54.

Topic IV: Developing Strategies for Prewriting

1. *Teacher Presentation.* Review with students the concept of prewriting (Topic I) and the types of preparation for writing that they have done (Topics 2 and 3). It should be evident to them that the strategy of collecting ideas from their own daily experiences will not be helpful when they are assigned an impersonal topic relating to, say, a character or situation in literature or when they are doing an in-class assignment for which writing time is quite limited. For such situations, which are quite common in schools, it is useful for students to know some strategies that will help them get ideas quickly.

2. *Activity.* Explain to students that an effective strategy for getting ideas about a topic is to relate themselves to the topic they are to write about. Suggest that they ask themselves, "Am I like one of the characters in this story (poem, movie, play,

picture)? Is there a character I identify with, feel hostile to? Have I ever been in a similar situation? Would I have behaved as the character behaved? Do I feel sympathy for the character? Do I disagree with, or disapprove of, him or her? Do the people I know behave like the people in the story?"

Assign students a very short story or poem to examine in this way, and then ask them to write a paragraph relating themselves in some way to the story or poem. Idries Shah's Sufi stories are ideal for this assignment. They can be found in a number of his books, including *The Exploits of the Incomparable Mullah Nasrudin.* (Dutton Paperbacks 1972).

3. *Activity.* Ask students to look at Reproduction Page 2. You can use a copy machine either to reproduce it or to make a transparency to use on an overhead projector. Discuss with students each of the five questions and ask them to memorize the five key words. Apply the strategy to analyzing a picture. Then assign students to use the strategy in developing compositions about other pictures, poems, or short stories that you have selected.

4. *Activity.* Ask students to look at the problem-solving strategy described on Reproduction Page 3. Discuss each step of the strategy with students. Then demonstrate the use of this strategy in writing an essay by going through the process of developing ideas for an essay with the students. Put these ideas on the board or use an overhead projector. For a sample essay you can make a transparency of Reproduction Page 4 to use on an overhead projector.

ASSESSING ACHIEVEMENT OF OBJECTIVES

On-Going Evaluation

Individual activities can be submitted for grading. The teacher can also observe the behavior of students as they begin writing assignments to determine the extent to which they are more effectively practicing the processes of prewriting.

Final Evaluation

Give students a writing assignment and require them to submit to you all the written materials they used in planning the writing. In addition, require students to submit a diary in which they briefly describe all the prewriting thinking they did. Evaluate their success in using prewriting skills with the following criteria.

1. Was the student able to begin promptly? Did the student know how to begin work?

2. Did the student have a source of ideas to use?

3. Did the student do adequate preparation for writing?

4. Did the student follow a strategy in prewriting or just flounder around hoping for ideas?

5. Does the final product show the adequate development that should result from prewriting?

RESOURCES FOR TEACHING THE SKILLS OF PREWRITING

The following is a selected list of materials useful for teaching prewriting skills. Addresses of publishers can be found in Appendix A.

Composition for Personal Growth by Robert C. Hawley, Sidney B. Simon and D. D. Britton. Hart Publishing Company. A collection of ideas for using personal growth skills as subject matter for writing. Most of the activities would serve as good prewriting strategies.

Designs for English by Martha Pomainville, Cynthia Blankenship, and Barbara Stanford. Designs for English. A fifteen-unit teaching kit in which reading, discussion, and other activities are used as prewriting exercises. The units are designed to provide students with the opportunity to explore ideas before they begin writing. Some of the units also instruct students in prewriting activities. The kit includes a teacher's guide, ten of each of the fifteen student guides, spirit masters, and a tape. Components are also available individually.

Strategies for Teaching the Composition Process by Carl Koch and James M. Brazil. National Council of Teachers of English. A collection of teaching strategies for each stage of the composition process. The strategies in the first two chapters, "The Comfort Zone" and "Prewriting," expand on the material in this chapter.

A Student-Centered Language Arts Curriculum: Grades K-13: A Handbook for Teachers by James Moffett. Houghton Mifflin Co. This classic work, which emphasizes drawing out children's ideas, contains a wealth of materials that are useful in the prewriting stage.

Writing to be Read by Ken Macrorie. Hayden Book Co., Inc. A student text that emphasizes the intuitive thinking skills that are important in prewriting. The text is lively and interesting and contains a number of student samples.

3

Teaching Students to Write Paragraphs

In the usual progress of learning, the baby learns to say words, the small child learns to speak short sentences, and the early schoolchild learns to write in sentences. The student writer then reaches the point of learning to communicate by paragraphs, and it is here that the die will be cast: he or she becomes an effective writer or does not, depending on whether he or she learns to write by paragraphs.

In order for students to master paragraph writing, they must first understand what a paragraph is and how it functions in writing. They must see that a paragraph is the basic formal unit by which writers convey their ideas. It is in the paragraph that the writer's generalizations are finally expressed on the detailed level and are finally made specific and complete for the benefit of the reader.

Students must understand that a paragraph consists of a single limited statement formulated with care and developed in detail. To say it in another way, it is a general statement illuminated or elaborated by specific statements. It is the building block of larger writings such as essays, reports, new stories, novels and short stories. The paragraph, in short, is where writing happens.

A good paragraph doesn't just happen, however. Good writers know what they are doing and make deliberate choices rather than put down sentences as they come to mind with no conscious reason. Making the proper choices as one constructs a paragraph is a skill that can be taught rather than left to chance. The lessons and activities in this chapter teach students how to make the right choices in composing paragraphs. They are presented here in logical sequence, beginning with more rudimentary skills and proceeding to more sophisticated ones. In general, we suggest that you schedule the activities in the order in which they are presented. However, as some are likely to be too difficult for younger or less able students, not all may be suitable for any particular class.

> **OBJECTIVES**
>
> As a result of the learning experiences in this chapter, students should be able to:
>
> 1. Construct a topic sentence that is limited enough to be developed in one paragraph.
>
> 2. Construct a topic sentence that summarizes a given set of details.
>
> 3. Choose an appropriate means for developing a topic sentence with specific statements.
>
> 4. Eliminate any specific details that do not support, explain, or illustrate the topic sentence.
>
> 5. Arrange the specific details in the best order.
>
> 6. Improve the coherence of their paragraphs.
>
> 7. Write paragraphs that are well developed, logically organized, unified, and coherent.

LEARNING EXPERIENCES

Topic I: Topic Sentences

1. *Teacher Presentation.* Explain to students that a topic sentence is so called because it is a sentence about a topic. It is *one* topic, *one* subject. And it is a sufficiently limited statement that it can be completely developed in detail in one paragraph. The function of the paragraph is to do just that—to develop the topic sentence in complete detail. Students need to know that the topic sentence determines what can go into a paragraph, and that no statement can go into the paragraph that is not related to the topic sentence. Reproduction Page 5 provides topic sentences that you might find useful in discussing the nature of the topic sentence with your students or that you can use for some of the suggested activities or for assignments as you desire. Reproduction Page 5 can be used to make a spirit master for duplicating the list to distribute to students or to make a transparency for use with an overhead projector.

2. *Activity.* Since a topic sentence is a *general* statement supported, explained, or illustrated by *specific* statements, it is essential that students understand fully the concept of general versus specific. After explaining the concept, give the class several pairs of words, one of which is more general than the other: car/Ford, and language/French, for example. Have students decide which word is more specific than the other. Then read or write on the board pairs of phrases, one of which is more specific than the other: getting dressed/putting on my socks, my grandfather/elderly persons I have admired, and the view from my bedroom window/an apple tree in my neighbor's yard, for example. If students need still more practice, give them a list of pairs of sentences, one of which is more general than the other: My mother spent an hour doing the grocery shopping/It took her ten minutes to decide between ground beef and ground veal, for example.

3. *Activity.* A list of topic sentences appears on Reproduction Page 6. Make copies of this page and distribute them to the students or make a transparency and show it with the overhead projector. Working with the class as a whole, discuss and evaluate the topic sentences on the list. Some of them are sufficiently specific to be developed in detail in one paragraph. Others are too broad and general, and would require an entire essay or even a book. Some make two or more statements in one sentence and are therefore poor topic sentences. Have students identify the poor topic sentences and choose the good ones. Answers can be found in Appendix B.

4. *Activity.* Assign students to take the subjects labeled "too broad" in Activity 3 and identify one part or aspect that could be the subject of a paragraph.

5. *Activity.* Divide the class into small groups (about three or four students to a group). Perhaps the best way to do this is to divide the number of students in the class by either three or four. The answer you get is the highest number that students should "number off" to. Have students number off, and then have all the 1's get together, all the 2's get together, all the 3's, and so on. This procedure assigns students randomly so you do not have the same students working together all the time. Explain to the class that you will give all the groups the same subject and that in five minutes (or longer if you wish) you want each group to come up with as many specific details about the subject as they can. Less able students may profit from your doing one subject with the total class as an example. Here are some subjects to assign:

a fall day	cafeteria after lunch
a friendship's ending	first day of school
an overcrowded school	going out to dinner
a warmly hospitable family	a dilapidated building
a summer walk in the woods	a day at the beach

As the groups are working, circulate among them to make sure they are arriving at details (the lockers have been painted blue), not general statements (everything was colorful). When groups have finished listing all the details they can, have them write a statement about the subject that includes one group of related details. Point out to your students that they may have material for a number of topic sentences if their list of details is extensive. For instance, "an overcrowded school" can generate details having to do with discomfort of students, safety problems, negative influences on quality of education, or decline of the school environment.

When all groups have finished, let them read their general statements (topic sentences) and selected lists of details to the total class. At the end of the lesson, assign students to choose one of the general statements and its list of related details and to develop them into a paragraph.

Another way to use this exercise is to ask each group to come up with as many topic sentences and lists of related details as possible. Give special praise to the group that does the best job of developing every aspect of the subject. (The awareness that even a limited subject can be developed into a number of different paragraphs is a big step toward understanding how a subject can be turned into an essay, a task to be studied in the next chapter.)

6. *Activity.* Assign each student to prepare a list of details about the view out of his or her bedroom window. As each student reads the list of details to the class, have the

other students try to make a statement about each view based on the details read. These could be written on the board, and the student who generated the descriptive details could choose the sentence that best summarizes his or her list. Other subjects suitable for this activity include my little brother (or sister), my favorite person, my new car, and my favorite after-school activity. Be sure the students understand they are to bring to class a list of details, not statements that could themselves be topic sentences. Here is an example of a topic sentence using "my little brother" as the subject: my little brother has every annoying trait an eight-year-old can have.

7. *Activity.* Divide the class into groups of three to five students each, using the procedure suggested in Activity 4. Have each group make a list of details relating to some event, situation, feeling, or controversy that is familiar to all members of the class. The students should have a topic sentence in mind and make sure that every detail on their list relates to that topic sentence. The students will, of course, not reveal their topic sentence, but instead, after they have made their lists, exchange them with another group to see if it can guess the topic and construct a topic sentence that embraces all the details on the list. For example, one group might list the following details: the team was overconfident; we fumbled a lot; the opponents intercepted three of our passes; the final score was embarrassing; and we had many penalties. Another group might guess that the details all relate to "a game where everything went wrong" and might construct the following topic sentence: The football game was a disaster for us. *Another example of details:* The dogs howl at night; there are lights on at all hours of the night; car doors slamming wake me up; when the wind blows our way the odor is bad; and our property value has gone down. *Topic sentence:* It is not always pleasant living next door to a dog kennel. This activity gives the students an enjoyable opportunity to try to trick one another with relevant but misleading details.

8. *Activity.* Have the class interview one member (a volunteer) about how he or she spends spare time (or what the person likes on TV, what kind of music he or she prefers, or what the person thinks a perfect friend is). Make a list of the details the interviewee reveals. Put it on the board for all the class to see.

   Then ask each student to write a topic sentence that makes a statement about how the interviewee spends spare time (or whatever). The statement should include as many of the details as possible and should be suitable for development in one paragraph. For example, if the list of how George spends his leisure time is as follows: "listens to records, reads, daydreams, rides exercise bicycle, plays guitar, and writes letters," the topic sentence might be "George doesn't need companionship to help him spend his free time." After several students have read their topic sentences, have the class interview a different person and repeat the exercise.

Topic II: Developing a Topic Sentence into a Complete, Unified Paragraph

1. *Teacher Presentation.* Remind students that the topic sentence determines what the development of a paragraph will be, since only detailed statements that support, prove, and specify the topic sentence can be included. All other details must be eliminated (perhaps to go into another paragraph with a different topic sentence). A very common way of developing a topic sentence is simply to break it into its

logical parts such as ways, reasons, causes, results, components, steps, and facts. Here are some examples to use in clarifying this kind of development for your students. The important thing to remember is that it is the topic sentence that determines what goes into the paragraph because it is its parts which make up the development.

Topic Sentence	*Parts*
It was my fault we were not friends.	things I did that were my fault
There are three ways to knead bread.	the three ways
Grass is greener on the other side of the fence.	reasons why
The apple is unusually nutritious.	ways it contributes to nutrition
We learned important lessons on our vacation.	important lessons we learned
There are many fascinating people in my class.	examples of fascinating people.

2. *Activity.* Reproduce for the class Reproduction Page 7. Have the class, with you supervising, take the list of topic sentences and name what the developmental parts would be if they were writing a paragraph about the topic sentences. (Sample answers are given in Appendix B.) Don't encourage students to come up with the actual details (content) of the paragraph. Simply have them specify what type of content the topic sentence calls for. For example, for the first topic sentence in the list, a correct response would be, "The reasons why the writer doesn't like frogs."

3. *Activity.* Choose three topic sentences from the list on Reproduction Page 7. Review the developmental parts that the class agreed upon, and ask the students to suggest the actual detailed sentences that could make up the paragraph. Students could work as a class, under your supervision, or could divide into small groups, devise their lists of sentences, and then come back together to share. Of course, in this activity students will have to use their imaginations and make up details they feel are suitable.

Example

Topic Sentence: His fear of dogs is deeply rooted in past experiences.

Detailed Statements: A dead dog fell into Mike's baby carriage. A wolf that looked like a dog lunged at his stroller when Mike was between one and two. When Mike was three, he was attacked by a large Siberian husky. The neighbor's dog ate his pet cat when Mike was seven.

4. *Activity.* Ask students to choose three different topic sentences from Reproduction Page 7. Have them devise a list of developing sentences as they did for Activity 3, but this time include both statements that belong in the paragraph and a few statements that do *not.* In other words, they are to deliberately violate the principle of unity by putting in statements that do not belong. Then have students, working

in pairs or small groups, exchange their lists of sentences to see if they can identify and eliminate sentences that violate unity or that do not really pertain to the topic sentence.

5. *Teacher Presentation.* Tell students that there are a number of other ways to develop a topic sentence into a paragraph besides breaking the topic sentence into its logical parts. Nevertheless, it is the topic sentence, again, that determines the most suitable means of development. Depending on what method will most effectively specify the topic sentence, the writer may choose from these means of development: explanation, factual data, description, narrative, and examples. Numerous other methods of development could also be considered, but these are the most useful.

6. *Activity.* Make copies of Reproduction Page 8. Give a copy to each student and ask each to determine which of the main methods of developing a paragraph (explanation, facts, description, narrative, or examples) is used in each paragraph. Suggested answers are given in Appendix B.

7. *Activity.* Remind students of all the usual means of developing a topic sentence into a paragraph, including the one discussed in Teacher Presentation 1 (analysis) as well as the five introduced in Teacher Presentation 5. Have students, working as a total class or in groups, study the list of topic sentences on Reproduction Page 9 and agree on the best means of development for each one. (Answers are given in Appendix B.) It is less important that the students agree on the means of development than that they understand that numerous means are available to develop all kinds of topic sentences. Thus students may have correct answers other than those listed in Appendix B.

8. *Activity.* Divide the class at random into pairs or groups of three and assign each a topic sentence from the list on Reproduction Page 9. Have students come up with as many specifying statements as possible to develop the topic sentence in the manner designated. Have the students share their lists with the class.

9. *Evaluation.* As a means of checking how well students have mastered the skills taught by the preceding learning experiences (or as an additional practice exercise), assign the same topic sentence to each student. (See Teacher Presentation 1 for suggestions or prepare one that is better suited to your class.) Have students, working individually, determine the best means of development, make a list of developing parts and statements and, finally, write a completely detailed paragraph. It would be helpful to collect the paragraphs and lists and reproduce them by spirit duplicator or overhead projector. Or, if necessary, read them aloud and let the class critique the lists and paragraphs and choose those that they feel were done most satisfactorily. Unless the trust level in the class is high, do not identify the writer of each paragraph. (If no means of reproducing are available, you might circulate the papers in class, having students evaluate the papers on a point scale as in a diving match. Of course, if you have some students whose ability is markedly below the general level of the class, this approach would pose a problem, and you might prefer not to circulate the papers.)

10. *Teacher Presentation.* Tell students: you, as a writer, are often faced not with a list of specifying details or a topic sentence but with a complex and often confusing situation, thing, event, or person to write about. It is *your* task to reduce this experience with all its random parts and details to a clearly understood paragraph.

You will have to unify these details in one topic sentence, and *you* must decide what means of developing best suits *your* purpose. Your task is to find a common element or theme in all (or most) of the details before you and to express this theme or element in a statement that becomes your topic sentence. You will then eliminate the details that cannot be included under your topic sentence, choose the means of development that you see best suits your purpose and proceed with the writing of your paragraph.

Review with students the steps in the process:

a. Jot down all the ideas and details on the subject you can.
   Example: messy hair, dirty shirt, untied shoes, cutoffs, sharp eyes, etc.

b. Identify common element.
   Example: sloppy appearance (eliminate "sharp eyes")

c. State topic sentence.
   Example: My friend Charlie always seems to look sloppy.

d. Decide on method of development.
   Example: description

e. List specific details that you plan to use.
   Example: all from above list except "sharp eyes"

f. Write paragraph.

If you need to provide students with another example of how to turn a bewildering mass of details into a paragraph, utilize the following:

Details: horns, streamers, whistles, snake dances, perspiring delegates, harried sergeants-at-arms, democratic caucus in a corner, demonstration under the stage, etc.

Topic Sentence: The convention floor was a noisy, seething mass of nonsense and serious political business.

Method of Development: Analysis and description.

11. *Activity.* Working together as a class under your supervision, students should follow the six-step process suggested in Teacher Presentation 10. Have them choose a place, person, situation, object, or event and develop an extensive list of supporting details. Then have them devise a topic sentence that includes a sufficient number of details so that it can be developed into a paragraph. They should then decide on a method of development and settle on a final list of details that develop the topic sentence. You might even have students write the complete paragraph as a group.

12. *Activity.* A list of random details appears on Reproduction Page 10. Duplicate it to distribute to students (if you prefer them to work individually or in small groups), or use the opaque projector or overhead projector or chalk board (if you prefer them to work as a total class). Tell students to find a unifying principle or theme in the list of details and to state a topic sentence covering as many of the given details as possible. Have them draw lines through details that do not fit their topic sentence and determine which method of development is most appropriate for their topic sentence. (Possible answers are given in Appendix B.)

13. *Activity.* Assign the class one place, person, event, or situation to consider. Tell

students to make a list of the elements they identify, to look for a unifying theme or principle, to state a topic sentence and to eliminate all irrelevant details, to choose the method of development that is most suitable, and to write a paragraph. This is probably best done with students working individually, especially if they have done most of the preceding activities as a total group. Then have students share their paragraphs by reading them aloud in class so they can compare to see how similarly or differently they perceived the same assigned subject.

Topic III: Putting Developmental Details in the Best Order

1. *Teacher Presentation.* Remind students that the developmental details of a paragraph consist of such things as statements of fact, reasons why, examples, causes, effects, steps in a sequence, component parts, explanatory statements, logical arguments, descriptive details, and events that form a narrative. Call to their attention that since only one statement can be written or read at a time, a writer must choose the order in which statements will appear in the paragraph, and the choice should be based on some reason. In choosing an order for developmental details, many writers are guided by the following principles:

    Climactic Order: small to large, trivial to significant, inconspicuous to conspicuous, lacking in value to very valuable, fairly persuasive to absolutely clinching, etc.

    Sequential: chronological, steps in a process, numbers in a series, logical structure built argument by argument as in causation, etc.

    Spatial: from place to place in order, from one element to those surrounding it, from near to far, from left to right, etc.

    Contrast: either all aspects of one thing and then all of the other or a point-by-point alternation.

2. *Activity.* Working with the class as a whole, give students copies of Reproduction Page 11. Have students read the topic sentence and decide what type of order might be the best for the developmental details under each. Then have them number the details in order. There may well be some legitimate disagreement, and this is to be expected. The important thing is that students learn to consciously order details. (Answers are given in Appendix B.)

3. *Activity.* Have students (either as an entire class or working in twos and threes) read the paragraphs on Reproduction Page 12 and determine what weaknesses they contain in the order of the details. Have students decide on a better order for the details and number them accordingly. When all have finished, have the groups or individuals compare what they have done and see if they agree.

4. *Activity.* Assign students at random to groups of two or three and provide them with a subject or a list of subjects from which to choose. Ask them to:

    a. List developmental details about the subject they choose.

    b. Arrive at a topic sentence, and then

c. List the usable details *in order*, eliminating any details that do not pertain to the topic sentence.

Then you may wish to have students, working individually from this point, write a paragraph based on the ordered list of developmental details prepared by their group. The paragraphs could be read aloud and compared.

5. *Activity.* Have each student make a list of details that describe his or her bedroom and then find a unifying theme or principle and state this in a topic sentence. Each student should then place the list of usable details in order (identifying the ordering principle) and write a paragraph to be shared with the class or with one other student.

6. *Activity.* Have each student write a paragraph telling how to wash a car or perform some other common operation. Require students to follow the usual steps in writing the paragraph:

   a. Make a list of details.

   b. Compose a topic sentence.

   c. List the usable details in a logical order (in this case students will probably use sequential or chronological order).

   d. Write the paragraph.

7. *Activity.* Have each student write a paragraph giving examples of people who have had a great influence on him or her. Suggest that students follow these steps:

   a. Make a list of people who have been influential in their lives.

   b. Arrive at a topic sentence that includes most of the people named.

   c. Decide on an appropriate order (that is, climactic or chronological).

   d. List the usable examples in the proper order, eliminating those that are not included in the topic sentence.

   e. Write the paragraph.

8. *Activity.* Have students write a paragraph using one of the sentences below as their topic sentence:

   Basketball is more exciting than football for the spectators (or vice versa).

   The duties of the guards differ from those of the tackles.

   British rock groups have a musical style that is noticeably different from that of American groups.

   Cats make better pets than dogs (or vice versa).

   Require them to choose a means of organizing the details that makes the contrast clearly apparent.

9. *Activity.* Have students list, in writing, the steps one must go through to write a completely detailed and orderly paragraph about a place, person, thing, event, or situation. Have them meet in small groups to discuss how their lists differ and to reach an agreement on one list of steps.

10. *Evaluation.* Have students choose one topic sentence from the list on Reproduction Page 5 and write a properly developed paragraph with details in a consciously chosen order. Have them exchange papers and evaluate the extent to which the principles learned so far were applied in writing the paragraph or have them submit papers to you for grading.

Topic IV: Making the Paragraph Flow Smoothly

1. *Teacher Presentation.* Once students have learned to formulate a topic sentence and list developmental details in logical order, the paragraphs they write will be much improved, but often they will lack coherence. That is, the student writer will produce something that sounds more like a grocery list than a paragraph. Thus it is important to show students how to tie their sentences together and fill in the awkward gaps that sometimes occur between one statement and the next.

    Perhaps the most common means of achieving coherence—and luckily, the easiest to learn—is the use of logical connections and linking constructions. These are simply words or phrases that emphasize the logic of what is expressed while tying sentences and parts of sentences more closely together. The following list of examples of various types of connecting expressions can be written on the board or projected for students to copy and add to, or it can be reproduced and distributed to them. A good writer will make conscious use of connectors when checking and revising his or her work.

    - *Connectors Indicating Time:* soon, next, then, later, finally, first, and second
    - *Connectors Indicating Contrast:* but, on the other hand, however, nevertheless, otherwise, and yet
    - *Connectors Indicating a Sequence:* in addition, also, furthermore, moreover, another, likewise, similarly, next, finally, besides, first, and second
    - *Connectors Indicating Results:* therefore, hence, because, thus, consequently, as a result, and for
    - *Connectors Indicating Examples:* for instance, an example of this, for example, and take the case of

2. *Activity.* Use the paragraph on Reproduction Page 13, written by twelfth grade student Joe Finkelstein. Have students circle all the connecting devices that they can identify in the paragraph. Then go through the paragraph pointing out each connector and discussing with the class how it functions in the paragraph.

3. *Activity.* Have students study the paragraph on Reproduction Page 14, which is badly in need of logical connectors. Ask them, working in pairs or individually as you prefer, to put in links wherever they think connectors are needed. Then have the class share and discuss their answers. Reproduction Page 15 illustrates a possible revision of the paragraph with the connectors underlined.

4. *Activity.* Have students examine paragraphs that they have written for previous activities to see if the writing would profit from the insertion of logical connectors. Ask them to put a check at any point in the text where a connector would help and to write the connecting word or phrase in the margin at the end of the line.

(It might be helpful to have students keep all written work in a folder so that early work can be used for activities such as this one.)

5. *Teacher Presentation.* If writing is to be coherent and easy to read, writers must develop the habit of consistency. They must be consistent in the use of the same subject throughout the paragraph, in the words used to refer to the same subject, and in the verb tense in which the subject of the paragraph is placed. They must, for example, avoid starting out with "Students are..." and then switching to "The student is..." and to "He was...." If they start out with a plural form of the subject, they must continue with plural forms. And if they are telling a story or summarizing a plot in the present tense, they must stick to the present tense throughout. If students find it difficult to control these inconsistencies in their writing, they will profit from learning to correct them consciously as part of the process of revising.

6. *Activity.* Paragraph A on Reproduction Page 16 is incoherent because there is a different grammatical subject in almost every sentence. Reproduce or project it and read it aloud with the students so they can "hear" the incoherence. Then ask students (either individually or as part of a total-class discussion) to choose the subject on which the paragraph should focus and then rewrite the paragraph adhering to that subject throughout. When they have finished rewriting, have some students read their revisions aloud to see if the coherence has been improved. Paragraph B on Reproduction Page 17 can be used as an example of one way of revising paragraph A to improve the coherence. Repeat the procedure with paragraph C on Reproduction Page 18 in which the subject changes so many times that the paragraph moves away from the subject of the topic sentence. After students have rewritten paragraph C, you may wish to show them paragraph D on Reproduction Page 19 in which the writer sticks more closely to the subject of the topic sentence.

   Paragraph E on Reproduction Page 20 and its revision, paragraph F on Reproduction Page 21, may be used with less advanced classes.

   Be sure your students observe that throughout revised paragraph B on Reproduction Page 17 the subject of every sentence is either "the experienced hostess," "the hostess," "the skilled party giver" or "she." The focus remains on the hostess throughout the paragraph. If your students complain that it sounds awful to repeat "she" so often, you may reassure them that they probably would not have noticed the repetition of the pronoun if it had not been called to their attention. In one's usual writing, you may wish to explain, one may choose from a variety of means for achieving coherence and need not use one technique so exclusively that it becomes conspicuous.

   Have your students observe that in Paragraph C on Reproduction Page 18 no two sentences have the same subject and, as a result, the paragraph moves away from "the police officers," the subject of the topic sentence. Your students should count the subjects in paragraph C and then observe that in revised paragraph D on Reproduction Page 19, the focus remains throughout on "the police officers" or "they."

7. *Activity.* Paragraph A on Reproduction Page 22 is incoherent because there are a number of verbs in the passive voice. As a result the reader is kept in the dark about the *subject* of the verb and the coherent flow of meaning is impeded. Reproduce paragraph A or project it and read it aloud with the students so they can "hear"

the incoherence. Then ask students (either individually or as part of a total-class discussion) to rewrite the paragraph, putting all verbs in the active form and providing a subject for each verb. When they have finished rewriting, have some students read their revisions aloud to see if the coherence has been improved. Paragraph B on Reproduction Page 23 illustrates one way of revising paragraph A to improve the coherence by eliminating passive verbs. Point out that it is not always desirable to eliminate all passive verbs, as use of the passive voice sometimes allows the writer to avoid bringing in other subjects: "The moment he put his hand into the hole it was seized by...." Repeat the procedure with paragraph C on Reproduction Page 24, which also lacks coherence because of frequent use of passive voice. After students have rewritten paragraph C, you may wish to show them paragraph D on Reproduction Page 25, which indicates one way the coherence could be improved.

Point out to your students that they should choose a subject to be the focus of their paragraph and introduce it as the subject of their topic sentence. If they consistently use their subject throughout their paragraph, they will be less likely to over-use verbs in the passive voice. Note how, in paragraph B, "we" serves consistently as the subject and in paragraph D "some gardeners" or "they" is the subject, which helps to eliminate passive verbs and makes the paragraph more coherent.

8. *Activity.* Paragraph A on Reproduction Page 26 is incoherent because it contains so many errors in point of view. The writer did not choose the person and number of the subject and adhere to them faithfully throughout. Read paragraph A aloud with the students so they can "hear" the incoherence. Then ask them (either individually or as part of a total class discussion) to rewrite the paragraph with a consistent point of view. When they have finished rewriting, have some students read their revisions aloud to see if the coherence is improved. Paragraph B on Reproduction Page 27 illustrates one way of revising paragraph A to improve the coherence by making point of view consistent. Repeat the procedure with paragraph C on Reproduction Page 28, which also lacks coherence because of frequent shifts in point of view. After students have rewritten paragraph C, you may wish to show them paragraph D on Reproduction Page 29, which indicates one way the coherence could be improved.

9. *Activity.* Paragraph A on Reproduction Page 30 demonstrates how inconsistency in verb tense can reduce coherence. This problem often arises when students are summarizing the plot of a story or movie or when they are narrating an episode from their own experience. You might wish to remind them that it is customary to write plot summaries in the present tense. Read paragraph A aloud with the students so they can "hear" the incoherence. Then ask them (either individually or as part of a total class discussion) to rewrite the paragraph, correcting the inconsistencies in verb tense. When they have finished rewriting, have some students read their revisions aloud to see if the coherence has been improved. Paragraph B on Reproduction Page 31 illustrates one way of revising paragraph A to improve the coherence by making verb tense consistent. Repeat the procedure with paragraph C on Reproduction Page 32, which also lacks coherence because of frequent shifts in verb tense. After students have rewritten paragraph C, you may wish to show them paragraph D on Reproduction Page 33, which indicates one way the coherence could be improved. Paragraphs E and F on Reproduction Pages 34 and 35 can be used in the same way for less able students.

10. *Teacher Presentation.* Point out to students that one sure way to produce incoherent writing is to put together a succession of short, simple sentences as children do. This makes for rough, choppy reading that simply cannot hold a reader's interest for very long. Since not all sentences in a paragraph are of equal importance, there is no need for the writer to give them equal emphasis. When one sentence is less important than another sentence, the less important statement can be made subordinate to the statement that should be emphasized. And in the case of statements of equal importance, it is often good to connect them rather than let each statement stand as a short, simple sentence. It is by a judicious combination of connection and subordination that the skillful writer avoids the effect of choppy, childish writing. Demonstrate this principle to students by reproducing by spirit duplicator or projecting paragraph A on Reproduction Page 36, which contains no connection or subordination. Help students see how awkward and choppy the paragraph is. Then show them paragraph B on Reproduction Page 37, in which connection and subordination have been utilized to improve coherence.

11. *Activity.* Have students, working individually or in pairs, rewrite the paragraph of short simple sentences on Reproduction Page 38, using subordination and connection to improve coherence.

12. *Activity.* Put students in pairs or small groups and select one topic sentence for all to use. (See the list on Reproduction Page 5.) Instruct students to list developmental details that support or specify the topic sentence and put them in logical order for a paragraph. Then have students, working individually, write the paragraph in short simple sentences. Ask them to exchange papers with one another and have each student rewrite the paragraph, using subordination and connection and other means of improving coherence. Students may be interested in hearing or reading some of the most dramatically improved paragraphs.

13. *Activity.* Have students review their file of previously written paragraphs to see whether they could be improved with connection and subordination techniques. Distribute the rewritten paragraphs for class members to study.

14. *Teacher Presentation.* Explain to students that a basic way for the writer to achieve coherence is to make sure that he or she leaves no gaps in thought. The reader can move successfully and smoothly through the sequence of thoughts if the writer has been sure to say exactly and completely what he or she means instead of assuming that the reader will be glad to figure it out and fill in the gaps. Only a few readers are willing to go to that trouble (and most of them are English teachers). Few will be interested in a paragraph full of "holes"—places between sentences where more needs to be said. At best, the reader will know *generally*, rather than *exactly*, what the writer means, and the paragraph will stagger and stutter along rather than flow smoothly and coherently.

15. *Activity.* Have students discuss and agree, if possible, on exactly what the writer meant in paragraphs A and B on Reproduction Page 39. Help them see that because the writer has left glaring gaps in thought, the reader must do much guesswork. You might wish to have students work in pairs in trying to figure out the writer's meaning and then have the pairs share their opinions with the class and see if there is agreement. Note that paragraphs C and D on Reproduction Page 40 indicate how the gaps might be filled in.

16. *Activity.* Duplicate Reproduction Page 41 and have students rewrite paragraphs A and B, filling in gaps in thought to improve coherence. Paragraphs C and D on Reproduction Page 42 illustrate how the revisions might be made.

17. *Activity.* Distribute copies of Reproduction Page 43. Read paragraph A, warning students to be aware of the incoherence caused by gaps in thought. Then read paragraph B so that students can see how the gaps in thought have been filled with "extender sentences" that make the writing both more coherent and more complete. Then pass out copies of paragraph C on Reproduction Page 44, which has places provided for students to insert sentences further specifying and extending the sentences they follow. After students have finished, read some of their efforts aloud and emphasize the improvement in both completeness and coherence. Urge the use of extender sentences to help students avoid the effect of a "grocery list" when they put together in final form the list of developmental details they have decided on. Point out that this is developing, not just *listing*. Reproduction Page 45 can be used in the same way.

18. *Activity.* Have students choose a topic sentence from the list on Reproduction Page 5 and write a paragraph, following all the steps outlined previously except that they are to make their paragraphs as incoherent as possible. Have students exchange papers and revise the work of their partners. Then pass the papers back to the original writers and have them evaluate how well their partners caught the deliberate errors.

19. *Activity.* Divide the class at random into small groups of three to five students each. Have them work together to write a paragraph (one paragraph per group), following the steps below. (Write steps on board or distribute this list to each student in the group.)

    a. Choose a subject that all in the group know something about.

    b. Compose a topic sentence about this subject, making sure it is narrow enough to be covered in detail in one paragraph.

    c. Jointly make a list of developing details that support, explain, illustrate, or illuminate the topic sentence.

    d. Agree on the best order for these details.

    e. Check to make sure all details are relevant to the topic sentence.

    f. Compose the sentences containing the developmental details.

    g. Have one member of the group check the paragraph for completeness, adding details where needed.

    h. Have one member of the group check the paragraph for coherence, adding connectors and filling in gaps with extender sentences.

    i. Have one member of the group check the paragraph for spelling, punctuation, usage, and final form. Then have groups exchange paragraphs and evaluate the work of another group.

ASSESSING ACHIEVEMENT OF OBJECTIVES

On-Going Evaluation

The extent to which students have mastered the individual skills covered under each topic in this chapter can be measured by the procedures headed "Evaluation" that appear periodically. Almost any of the activities suggested in each section could also be submitted for evaluation.

Final Evaluation

For an overall evaluation of students' ability to write paragraphs, assign a paragraph to be written in class. List on the board several general subjects from which students can choose and announce that they are to write a paragraph on some aspect of that subject. Depending on the age and ability level of the students, length requirements can vary from 50 to 200 words. Grade the paragraphs according to criteria such as the following:

1. Has the writer chosen an aspect of the subject that is narrow enough to be developed in detail in one paragraph?

2. Does the paragraph consist of a general statement supported (specified, developed, examined, and illuminated) by a series of more specific statements?

3. Are all the specific statements directly related to the general statement?

4. Has the writer arranged the developmental details in a logical order?

5. Has the writer utilized logical connectors and other devices as needed to improve coherence?

RESOURCES FOR TEACHING PARAGRAPH WRITING

The following is a selected list of resources useful for teaching the skills of paragraph writing. Addresses of publishers can be found in Appendix A.

Audio-Visual Materials

All about Paragraphs and *Paragraphs That Work* by Thomas Gaston. Thomas Klise Company. Two filmstrips with records (or cassettes) and guides. Presents the evolution and progression of the paragraph—how and why it became the basic unit of all expository writing. Discussion of topic sentences, the need to substantiate general contentions, and paragraph structure and strategy. Examination of organizational formula (Tell, Explain, Support, Transition). Amusing, entertaining cartoon characters. Suitable for all students as foundation material.

Communication Skills: Write it Right. The Center for the Humanities. Two hundred slides in three carousel cartridges, three tape cassettes, three LP records, teacher's guide, and library-processing kit. Examples and exercises provide students with a well-delineated step-by-step approach to organizing ideas into words, words into an outline, and the outline into a clear, well-written paragraph. Very effective for all students.

Fundamentals of Writing. Applause Productions. This six-filmstrip set provides instruction in outlining, choosing a topic, examining sentence and paragraph relations, writing introductions and conclusions, the use of transitional devices, and establishing unity and creating variety through style. Set includes teacher notes and five sets of student worksheets for use with writing exercises.

Organizing Your Writing. Encyclopedia Britannica Educational Corp. Series of eight filmstrips. Covers key factors of the composition: the five steps in writing, outlining, the introduction, the body, and the conclusion as well as pattern of paragraphs and how to make transitions between paragraphs.

The Paragraph. Filmstrip House. Four color filmstrips. Discusses paragraph sense, topic development, unity and coherence, transitions, and connectives.

Paragraph Power. Filmstrip House. Four full-color filmstrips: "Thinking in Paragraphs," "Topic Sentence Power," "Paragraph Unity," and "Paragraph Development"; four LP record sides (or tape cassettes); sixteen spirit duplicating masters; and script book. Designed with a developmental emphasis to guide students from basic ideas to practical application. Very effective—a fine skill-oriented teaching tool. Appropriate for all students.

Paragraphs. Encyclopedia Britannica Educational Corp. One part of *Composition Skills*, an overhead transparency program. Consists of thirty-eight transparencies in plastic case, duplicating masters, and teacher's guide. Excellent materials, appropriate for all students.

Paragraph Techniques. Filmstrip House. Four full-color filmstrips, two LP records (or cassettes), four scripts, and catalog card kits. Covers "Focusing on a Topic," "Developing a Topic," "Unifying," and "Writing Transitions." The filmstrip features a fifteen-year-old student learning and modeling, step by step, how to write an effective paragraph. Provides good foundation in paragraph writing.

The Specific Is Terrific. Centron Films. In this twelve-minute color film, Pvt. Splunk learns to write interesting letters home by communicating specific information with specific words. The importance of specific writing is also shown to be important in other settings.

Techniques of Paragraph Writing. Eye-Gate. Four filmstrips, two cassettes, and study guide. Filmstrips on "Planning a Paragraph and Creating a Topic Sentence," "Methods of Developing a Paragraph," "Methods of Organizing a Paragraph, I," and "Methods of Organizing a Paragraph, II." Suggested activities and discussion materials included.

Writing a Good Paragraph. RMI Educational Films, Inc. Color filmstrip. Emphasizes unity, clarity, coherence, and ways to achieve them. Provides detailed explanations of topic sentences, main idea, order of interest, and cause-effect relationships.

Writing: From Assignment to Composition by Arlene Oraby, consultant. Guidance Associates. Two full-color filmstrips plus discussion guide with instructions on how to use the program, discussion questions, and related activities. Outlining, revising and composition are discussed. A thorough, practical teaching aid.

Print Materials

The Art of Composition by Barbara Pannwitt. Silver Burdett Company. One of six books on composition in the Contemporary English Modules series. Excellent format—helpful diagrams, examples, charts, and explanations. Teacher's manual available. Complete with lesson plans.

Better Writing: From Paragraph to Essay by Gene Stanford and Marie N. Smith. Holt, Rinehart & Winston. A self-teaching, self-correcting basic composition workbook that teaches paragraph and essay writing in small, incremental steps.

Composing with Paragraphs by Sister Agnes Ann Pastva. Cambridge Book Company. Exceptional in its visual attractiveness. Includes sections on words, sensory awareness, communication, description, expressive impact, style, and composition. An interesting and stimulating work that will motivate students and facilitate learning.

Composition I by Sara Hickman. Educators Publishing Service, Inc. Excellent source of materials on a wide variety of paragraph types—descriptive, instructionsal, factual, narrative, and developmental. Related exercises in paragraph unity, coherence, and emphasis. Flexible, versatile —appropriate for average and advanced students.

Composition: Models and Exercises by Desmond J. Nunan and Philip McFarland. Harcourt Brace Jovanovich. A five-book series. Each book contains models, explanations, and exercises richly augmented by interesting suggestions for possible writing activities. Consistent instructional format, concise, well-delineated, easy-to-follow framework.

Confront, Construct, Complete: A Comprehensive Approach to Writing. Books 1 and 2 by Jack Easterling and Jack Pasanen. Hayden Book Co., Inc. This two-volume writing program views discovering and explaining relationships as the basis of sound thinking and writing. Through these relationships students discover content and the guidance they need for organizing and revising. Each book contains approximately one hundred exercises and assignments.

Developing Ideas by Paul O'Dea. Science Research Associates. Aimed primarily at grade nine. Sequential format provides opportunities for students to become actively involved in learning. Contains models, explanations, assignments, and evaluation devices. Incorporates twelve important composition principles on the paragraph.

The Five-Hundred-Word Theme by Lee J. Martin, revised by Harry P. Kroitor. Prentice-Hall, Inc. Complete, comprehensive chapters on paragraphs, putting the paper together, and maintaining unity and coherence. Outstanding in clarity.

Language Building by Jess G. Berman. J. Weston Walch, Publisher. Helpful incremental format beginning with parts of speech and then proceeding to sentence structure, to writing paragraphs, to writing compositions, to proofreading and ending with writing stories. Information on types of paragraphs—informative, instructional, expository, didactic, descriptive, and subjective. Visually attractive, clear and direct. Suitable for slower and average students.

Paragraph Writing by Frank Chaplen. Oxford University Press. An excitingly concise and illustrative text on paragraph writing. Complete with model paragraphs, informative instructional notes, and tips on how to compose a good paragraph. Excellent exercises, explanations, assignments, notes, and diagrams. Contains substantial sections on "The Controlling Idea and Its Development" along with information on selectivity, scope, content, and emphasis. Appropriate for average and advanced students.

Planned Paragraphs by J. Rowe Webster. Educators Publishing Service, Inc. Contains numerous examples of effective well-written paragraphs and provides fundamental principles and suggested steps toward putting them into practice. Helpful to students in grades seven to twelve.

Steps to Better Writing by Gene Stanford. Holt, Rinehart & Winston. A self-teaching, self-checking workbook similar to but more basic than *Better Writing*. Contains all the instructions and explanations that students require and allows them to check their own work against an answer key. Breaks down basic writing skills into small, logical steps: the student practices each step before moving on to the next. Especially suitable for grades seven through ten or for slower and average students in upper grades.

Twenty Steps to Better Composition: How to Write Clear and Readable Themes, Reports, Letters, and Stories by the staff of *READ* magazine. Xerox Educational Publications. A short, informative guide with brief, condensed explanations and practice exercises. Workbook format. Especially useful for average or slow students.

The Writer's Handbook by John B. Karls and Ronald Szymanski. Laidlaw Brothers. A comprehensive writer's guide with sections on paragraphing and paragraph structures and types: introductory, developmental, transitional, and concluding. Succinct definitions and effective explanations. Practice section included. Primarily for better students.

Writing Sentences and Paragraphs by Bernard R. Tanner and Craig Vittetoe. Addison Wesley Publishing Company. Contains a section on paragraphs and paragraph structures. Clear and precise explanations and good learning activities.

4

Teaching Students to Write Expository Essays

This chapter focuses on the skills needed for writing the kind of composition most frequently assigned in high schools—the multiparagraph essay of opinion. The activities in this chapter follow logically those of the preceding chapter on paragraph writing. In fact, it is assumed that the student has mastered paragraphs before beginning work on essays.

The process of writing an essay should be a fairly orderly one, with the student consciously undertaking each step, rather than simply putting ideas down on paper as they occur. First of all, assuming that students have freedom to choose their own topics, they should choose something to write about which they know well. They then must settle on a thesis (an idea *about* the subject) and restrict it to manageable size. Next, students must organize the paper in a way that is logically consistent with its thesis. They then write the paragraphs for the paper, using transitional devices to help readers find their way through the essay and giving special attention to the introductory and concluding paragraphs.

The activities in this chapter are arranged in a sequence parallel to the steps writers must take in planning and writing the essay. Some parts of the sequence—or some individual activities—are likely to be too difficult for less mature or less able students and can be omitted at the teacher's discretion. In general, however, following the activities sequentially will provide most students with thorough instruction in expository writing.

OBJECTIVES

As a result of the learning experiences in this chapter, students should be able to:

1. List at least ten topics that are appropriate for a paper of five to ten paragraphs and that they know thoroughly enough to write about.
2. Restrict a subject to a size appropriate for the length of paper to be written.
3. Explain the difference between a subject and an idea about a subject.

4. Compose a thesis statement that is limited, precise, and unified.

5. Analyze a thesis into its parts.

6. Organize an essay in a way that derives logically from the thesis.

7. Supply transitional devices as needed to make the organization of the essay apparent and improve its coherence.

8. Write an introduction of the anecdotal type, the outline type, and the funnel type.

9. Write at least two kinds of concluding paragraphs.

10. Describe, step-by-step, how one goes about writing an essay.

11. Write an effective essay of at least five paragraphs.

LEARNING EXPERIENCES

Topic I: Choosing a Subject

1. *Activity.* Divide the class into small groups of no more than five students each. Challenge each group to make a list of things they know about and could write about. Here are some topics to get the groups started:

early memories of home	teachers one can learn from
starting to school	teachers one can't learn from
grade school	having to take subjects I don't like
junior high	getting into trouble
senior high	discipline
problems of school	family
pleasures of school	

   Suggest that the groups attempt to generate as long a list as possible without commenting on or evaluating one another's contributions. After fifteen or twenty minutes, reconvene the entire class and have groups share their lists. Instruct one student to write the lists down as they are read or have the groups submit their lists to you so that you can reproduce them and give a copy to each student. Instruct students to keep the list in their notebooks or in a folder in the classroom to be referred to later.

2. *Activity.* Divide the class into small groups of three to five students each. Give all groups a subject (such as "problems of school") from the list generated in Activity 1. Challenge the groups to list *everything* they know about this subject. After ten or fifteen minutes (or longer), reconvene the total class and see which group has the most items on its list. Continue to brainstorm in the total class for even more items on the same topic. Reproduce the total list of items, as you did above, and distribute it to students to keep for use in a later activity.

Here is a sample list, using "problems of school" as the topic:

Having to take required courses

Not being allowed to choose preferred teachers

Too much homework

Absence of places to be alone

Difficulty of making friends

Time schedule too tight—no free times

Behavior at assemblies

Vandalism

Overcrowded library

No facility for student smoking

Inadequate parking

Unfair grading by many teachers

Thefts from gym lockers

Conflict between "jocks" and "freaks"

Poor food in the cafeteria

Only seniors being able to have one pass-fail course

Closed campus

Difficulty in getting permission for independent study

All teachers giving tests at midterm or term end

Too much emphasis on grades

Too much emphasis on college prep only

Failure to provide career advice or training

Discriminatory enforcement of rules

Refusal to encourage student participation in curriculum planning

Student behavior and sloppiness in cafeteria

Inadequacy of homeroom system

Topic II: Restricting the Subject

1. *Activity.* Point out to students that this long list of subtopics indicates that there is a lot they can "say" about the subject. Suggest that they discuss for a few moments how they would go about writing an essay on all this material. They may conclude that it is simply too much for one paper.

    Then ask the students what problems they would have if you assigned them to write one paragraph on the subject. They will realize, one hopes, that there is far too much for one paragraph. Therefore, suggest that they fine one piece of information in their list that might be suitable for one paragraph. Have them compose a sample topic sentence or two and quickly brainstorm how that topic sentence might be developed.

Next, have the group find a larger "piece" of the material they have listed that could be developed into a three-paragraph essay.

2. *Teacher Presentation.* Use the diagram on Reproduction Page 46 to explain how a large (very abstract) subject can be broken down into a small (less abstract) subject by becoming increasingly specific. For example, you might label the largest square "books" and the next smaller square in the lower left corner "children's books," pointing out that you've chosen one aspect of the large topic and thus have become more specific. Then label the next smaller square with an even more specific subject, such as "heroes and heroines in children's books." Finally, label the smallest square with a still more specific subject, such as "values transmitted through the example set by heroes and heroines in children's books."

Give students another example of how a large subject can become ever more specific: cars–Fords–old Fords–1927 Ford–engine of 1927 Ford–ignition system of 1927 Ford. (You may have to draw still smaller squares to accommodate the most specific subjects.)

Then suggest a very general topic—such as education—and have students suggest how it can be cut down in size by becoming progressively more specific. Label the squares in the diagram with their contributions.

3. *Activity.* Give students, individually or in small groups, several large subjects (cars, education, pets, family, etc.) and tell them to change each to a small subject suitable for a short essay.

4. *Activity.* Challenge students to reduce the ideas on Reproduction Page 47 to the scope desirable for a paper with only three or four developed paragraphs. You might wish to have students work in two or threes and then come together to share their answers with the total class. Possible restricted ideas for each of the general ideas are given in Appendix B.

5. *Activity.* Give students Reproduction Page 48 with its list of ideas that are limited enough to be the topic sentence of a paragraph. Challenge them (perhaps working in twos or threes) to enlarge them to ideas big enough for a five- or ten-paragraph paper. Possible enlargements are given in Appendix B.

6. *Activity.* Give students the ideas on Reproduction Page 49 and have them indicate what size composition it would take to develop each: (a) a library, (b) a shelf of books, (c) a book, (d) a chapter, (e) a five-to-ten paragraph essay, (f) a three-paragraph essay, (g) one paragraph. (Answers are given in Appendix B.)

Topic III: Turning a Subject into a Thesis

1. *Teacher Presentation.* Point out to students that even though a subject has been cut down to a manageable size (that is, reduced in abstractness), it is still not suitable for an essay until the writer takes a stand with relation to the subject. For example, the general subject of cars could be reduced in size as follows: cars–old cars–old cars

on major highways with high speed traffic-accidents caused by old cars. But then the writer must take one more step and convert the subject into an idea *about* the subject. For example: Cars older than fifteen years should not be allowed on express highways with high speed limits. This statement of the writer's point of view toward the subject can be called a *thesis sentence* or simply a *thesis*.

To clarify the difference between a subject and a thesis, use Reproduction Page 50 to make a transparency for an overhead projector. Explain to students (if you did not use Reproduction page 46) that the largest square represents a large subject. Label the large square with some very general subject, such as "education." Then point out that the next smaller square represents a somewhat restricted subject related to the general subject, for example, "high schools." Write "high schools" in the square labeled "somewhat restricted subject." Then point out that the next smaller square represents even smaller subjects related to high schools, perhaps your own high school. Write the name of your school in the square labeled "even smaller subject." Then point out the smallest square is a very restricted topic, such as "this composition class," which is a small part of the larger topics. Label the smallest square accordingly.

Then explain that the next step for the writer after he or she has reduced the subject in size is to take a stand in relation to that small subject. Write a thesis such as "People who don't learn to write are handicapped in their future lives."

Give the class another example of how the writer must take a stand in relation to the subject after cutting it down to size. Again label the squares with increasingly specific topics, such as dogs–little dogs–dachshunds–pet dachshunds–children's pet dachshunds. Then label the arrow with a statement that shows the writer's point of view on the small subject. For example, "Dachshunds make playful pets for active little boys who like to wrestle."

Point out that the thesis should have the following characteristics:

a. It should be expressed as a declarative sentence, not as a question or merely a word or phrase.

b. It should not be simply a self-evident fact ("Many Americans enjoy apple pie"), but should be at least somewhat arguable ("Apple pie is America's favorite dessert").

c. It should not be simply a statement of personal preference ("I like apple pie") but should be a statement of the writer's opinion on an issue that includes more people than just the writer ("Americans should eat more apple pie in order to stay healthy").

2. *Activity.* Give the class a general subject from the list below and have them first reduce it in size (perhaps by drawing successively smaller squares as you did in Teacher Presentation 1) and then compose a thesis indicating a point of view toward the smallest subject. Or divide the class into two groups, one to reduce the subject in size, the other to compose the idea about the restricted subject. Use these general subjects:

education	music	motorcycles
politics	cars	varsity sports
canoeing	camping	religion

food	dating	dieting
fashion	gardening	health
war	hair	travel
aviation	poverty	law and order
human relations	free enterprise	communications
art	vacations	city life

3. *Activity.* Have students individually choose a large abstract term from the following list and reduce it to a thesis by cutting its size and then indicating a point of view toward the smallest subject. Have them write down each step in this progression, in the manner shown:

Abstract term: education

Steps in reducing the subject in size:

    secondary education

    my high school

    my sophomore year

    my sophomore math class

    sophomore math was a waste to me

    the teacher was always hurrying so we could finish the book

Thesis: The teacher of beginning math should allow the student time for full comprehension rather than be concerned with finishing the book.

Then allow students to share and compare their steps and their resulting thesis sentences. They will probably be surprised at the similarities of their thought processes in some cases and the difference in others. Have students save the results of this activity in their folders for later reference. Use one or more of the following terms:

loyalty	hope	death
love	courage	goodness
justice	hatred	faith
maturity	prejudice	security
peace	friendship	pain
loneliness	happiness	fear

4. *Activity.* Give students Reproduction Page 51, which lists subjects that have already been restricted in size and have them compose a thesis sentence based on each. Then have them share their results with the total class. It will be interesting to see the similarities or differences in the final statements arrived at by the different students. Or, if you prefer, have students work in small groups and arrive at thesis sentences cooperatively. Make sure students save the results of this activity for use in a later activity.

5. *Activity.* Working with the total class, take an abstract term, write it on the board, and have the class take the steps necessary to turn it into a usable thesis statement. See how many times and in how many directions they can do this for the same term, arriving each time at a thesis sentence suitable for a paper with three or four developed paragraphs. Let the students choose the beginning abstraction or general subject area or give it to them from this list: politics, sports, dating, parent/child relationships, growing up, love. Have students save the results of this activity.

6. *Activity.* Divide the class into small groups of three to five persons each. Give each group this list of general subjects:

apples	being sick	friends
telephoning	getting up early	television
movies	going steady	being popular
drag racing	teachers	swimming
backpacking	parents	seafood
New York City	good grades	tourists

Ask each group to come up with two ideas (thesis statements) about each subject or some aspect of each subject. Supervise the work of the groups closely to be sure they have learned the difference between a thesis and a personal expression of like or dislike. Save the lists of ideas for use in Activity 7.

7. *Activity.* With the lists generated in Activity 6, have each group decide which of the two theses about each subject is "bigger" and thus would require the longer essay to develop it in detail. Or have students determine the length required of each essay in order to cover the idea completely.

8. *Activity.* Explain to students that an easy way to arrive at a thesis about a subject is to relate it to another subject. For example, the subject "loving families" can be related to the second subject "crime" to produce the thesis, "A loving family is a major preventive to crime." Give students Reproduction Page 52 and have them name the second subject that has been related to the first subject to produce the thesis. (Answers are found in Appendix B.)

9. *Activity.* Give students, working in twos or threes or individually, the pairs of subjects found on Reproduction Page 53 and ask them to construct a thesis for each that relates the two subjects. (Sample answers are found in Appendix B.)

10. *Activity.* Reproduce Reproduction Page 54 to give students a list of thesis sentences composed by joining two subjects. Have them identify the two subjects that have been joined, by drawing a line under each. (Answers are found in Appendix B.)

11. *Teacher Presentation.* Explain to students that a thesis sentence should be checked to make sure it is *limited.* That is, a good thesis covers only what the writer intends to discuss in the essay. The writer should examine the thesis sentence carefully and qualify any statements that are too sweeping to be supported. For example, the thesis sentence "Missouri is a great vacation state" is probably too sweeping for most essays (although it might make an excellent headline for a travel promotion leaflet). The writer of this thesis should ask questions such as: all of Missouri? for everyone?

all kinds of vacations? and all the time? After asking such questions, the writer might arrive at a better thesis: "The Ozark country in southern Missouri is an excellent summer vacation spot for those hardy souls who enjoy hot weather, camping, canoeing, and hiking."

Give students another example of a fairly sweeping thesis sentence, such as "Dogs are wonderful pets," and help them ask the necessary questions to limit and qualify the statement: all dogs? for all people? in all ways? Then have students formulate a more qualified thesis as a result of answering these questions. One such sentence would be: "The poodle makes a companionable pet for an elderly person living in a small apartment." You may want to note that vague, general, or ambiguous phrases are frequently used in political speeches or songs where the goal is to stir the emotions without engaging the mind, but they are not appropriate in expository writing.

12. *Activity.* Give students the list of sweeping thesis statements on Reproduction Page 55. Have them limit and qualify them by asking questions such as: all? everyone? always? everywhere? and all kinds? (Possible answers are given in Appendix B.)

13. *Teacher Presentation.* Explain to students that they should check a thesis sentence to make sure it is precisely worded. They should be sure that every word in the thesis can be interpreted only in the way it is meant by the writer. For example, "St. Louis is an exciting town for sports lovers" is a precise thesis only if the writer intends to deal with both excitement of spectator sports in St. Louis and excitement of participation in sports in St. Louis. If the writer intends to deal with only the excitement of spectator sports, the phrase "sports lovers" should be replaced with the more precise term "fans." Students should see that precise wording is simply one more way of limiting the thesis until it is an *exact* expression of what the writer intends to cover in his or her paper.

14. *Activity.* Give students the list of imprecise, and hence misleading, thesis sentences on Reproduction Page 56. Ask them, working as a total class, in small groups, or individually, to identify the weak spots (words that could be taken more than one way or unqualified terms about which they have questions) and then to rewrite each sentence to make it more precise. (Sample answers are found in Appendix B.)

15. *Teacher Presentation.* Explain to students that an essay should deal with only one overall idea. If a thesis sentence contains two or more ideas, the writer has several options:

   a. Sever the two ideas and write two papers.

   b. Combine the two ideas through pointing out a causal relationship, making a comparison, contrasting them, subordinating one to the other, or otherwise making the two ideas into one.

   c. Subordinate both of the ideas to a larger thesis that is general enough to include both ideas.

   For example, the thesis "Tennis began as a rich man's game and also has caused the rise of a profitable industry" can be handled by:

   a. *Severing:* One paper on "Tennis began...." and another on "Tennis has caused the rise of...."

b. *Combining:* "Tennis has come a long way from a rich man's pastime to a game so popular that it forms the foundation of a million dollar industry."

As another example, the thesis "Dogs are man's best friends, and cats are good friends, too" can be handled by:

a. *Severing:* One paper on "A dog is man's best friend" and another on "Cats are good friends to their owners."

b. *Subordinating one part to the other:* "Contrary to the old saying about dogs, cat lovers insist that it is actually the cat who is a person's best friend."

c. *Contrasting:* "Dogs may stay with you to the bitter end, but cats keep you on your toes."

d. *Comparing:* "The much maligned cat has many of the same arts of friendship that make the dog so popular as a pet."

e. *Subordinating both to a larger generalization:* "There are only two animals who have developed sufficient adaptability to human beings' urban life style to be safely and conveniently kept as house pets." Or "The pet industry of America is dominated by two animals, the dog and the cat." Or "The slang of America would be much poorer if it were not for cats and dogs."

16. *Activity.* Provide the class—working as a total group, in pairs, in small groups, or individually—with the list of both unified and ununified thesis sentences on Reproduction Page 57. Have students identify the unified ones and correct the ununified ones by severing them, unifying them by finding a relationship between the various parts, or by subordinating both parts to a higher generalization large enough to include them both. (Sample answers are given in Appendix B.)

17. *Activity.* Have students bring to class three or more thesis sentences that they have made either unified or ununified. (They might wish to base their work on thesis sentences constructed for previous activities and filed away for future use.) Have students, one at a time, put the sentences on the board so the class can approve or correct them. Or, if you prefer, students could work in pairs, exchanging papers, signing their names on their own thesis statements and on their corrections or acceptances of their partner's statements. These would then be handed in for grading.

18. *Teacher Presentation.* Summarize for students the characteristics of a good thesis sentence:

a. It is a general statement with which there can be disagreement. In other words, it is not a simple statement of fact that needs no support, nor a personal observation with which no one can disagree, nor a statement of truth so self-evident that there is really no reason even to say it.

b. It is restricted. That is, it is cut down in size to fit the scope of the assignment. Remember that the task of the writer is to develop in detail. If the subject is large and the assignment asks for only three paragraphs, it will be impossible to cover the subject in complete detail.

c. It reflects the author's point of view. The author takes a stand in relationship to the subject rather than just planning to write about it in general.

d. It is unified. It introduces one and only one idea.

e. It is precise. It is stated in words that can be interpreted in only one way.

19. *Activity.* Give students the list of thesis sentences on Reproduction Page 58 and have them determine whether they meet the criteria for a good thesis. (Answers are found in Appendix B.)

20. *Activity.* Have students revise each of the thesis sentences from Activity 19 that they considered to violate the criteria of a good thesis sentence.

21. *Evaluation.* Many of the previous activities could be submitted for grading, if you wish. However, since many of them may be assigned as homework or may be completed by students working in small groups, a more carefully controlled measure of the individual student's ability to construct an effective thesis sentence may be desirable. To assess students' ability to construct an effective thesis sentence, write on the board a list of general subjects, such as parents, hobbies, personal qualities, and good citizenship, and give the following instructions:

> Imagine that you have been assigned to write an essay of approximately five paragraphs on one of these topics. Choose a topic, and construct a thesis sentence for that essay, applying everything we have discussed about what makes an effective thesis sentence. You will have no more than twenty minutes to write and turn in your thesis sentence.

Apply the following criteria when grading:

a. Has the student chosen a topic for an essay about which he or she has sufficient knowledge?

b. Is the thesis sentence a complete declarative sentence and not a phrase or question?

c. Is the thesis sentence limited enough in scope to be developed in detail in an essay of approximately five paragraphs?

d. Is the thesis sentence broad enough in scope to require an essay to develop, or is it merely a good topic sentence for a single paragraph?

e. Does the thesis sentence indicate that the writer has taken a stand in relation to the subject? That is, is it at least somewhat arguable? Or has the writer simply stated a fact, a self-evident truth, or a personal preference?

f. Is the thesis sentence unified? That is, does it introduce only one subject?

g. Is the thesis sentence precise? That is, does it contain no words that can be interpreted in more than one way?

Topic IV: Organizing the Paper

1. *Teacher Presentation.* Explain to the class that after they have formulated a proper thesis sentence, the next step is to plan how they are going to explain, support, amplify, and develop that thesis. To do so, writers must ask themselves, "What are the parts that I must develop to cover my thesis entirely?" The thesis statement

itself will determine the proper technique of division. Sometimes a thesis sentence clearly reveals its parts, for example, when it asserts that there are many *causes* of something or many *ways* to do something or many *results* or a number of *great women*. One knows at once what will be the parts of each of these thesis sentences.

Not so simple are statements of ideas dealing with concepts or extrapolations rather than facts. For instance, a thesis statement such as, "If humanity is to survive, we must develop techniques or institutions for the purpose of effecting anticipatory change, a task for which we have shown little or no capacity in the past," must be carefully examined to identify the parts that must be covered in an essay. A little study makes clear that here is a recommendation based on an observation of humankind's past history and an evaluation of our present situation. The parts include: (1) How human beings have failed to achieve change in the past before great catastrophes forced them to do so, (2) a look at present circumstances that will no longer permit such behavior if humanity is to survive, and (3) suggestions for ways of developing the means for anticipatory change. Following is a simpler example of such a thesis statement and its parts, which might be useful for less advanced students: "The student who wishes to improve a weak academic record must eliminate the poor study habits that hamper achievement." The parts include: (1) a description of the weak academic record, (2) analysis of the poor study habits that cause poor grades, and (3) recommendations for changes.

2. *Activity.* Put on the board as many of the following thesis statements as you believe suitable for the level of your class. Help students see the parts into which each one must be divided if a complete essay is to be written.

   a. The Civil War had many causes besides the move to free the slaves.

   Parts: causes—probably categorized as economic, social, and political.

   b. Uninterested high school students might devote themselves more seriously to their school work if they were allowed to participate more in planning their own courses of study.

   Parts: 1) facts and statistics indicating the problem of uninterested students.

   2) evaluation of why students are uninterested.

   3) recommendation of how to re-interest them.

   4) prediction of favorable results.

   c. The dachshund is a better apartment pet than the collie.

   Parts: lists of qualities making up the difference, such as size, kind of hair, and living habits.

   d. It is a wise parent who knows how much freedom to grant an adolescent offspring.

   Parts: 1) pitfalls of giving too little freedom.

   2) pitfalls of giving too much freedom.

   3) wisdom of falling in between—giving enough freedom to show trust and develop maturity but not enough to convey neglect and encourage dangerous or unacceptable behavior.

e. There are many techniques for. . . .

   Parts: different techniques.

f. There are many reasons why the birth rate declines in an industrial society.

   Parts: reasons.

g. Complete and honest communication among all members of a family is essential if they are to have a happy life together.

   Parts:
   1) description of unhappy status of family when communication is poor.
   2) description of happy status of family when communication is good.
   3) suggestions for improving communication in order to achieve happier family relationships.

h. One sure way to win friends is to become a person people are comfortable around.

   Parts:
   1) why we feel uncomfortable with some people and try to avoid them.
   2) why we feel comfortable with others and seek their company.
   3) how to make people feel comfortable so they will seek us.

i. A smoking lounge should have been provided at the high school several years ago.

   Parts:
   1) present situation concerning the smoking lounge.
   2) occurrences and situations of the past years that could have been avoided.

3. *Activity.* Ask students, one by one, to put on the board thesis sentences they have written (perhaps those from a previous activity that they have saved in their folders) and see if class members can divide each into the proper parts for a complete essay.

4. *Evaluation.* To test students' understanding of this important skill (or to give them further practice), give them the list of thesis statements on Reproduction Page 59 and see if they can successfully divide the sentences into the parts that must be covered if a complete essay is to be written. Point out that they need not know anything about the subject matter being introduced to identify the parts of each thesis. (Sample answers are included in Appendix B.)

5. *Teacher Presentation.* Explain to the class that once the writer has determined the parts of a thesis, the next step is to arrange those parts in the best order. The writer attempts to arrange the parts in an order that will be logical to the reader while fulfilling the purpose of the author. Thus, the best internal organization of each essay will depend on the nature of the thesis. For example:

   a. If the thesis indicates parts such as examples of ways or methods, reasons, causes, results, or arguments, then the author's task is to arrange these parts in a climactic order, that is, from least to greatest in terms of length, interest, significance, complexity or persuasiveness. Thus, the writer builds the reader's response throughout the essay to a climax at the end.

b. If the thesis is one in which the parts are not explicitly identified but are implied by the meaning of the statement, a general rule might be to move in the order of:

1) facts

2) evaluation or opinion

3) suggestion or recommendation

Thus, one builds support on a foundation of fact and prepares the reader for agreement. A good example is the thesis sentence about uninterested students that was introduced in Activity 2.

c. If the thesis is one indicating that a contrast is to be developed, the author should determine the common elements of the subjects that are to be contrasted and arrange them in an appropriate climactic order. Example: "Most high school seniors look back at themselves as ninth graders and are amazed at the changes in themselves." Parts arranged in order of increasing importance: (1) physical, (2) social, (3) values and interests, (4) intellectual, (5) self-concept.

d. If the thesis is highly argumentative, the author should be prepared to identify the contrary arguments and dispose of them adequately by developing his or her own arguments. Otherwise, the author may well leave readers unconvinced, with unanswered questions and unrefuted arguments. Two ways to organize such a paper are:

1) Identify the major opposing arguments in at most two paragraphs at the beginning of the essay and devote the remaining, major portion of the essay to developing your own arguments that refute all of these.

2) Identify each contrary argument and develop your own argument opposing it in separate paragraphs throughout the essay, as in a debate. Sample paragraph: "While there are reasonable people who assert that . . . it is my contention that they overlook a major flaw in this view. . . ."

If the author will keep the reader in mind at all times, as well as his or her own exact purpose in approaching the reader, it should not be too difficult to put the parts of an essay in an order which will satisfy both writer and reader.

6. *Activity.* Provide students with the list of thesis sentences and their parts on Reproduction Page 60 and have them, working in groups of three or four, determine what they consider to be the most climactic order. You may, of course, prefer to have students work individually so you may more surely ascertain the grasp of each student. The ranking of these parts will vary from person to person of course, since judgments will be based on individual values. One possible set of answers is given in Appendix B.

7. *Activity.* Put students into groups of three to five or work with the total class in one group. Ask each student to prepare a thesis sentence that explicitly indicates its parts. For example: "Being an only child has its advantages" or "To be a successful baseball player, one must master at least four different skills." Students may wish to utilize a thesis they constructed for a previous activity. Then ask the students to list four to six parts for their thesis statements on their papers in random

order as in Activity 6. Finally, have students exchange papers and arrange the list of parts in an order that agrees with what each author intended. If you have an opaque projector, you could project each thesis and its parts and let the entire class choose the best order.

8. *Activity.* Distribute to students the list of thesis sentences with parts that are *not* explicitly identified on Reproduction Page 61. Do one or two as examples on the board for the benefit of the whole class and then let students work at dividing the statements into their logical parts and listing them in proper order. They may work individually or in pairs, as you prefer. Then let the entire class go over the list together to check each student's understanding.

9. *Evaluation.* Repeat the procedure in Activity 8, but use the list of thesis sentences on Reproduction Page 62. Have students work individually.

Topic V: Providing Transitions

1. *Teacher Presentation.* Explain to the students that it is the author's task to provide as much assistance as possible to the reader working his or her way through an essay. The author must ensure that the reader does not get lost among the developmental details and fail to follow the idea sequence. That is, the author must strive to keep the reader informed about the organization of the paper. Perhaps the best way to keep the reader on the right path (aside from simple clarity and directness of language) is to provide "sign posts" wherever they might be helpful, much as the highway planner puts signs wherever there is a chance a driver might miss an important turn or overlook an intersection.

These signposts may take the form of deliberate transition sentences or even entire paragraphs at those points in the essay where the writer is concluding one section of the essay and moving to the next.

Such transitions may also be as simple as the addition of one word, such as the summing-up word "then" or the moving-on word "next." Or they may be an entire paragraph summing up the previous section and introducing the next. Whatever their form and length, these signposts should point the reader to the next part of the author's idea-structure and ensure the reader's easier comprehension of the essay.

One much used technique of achieving easy transitions through the structural framework of the essay is the use of leading questions. In the first part of her article "Let Us Speak to One Another," Ardis Whitman specifies at length the importance of communication in our lives. Reaching the second part of her essay, she asks, "Why, then, if communication is so important in our lives, are we unable to . . . ?" and after discussing barriers which keep us from freely communicating, she goes on to ask, "But is there nothing we can do to improve the quality of our . . . ?" Then she discusses possible ways to improve communication.

A list of possible wordings for transitions appears on Reproduction Page 63. You might want to duplicate and distribute this list to students for their study and use, put it on the board, or project it with the overhead projector and ask the class to discuss each example and take notes.

2. *Activity.* Have each student make up transition sentences and paragraphs like those on Reproduction Page 63 and share them with the class. Let the other students guess the place in an essay where the transition would be suitable.

3. *Activity.* Have students look in books and magazines that they have read recently or are reading now and identify transitional devices the author has used to ease the reader's passage through an idea-structure. Suggest that students choose expository prose for this assignment, since the transitions are likely to be more apparent here than in fiction. Have students bring their examples to class and explain them to one another. You might be wise to have some suitable material on hand in case students come unprepared.

4. *Evaluation.* To test students' ability to provide necessary transitions between the parts of an essay, administer the two-part test on Reproduction Page 64. (Answers are given in Appendix B.)

Topic VI: Constructing Introductions and Conclusions

1. *Teacher Presentation.* Explain to students that an introductory paragraph, like a transitional paragraph, is a *functional* paragraph and not a *developed* paragraph, which presents a topic sentence and develops it in detail. The introductory paragraph has the special function of introducing the reader to the central idea of the essay.

    Generally speaking, the length of an essay determines the length of the introduction. A thesis sentence that can be supported with only three or four developed paragraphs requires only a single introductory paragraph. However, an essay with six or eight major supporting points, each of which is explained in one or more paragraphs, may require two or even three paragraphs to introduce the thesis adequately.

    In any case, the introduction should contain the thesis sentence in some form. Thus, the reader knows at the very outset of the essay what point the writer is trying to make and is not kept in the dark as to the writer's purpose. On the other hand, the writer can be somewhat subtle in introducing the thesis and should avoid at all costs such awkward statements as, "In this essay I shall attempt to show that...." or "My thesis is that...."

    Reproduction Page 65 describes four common types of introductions and gives a sample of each. You may wish to duplicate this sheet and distribute it to students.

2. *Activity.* Give students Reproduction Page 66 and have them determine which methods were used for constructing the seven introductory paragraphs—anecdotal, contrast, funnel, or outline. (Answers can be found in Appendix B.)

3. *Activity.* Give students the pairs of sentences on Reproduction Page 67. In each pair, one sentence is a large generalization and the other is a thesis statement related to it. Have students connect the two into a properly constructed funnel introduction by supplying the intervening sentences. In small groups students might trace the steps needed to narrow the generalization down to the specificity of the thesis statement. Then each student can write his or her own version, and the papers can be compared for fluency and completeness.

4. *Activity.* Give students the funnel introductions on Reproduction Page 68, all of which contain flaws, and ask them to test the paragraphs for coherence (too big gaps in thought between the sentences) and consistent direction from the opening generalization to the thesis sentence. Also ask them to comment on the suitability of the opening generalization in terms of its actual relationship to the thesis: did the writer jump too far, and did he or she jump in an unnatural or unwarranted direction? (Sample answers are given in Appendix B.)

5. *Activity.* Give students the thesis statements on Reproduction Page 69 and have them construct anecdotal introductions leading to them. Caution students not to think of the thesis as a topic sentence and attempt to develop it with a narrative. Instead, they should narrate an incident that leads to the thesis; thus, the thesis sentence should usually be the last sentence, not the first, in their introductions.

6. *Activity.* Give students the outline for a rather complex essay on Reproduction Page 70 and have them construct an outline introduction for it. This assignment could be done as homework, with the students bringing their outline introductions to class to share with others. It may be interesting to them to see how similar and how different they are.

7. *Activity.* Give students the list of thesis sentences on Reproduction Page 71 and have them construct contrast introductions for each. (The assumptions that these statements contradict are found in Appendix B.)

8. *Activity.* Have students choose one of the thesis sentences they developed in previous activities or give them a list of thesis sentences from which to choose. Have them write an introduction for one thesis, using any method they wish. Then have students read their introductions to the class, and let the rest of the class determine which type of introduction the writer constructed. Have the writer justify the type of introduction chosen.

9. *Evaluation.* To test students' abilities to construct an effective introduction, have them choose one of the thesis statements on Reproduction Page 72 and write an introduction for it. After grading the introductions, return them to the students and have all students who wrote an introduction for the same thesis sentence move their desks into a circle, read their paragraphs to the group, and discuss similarities and differences in their approaches.

10. *Teacher Presentation.* Explain to students that the concluding paragraph, like the introductory paragraph, is a *functional* paragraph, not a *developed* one. That is, it does not present a topic sentence and develop it with details. The conclusion gives the essay a neat, rather than an abrupt, closing, so that the reader is not left hanging after the last supporting point has been made. Students often find conclusions difficult to write. The suggestions and sample conclusions on Reproduction Page 73 should be helpful to students.

11. *Activity.* Have students look at essays in their favorite newspapers and magazines and identify the ways the authors introduce their central ideas and the ways they conclude their essays.

12. *Activity.* Have students write a conclusion for an essay based on the thesis sentence they used for Activity 8 or Activity 9.

13 *Activity.* Distribute to each student a copy of an essay from which the conclusion has been omitted. Have students read it carefully and write a conclusion for it. Then show them the original conclusion and let them discuss how theirs differ from it.

Topic VII: Writing the Complete Essay

1. *Teacher Presentation.* Make a transparency of the essay on Reproduction Page 74 and project it with the overhead projector.
    Discuss each part of the essay, using the following questions.

    a. Which paragraph or paragraphs contain the introduction? What type of introduction is it?

    b. What is the thesis statement of the essay?

    c. Into what parts has the thesis been divided?

    d. What sentences, words, or phrases in the essay serve as transitions?

    e. Find the conclusion and tell what kind it is.

2. *Teacher Presentation.* Point out to students that so far they have concentrated on learning the various individual skills needed for writing a good essay. They are now ready to write an entire essay from beginning to end. Suggest that they help you list on the board the steps a writer should go through in writing an essay. Elicit answers from the total class. The result should be something like those on Reproduction Page 75.

3. *Activity.* Give the students a short list of general subjects—such as loneliness, space exploration, smoking, TV violence, and good teachers (or see the list in Activity 4 below). Instruct them to write an essay on some aspect of one of these subjects. For average students, you may wish to distribute the checklist on Reproduction Page 75 and suggest that students check off each step as they finish it. More advanced students may not need the checklist if they were attentive during the teacher presentation. This assignment can be done as homework, with students working entirely on their own. On the other hand, there is undoubtedly value in having students work together in class by pairing up and exchanging papers after completing each step so that they can get feedback from one another. Having students work together in this fashion is particularly valuable when they are just beginning to write complete essays.

4. *Activity.* Give the students the following list of general subjects to choose from and have them write an essay of at least five paragraphs. When the essays are finished, divide the class into groups of four or five students each. Have the members of each small group exchange papers until all members of each group have read the papers of all other group members. Instruct the small groups to make suggestions to improve the papers they have read and to make every paper from their group as good as possible. After all students have made suggestions, have the authors of the papers revise them and turn them in for grading.

vacations	required courses	religion
homework	popularity	pornography
summer jobs	human relations	censorship
public health	losing weight	self-discipline
self-reliance	advertising	propaganda
tropical fish	horsemanship	drag racing
honesty	communal life	country living
pollution	scenic rivers	white water
sky diving	public transporation	bigotry
float trips	backpacking	motorcycles

ASSESSING ACHIEVEMENT OF OBJECTIVES

On-Going Evaluation

The extent to which students have mastered the individual skills covered under each topic above can be measured by the procedures headed "Evaluation" in each section. Almost any of the Activities suggested in each section can also be submitted for grading.

Final Evaluation

For an overall evaluation of students' abilities to write an expository essay, assign a short essay to be written in class. List on the board several general subjects from which students can choose and instruct them to write an essay of four to six paragraphs. Require them to underline the thesis sentences in their essays before submitting them for grading. Grade the essays according to these criteria:

1. Has the writer chosen a topic he or she knows well?
2. Has the writer narrowed the subject adequately?
3. Does the thesis sentence indicate that the writer has taken a point of view in relation to the subject?
4. Is the thesis unified?
5. Is the thesis precise?
6. Is the essay logically organized?
7. Does the essay contain extraneous material that does not support or amplify the thesis?
8. Is the introduction effective?
9. Does each developed paragraph contain a topic sentence developed with specific details arranged in a logical order?
10. Does the essay have an effective conclusion?

RESOURCES FOR TEACHING THE EXPOSITORY ESSAY

Below is a selected list of resources useful for teaching the skills of expository writing. Addresses of publishers can be found in Appendix A.

Audio-Visual Materials

Composition Power by Educational Record Sales. Filmstrip House. Four color filmstrips and four cassettes entitled "Outline Power," "Opening," "The Meat of the Sandwich," and "Closing and Revising." The series emphasizes clear thinking as a prelude to good writing and stimulates students to emulate examples of good openings and endings.

Composition Starters: Argumentation and *Composition Starters: Exposition* by Bruce Reeves. Doubleday Multimedia. Two sets of four film loops (silent) and cards with questions and suggestions for writing. Students can choose from a number of possible assignments for each film loop. The loops are all taken from Walt Disney nature films and deal with topics such as "Lions Hunting Gnu," and "Hawk Attacking Rattlesnake."

How to Write an Effective Composition: Organizing and Writing an Essay by Morris Schreiber. Folkways Records. LP Record. Gives a concise summary of the steps in writing an essay, similar to those outlined in this chapter. Probably most useful for an individualized instruction program or small groups rather than the entire class.

Organizing an Outline, Writing an Opening Paragraph, Writing Paragraphs, Editing and Rewriting. Filmstrip House. This series of filmstrips, under the series title, Composition, is particularly suited to less capable students. Captions rather than recorded narration are used.

Organizing Your Writing. Encyclopedia Britannica Educational Corporation. A series of eight filmstrips with captions on the following topics: "The Five Steps in Writing a Composition," "Outlining a Written Composition," "The Main Parts of a Written Composition," "The Introduction of a Written Composition," "The Body of a Written Composition," "The Conclusion of a Written Composition," "The Patterns of Paragraphs," and "Making Transitions in Written Composition." Could be used for a presentation to the total class or for individualized instruction.

Steps to Better Writing. Thomas Klise Company. Series of five sound filmstrips (and records or cassettes) that present the essentials of composition in a clear, clever way. The five areas covered are as follows: "Writing Your Way to an Oscar" (establishes that writing must be approached as a systematic process), "Worrying Your Way to a Purpose" (clarifying subject, audience, purpose, role, and main point), "Planning Your Way to a Paper" (shows why and how to outline), "Writing Your Way to an End" (focuses on the first draft), and "Revising Your Way to an A" (discusses rewriting). Highly recommended.

The Techniques of Theme Writing. Eye-Gate. A series of four sound filmstrips (with two records or cassettes) that explore four aspects of expository writing: the beginning, the arrangement of paragraphs, the transitions between paragraphs, and the ending.

Writing a Good Theme. RMI Educational Films, Inc. Filmstrip with sound on record or cassette. Part One shows by examples how an essay is developed: the introduction, the body, and the conclusion. Part Two shows by examples the development of an essay in terms of unity and coherence.

Writing a Short Theme. Westwood Educational Productions. Sound filmstrip presenting a step-by-step procedure for organizing and writing a good essay. Establishes a number of criteria for evaluating a theme and shows by examples how to distinguish between good and bad themes.

Writing: From Assignment to Composition. Guidance Associates. Two sound filmstrips with records or cassettes. Part I, "Outlining the Composition," deals with selection and delineation of the topic, organizing an outline to suit content, achieving a logical flow of thought, and the major first-draft challenge of getting something down. Part II, "Rewriting the Composition," covers topic sentences and paragraph structure, sentence length and design, elimination of unnecessary thoughts and words, and means of achieving coherence, tone, unity. Discussion guide included.

Print Materials

The Art of Composition by Barbara Pannwitt. Silver Burdett Company. A brief introduction to basic aspects of expository writing. Packaged in a visually attractive, compact little paperback, it is one of a series of Contemporary English Modules with a single teacher's guide for all composition titles. Another title in the series, *The Persuasive Writer* by Deborah Stevens, is somewhat more substantial.

Better Writing: From Paragraph to Essay by Gene Stanford and Marie N. Smith. Holt, Rinehart & Winston. A self-teaching, self-correcting basic composition workbook that teaches paragraph and essay writing in small, incremental steps.

Composition: Models and Exercises, Heritage edition by John E. Warriner, Richard Ludwig, and Francis X. Connolly. Harcourt Brace Jovanovich. A series of five books covering roughly grades seven to twelve, but since they carry no grade-level designation, the teacher can be flexible in choosing the book appropriate for the needs of the class. Each book contains examples of professional writing, guided student analyses of the writing skills illustrated in these examples, and composition assignments applying these skills. Teacher's manual available for the series.

A Composition Practice Book by Zan L. Skelton, Jr. J. Weston Walch, Publisher. Provides, as the title suggests, opportunities for the student to write many compositions of various types, from paragraphs through the term paper. For most assignments space is provided in the book for the student to write responses, with the book serving as a convenient reference file of compositions and corrections. Suitable for average students from grade nine up.

Composition Skills. (Books 1–6.) Allan A. Glatthorn et al. Science Research Associates. A series of textbooks on composition that emphasize practical writing skills for all areas of life: school, work, and personal living. Numerous strands are developed through the series: the writing process, the elements of composition, the mode of discourse, and the revising process. Includes chapters on writing about literature, on argumentation and exposition, and on writing in various subjects of the curriculum.

Composition Workshop by Herbert M. Rothstein, Peter Beyer, and Frank Napolitano. Prentice-Hall, Inc. A series of small workbooks without grade-level designation so that they can be used for multilevel individualized learning programs. Includes explanations and activities dealing with words, sentences, paragraphs, and longer writing forms. Excellent for average students. Clearly delineates skills to be mastered and provides opportunity for practice. Students record their progress on a chart at the back of each workbook.

Designs for English by Martha Pomainville, Cynthia Blankenship, and Barbara Stanford. Designs for English. A student-centered composition, communication, and reading program. Students are guided to write paragraphs and essays on topics relevant to their concerns after their ideas have been stimulated by reading and discussion.

The Five-Hundred Word Theme by Lee J. Martin, revised by Harry P. Kroiter. Prentice-Hall, Inc. Intended for college freshmen but very appropriate for capable high school students. Takes much the same approach as the material in this chapter. Clear explanations, many examples, useful exercises, and activities. Useful as teacher resource if too difficult for students.

The Freshman Writer by Michele F. Cooper. Barnes and Noble. An excellent how-to-survive book that college-bound high school students may find useful. Includes sections on writing about literature, the term paper, and essay exams. Emphasis is on giving the reader the bare essentials rather than extensive practice. Useful as teacher resource if too difficult for students.

How to Write Themes and Term Papers by Barbara Lenmark Ellis. Barron's Educational Series, Inc. A survival guide, similar to *The Freshman Writer* but more appropriate for high school students. Contains only explanations, no exercises or assignments.

The Lively Art of Writing by Lucile Vaughan Payne. Follett Publishing Company. A superb basic composition text for high school students. Gives very little attention to paragraphs but treats all other aspects of expository writing thoroughly. May be somewhat difficult for slower students or those in grades below eleven.

Organization and Outlining by J. F. Pierce. Arco Publishing Company. Focuses chiefly on patterns of organization and the various types of outlines but also includes brief sections on other aspects of expository writing. Probably not useful as the only text in any composition course, but individual students could be referred to this book for extra explanation and practice.

A Short Guide to Writing Better Themes by Ann R. Morris. Everett/Edwards, Inc. Composed chiefly of college freshman essays that the student can use as models. Discussion questions call the student's attention to various aspects of each model; a writing assignment follows each. Suitable only for advanced students in upper grades. Useful also as teacher resource.

Steps: An Essay Writing Program on 3 Levels for English and Social Studies. Interact. Individualized program teaching techniques of essay writing on three levels for basic, intermediate, or advanced students. Students study a model and are led step-by-step through the writing process.

Steps to Better Writing by Gene Stanford. Holt, Rinehart & Winston. A self-teaching, self-checking workbook. Contains all the instructions and explanations that students require and allows them to check their own work against an answer key. Basic skills of writing are broken down into small, logical steps; the student practices each step before moving on to the next. Especially suitable for slower and average students.

Teaching Written English Today by W. K. Jones and A. J. Francis. J. Weston Walch, Publisher. A collection of teaching strategies useful for a variety of grade levels.

Twenty Steps to Better Composition by the staff of *READ* Magazine. Xerox Educational Publications. A real bargain, considering the low price and excellent contents. Covers all aspects of expository writing from word choice to paragraphs to essays. Workbook format lets students respond in the book itself to many assignments. Especially useful for average or slow students.

The Writer's Handbook by John B. Karls and Ronald Szymanski. Laidlaw Brothers. Opens with an extensive glossary of terms and topics related to writing, which students might find useful for reference purposes. More useful, though, is the Writer's Guide, which contains explanations of various aspects of the writing process and practice activities.

Writing Proficiency Program by Richard M. Bossone, Ph.D. CTB/McGraw-Hill. A diagnostic-prescriptive approach to the teaching of expository writing for grades nine through thirteen. The kit contains forty-five teacher resource files on topics such as "Prewriting the Essay," "Sentence Elements," and "Types of Essays." Also included are student activity cards, mastery tests, a teacher handbook and a class record sheet.

Writing with a Purpose by James M. McCrimmon, Houghton Mifflin Co. Textbook covering prewriting, writing and revising. Uses both good and bad student papers for illustration. For advanced students.

5

Teaching the Research Paper

At one time no student graduated from high school without writing at least one, usually several, formal research papers, complete with footnotes in MLA style. Today, the popularity of the research paper as a learning experience for all students is waning. Many teachers question whether it is the best way of using valuable time in the English class, time that might be utilized teaching more basic skills that all students—even those not going on to college—need to master. However, even teachers who question the importance of the formal research paper acknowledge that students need a rudimentary understanding of how to collect a wide range of information on a topic, how to organize that information into an effective presentation, and how to give credit for ideas that are not one's own.

This chapter,[1] therefore, focuses on introducing students to the process of compiling and presenting information on a topic but does not presume to give students the thorough, comprehensive mastery of research skills that are probably best taught at the college level. The emphasis is on finding information in the library, choosing and narrowing a topic, systematically collecting information on the topic, and presenting the information in a well-organized manner. Whether to have students master a particular system of footnoting, for example, is a decision that must be made by individual teachers, based on the system they prefer and their knowledge of their own students.

OBJECTIVES

As a result of the learning experiences in this chapter, the student should be able to:

1. Utilize the *Readers' Guide,* card catalog, Dewey Decimal System, dictionaries, encyclopedias, and other reference books to find information in the library.

2. Choose and narrow a topic for a research project.

3. Systematically gather information from a variety of sources.

---

1. Adapted from teaching materials prepared by Robert Evans, English Department, Ralph Perry Junior High School, New Hartford, New York, and used with permission.

> 4. Keep efficient records of the sources of information.
>
> 5. Organize the information he or she has collected into an informative or persuasive essay.
>
> 6. Utilize a logical system for giving credit for ideas that are not one's own.

LEARNING EXPERIENCES

Topic I: Locating Information in the Library

1. *Teacher Presentation.* Point out to students that there is simply too much knowledge for anyone to ever remember it all, but that if they develop the ability to locate information, particularly in the library, they can have easy access to much of the knowledge of the human race. To do this, they must have a working knowledge of the library—the way it is organized, sources of information, and location of information in the various areas. With this information, a student will find the library to be a tool at his or her disposal rather than a vast complicated jungle of books, magazines, shelves, chairs, and librarians.

    Begin with a presentation of the basic headings of the Dewey Decimal System (DDS) either by utilizing an overhead transparency made from the chart on Reproduction Page 76 or by distributing copies of the chart reproduced by spirit duplicator. As an example of how the DDS subdivides the general categories into subtopics, write the following chart on the board:

    900-999 History, Geography and Biography

    910 General Geography

    920 General Biography

    930 History of Ancient World

    940 History of Modern Europe

    950 History of Modern Asia

    960 History of Modern Africa

    970 History of North America

    980 History of South America

    990 History of Rest of the World

2. *Activity.* As an alternative to simply telling the students how the DDS is organized, ask students to divide all knowledge into 10 categories. See if they come up with any of the ones in the Dewey Decimal System. Point out similarities and differences.

3. *Actvity.* After presenting the ten major DDS categories to the class, have students, working individually or in small groups, try to expand on what would be found in

each category, perhaps by listing at least five topics that would be found in each one. Have students meet in small groups and compare their work, discussing any items in one another's lists that they think are out of place.

4. *Activity.* To help students remember the main categories of the DDS for their own use, have them compose a sentence of words that begin with the same letters as the DDS categories. For example: *G*eorge (General works, 000) *P*urdy (Philosophy and psychology, 100) *R*ode (Religion, 200) *S*ix (Social sciences, 300) *L*arge (Language, 400) *P*igs (Pure Science, 500) *A*cross (Applied science and useful arts, 600) *A*cres (Arts and recreation, 700) of *L*ovely (Literature, 800) *H*ills (History, geography and biography, 900).

5. *Activity.* Assign students at random to small groups of four to five each. Distribute copies of Reproduction Page 77 and have each group develop answers to the questions. These questions can also be utilized as a quiz to determine how well students have mastered the basic concepts of the Dewey Decimal System.

6. *Teacher Presentation.* Explain to students that in some large city libraries or in college libraries another classification system is often used. This system uses a combination of letters and numbers. Point out that most libraries have maps posted that label the subject area as well as its call number and that most large libraries have several librarians available to answer questions.

7. *Activity.* Arrange for a field trip to the nearest public library. Ask the librarian to provide your students with a tour. If the library does not use the Dewey Decimal classification system, ask the librarian to explain the system it does use. If possible, arrange for all your students who do not have them to receive library cards.

8. *Teacher Presentation.* Less able students may profit from an explanation of the parts of a book so that they will know how to find the information they seek in it. Choose a general nonfiction work and, using the opaque projector if possible, show students the title page; preface; chapter headings; illustrations; tables; maps; appendix; table of contents; glossary; bibliography; index; author, illustrator, and publisher credits; and copyright notice, explaining how each can be helpful to readers in finding what they are looking for.

9. *Activity.* For many of the Teacher Presentations about locating sources of information, the school librarian is an obvious choice of guest speaker. In inviting the librarian to visit the class, make sure to be specific about the particular skills you want the students to master and provide him or her with some idea of the ability and maturity level of the class. Even if you choose not to invite the librarian to speak to the class, enlist his or her cooperation when teaching the research paper, since many of the activities require the use of library facilities. After fully understanding what you are doing, the librarian is better able to be helpful to students learning about the library.

10. *Activity.* Bring to class reference books of the kinds found in the library. Hand these out to students, with the requirement that each student examine the book he or she has been given and report to the class the nature of that book, its title, makeup, and usefulness. The student will make a brief report. For example: "This is a book entitled *Roget's Thesaurus*. It is like a dictionary but it lists synonyms for all kinds of words. It would be useful for writing papers or creative writing when another word or better word is needed."

Encyclopedia Americana

Encyclopedia Britannica

Collier's Encyclopedia

National Geographic World Atlas

Guinness Book of World Records

Dunlop Illustrated Encyclopedia of Facts

The New York Times Encyclopedia Almanac

Information Please Almanac

Webster's Third International Dictionary (unabridged)

... and the card catalog

"After you have gathered the information, you should try to see if there is something important about the information. Be careful. Don't overlook something that may appear insignificant. The persons who can make the best conclusions from the information will be the ones to solve the mystery.

"After you have exhausted clues 1, 2, and 3, come to see me and I will give you your next clue. There are ten clues in all; I will give you one at a time. You may take an educated guess at any time, but each incorrect guess will cost you one point. You will start with ten points and work your way down from there.

"You must also keep very detailed notes of your information which must include the books you used as well as the process you used. These will be very helpful in reviewing your case.

"Interpol Case #101 does have a solution and you can find it if you get accurate information and then try to reason carefully.

"Good Luck! You have no time limit on this problem although I would like to talk with you each day to evaluate your progress. Also, please don't hesitate to come to me if you meet a problem."

The clues, their sources, and their meanings are as follows:

#1: GREENLAND, TRISTAN DA CUNHA, ST. HELENA (We wanted them to realize that these were all islands. Any encyclopedia.)

#2: THE NUMBER OF REVOLUTIONS AROUND THE EARTH MADE BY RUSSIAN SPACECRAFT VOSHUD 1 ON FEBRUARY 12, 1964.

#3: THE AVERAGE TEMPERATURE FOR FEBRUARY IN MOBILE, ALABAMA (The answer to this clue and the previous clue are the longitude and latitude of the place we were looking for. *The New York Times Encyclopedia Alamanc.*)

#4: MARJORY BARTLETT SANGER (Miss Sanger wrote a book entitled Mangrove Islands. This information was meant to reinforce the idea that we were looking for an island. Card catalog.)

#5: CARTOGRAPHY ("The study of maps and map making" was meant to put the students onto the idea that a map has more to it than land and water. *Webster's Third.*)

#6: THE HARPER ENCYCLOPEDIA OF SCIENCE, PP. 648-9 (These pages carry a definition and explanation of longitude and latitude.)

#7: OUT TO SEA WHERE IT IS COLD/YOU FIND THE WHITE GOLD (This corny rhyme was meant to tell them that we were looking for an island and that it was probably in the north.)

#8: WHAT GOES UP, MUST COME DOWN/WHAT OPENS MUST CLOSE:/LIKE A SUBWAY AND A WORLD'S FAIR/IN NEW YORK CITY (The subway in New

York City opened on October 27, 1904 and the World's Fair closed on the same date in 1940. This was the date of the pick up. *Information Please Almanac.*)

#9: IF YOU GO FARTHER THAN 300 KILOMETERS, YOU'VE GONE TOO FAR (The point of reference for this one is Berlin since that is where our action takes place. Atlas.)

#10: HALFWAY BETWEEN AARHUS AND MALBORK,/BUT CLOSER TO BOSTOCK AND KOTOBREZ (Again, the atlas will allow them to zero in on the correct location: Bornholm Island.)

12. *Teacher Presentation.* Make a transparency from Reproduction Page 78 or reproduce it and distribute it to students. Use the sample entries to introduce students to the purpose and use of the *Readers' Guide (RG)*. Include the following points in your explanation:

   a. The *RG* indexes magazine articles from approximately 130 magazines.

   b. It first appeared in 1900 and is now published twice monthly from September through June and monthly during July and August.

   c. The *RG* is cumulated quarterly, listing magazines of the current month only for two months, while the third month includes all entries for the previous two months.

   d. A bound edition at the end of the year that lists all magazines published for the last two years.

   e. An abridged *Readers' Guide* (begun in 1935) indexes approximately 40 magazines.

   f. Articles may be found under either an author entry or a subject entry.

   g. Often one subject may be followed by many divisions or subheadings.

   h. All abbreviations are found in the front of the book.

   i. To find events of a specific date, look in the *Readers' Guide* that contains that date.

   j. To find current topics or topics with unknown dates, begin with the latest issue and work back.

13. *Activity.* Have students complete the worksheet on Reproduction Page 79 either individually or in small groups.

14. *Evaluation.* To determine how well students understand the use of the *Readers' Guide,* give them the quiz on Reproduction Page 80 or conduct a class discussion of the questions.

15. *Teacher Presentation.* Explain to students the three types of cards found in the card catalog by using Reproduction Page 81. Students should be able to identify the three types of cards and should know the pertinent information found on each—author, title, subject, call number, pages, illustrations, publishers, and publishing date.

16. *Activity.* Use Reproduction Page 82 to give students practice in utilizing information about the card catalog. You will probably want them to work in pairs and then compare answers when they have finished, or you can give Reproduction Page 82 as a quiz.

17. *Activity.* Have students discuss in groups the things that happen in the school library that make studying difficult. Then have them consider the following list of ways to help others in the library and see if their ideas are reflected here:

   a. Do your work quietly.

   b. Return books on time.

   c. Return books to their proper place after using them (proper area, shelf, and alphabetical sequence, for example).

   d. Treat books with care.

   e. Do not mark or cut up magazines.

   f. Learn and follow the rules of your library.

   Then have the students draw up their own list of library user guidelines. This list could be done by the entire class and posted in the library as a reminder.

18. *Activity.* Draw on a spirit master a simple map or diagram of your school library. Place a number on the map at the location of each major source of information, such as card catalog, magazine section, *Readers' Guide,* magazine storage, newspapers, vertical file, atlases, almanacs, dictionaries, encyclopedias, other reference books, and each of the major categories of the Dewey Decimal System. Duplicate enough copies of the map for each student to have at least one. Utilize one or more of the following approaches to help students become familiar with the physical layout of the library:

   a. Have students fill in all the numbered areas of the map with the name of what is located there.

   b. Have students make a list of the various areas of the library that correspond to the numbers on the map. Have them match these with the proper number.

   c. Have students, working in teams, compete to see which group can correctly identify the areas of the library first.

19. *Activity.* Assign students to pairs or let them choose a partner. Have each student write down some topic that interests him or her and give it to his or her partner. The partner's job is to find a magazine article on that subject listed in the *Readers' Guide,* write down the information needed to locate the magazine, find the article, and give it to the partner. The other partner should then read the article and return it to the person who located it.

20. *Activity.* Assign students to pairs or let them choose a partner. Have each person choose a drawer from the card catalog and find a book listed therein that interests him or her, marking it with a piece of paper or a paper clip. Each student then gives the card drawer to his or her partner, who writes down the information from the card that is needed for finding the book. He or she looks for the book, turns it over to his or her partner, and at the same time receives the book the partner has been looking for.

21. *Activity.* Reproduction Page 83 asks one for twenty-five pieces of information that could be located fairly easily in one school's library. Check to see if this information

is available in your library. If not, prepare a similar list of information that can be found in your library. Utilize Reproduction Page 83 in one of the following ways:

    a. As an individual assignment, with each student finding the information on his or her own.

    b. As the focus for class discussion, deciding where the best place to look for each item would be.

    c. As a scavenger hunt, with the class divided into groups of five, with groups competing against one another to find the correct answers.

22. *Activity.* Have each student choose a topic that is of particular interest. Then tell students to locate all possible sources of information on that topic, using both the library and any outside sources. (The topic must be fairly narrow or the number will be too large). Have students either photocopy the source (if it is a magazine in the library) or submit the actual article itself (from old newspapers and magazines at home). The object is to compile a file of articles that can be utilized in the classroom by other students.

23. *Activity.* With the approval of your school librarian, have students work for a week in the library, either before or after school or during study halls or free time. They can be useful in returning cards to books, replacing books on the shelves, getting magazines for students, straightening the book shelves and magazine stacks, signing out books, adding to the vertical file, and many other activities.

24. *Activity.* An exciting, comprehensive approach to developing library skills can be found in *Search*, an "interaction unit" published by Interact. Students work in teams to complete a number of activities, similar to some of those suggested above, all the while accumulating points in a race against other teams to earn the highest number of points. Included is a "Problem-Solution Competition" in which teams create short library research problems for another team to solve. (See the resources list at the end of this chapter for further information.)

25. *Activity.* A good project for practicing library skills is to conduct a mock debate of the United Nations. A social studies teacher might want to cooperate with you on this project. Assign each student a different country to represent in the debate and choose an international issue that is currently in the news. Give students several days to prepare for the debate by researching their country, the issue, and the position their country has taken on that issue. Assign several of the brighter students to prepare resolutions supporting their country's position, which will be voted on. Give students copies of these resolutions several days in advance of the actual debate and encourage students to begin "politicking." Assign a student with leadership skills to research parliamentary procedure and to preside over the debate.

26. *Evaluation.* On Reproduction Pages 84 and 85 there are sample tests for measuring students' understanding of basic concepts related to finding information in the library. They can be used either as quizzes or as practices assigned to students to work on in small groups.

Topic II: Preparing for Research

1. *Teacher Presentation.* Explain to students that researching a topic is a process well described by the word "research" itself. It consists of searching and searching

again to find information necessary to explain or prove a point. The search is for information above and beyond what the writer already possesses. Writing a research paper is more of an organizational task than a writing task. The researcher must have a plan of action to assure that the job is done thoroughly and efficiently. By proceeding in a systematic, step-by-step fashion, the researcher will be successful in going from a vague idea of what he or she wants to write about to a finished paper which has been researched, organized, and put together in a proper form.

2. *Activity.* Ask students to help you list on the board the steps a writer needs to follow in preparing a research paper. Say to them, "Imagine that your science teacher assigned you to write a paper about pollution. How would you go about doing it?"

3. *Teacher Presentation.* Emphasize to students that they must have a clear idea of what their paper will deal with before they can write in earnest. If they have the freedom to choose a topic, the task is fairly easy. All that is required is to select something that they are interested in learning more about or feel strongly about. Activities 4 and 5 that follow suggest several ways of selecting a topic if one can choose freely. If the topic has been assigned by a teacher, the process is a little more difficult, however. What one has to do is to determine some aspect of the topic that is interesting or appealing. This will require some informal preliminary research.

4. *Activity.* To help students choose a topic for a research paper, have them answer the following questions:

   a. List three things you would like to be doing right now if you were not in school.

   b. What are some things you are curious about and would like to understand better?

   c. What are the three biggest problems facing the world today? our nation? our community? our school?

   d. What would you like to be able to do better?

   e. What have you always wanted to try?

   Any of these questions could be the basis of small group discussions in which students share and explore ideas and beliefs in more detail and are stimulated to consider new points of view. Several topics appropriate for research projects are likely to emerge.

5. *Activity.* Duplicate the list of topics on Reproduction Page 87. Instruct students to circle three topics they would like to investigate. Then have them place check marks next to three topics about which they hold strong opinions.

6. *Teacher Presentation.* Explain to students that whether a topic has been assigned to them or chosen by them, it is almost always necessary to narrow it to manageable size. For example, have students imagine they are assigned to write a paper about pollution. Point out that this topic is too broad, since it can encompass air pollution, water pollution, litter, oil spills, sewage, automobiles, factories, garbage disposals, glass recycling, and so forth. Then have them choose one subtopic and break it down even further by thinking of a particular aspect of it. For example, for "oil spills," they might mention "Whose responsibility is it to clean up oil spilled by a tanker in the ocean?" For "glass recycling" they might mention "Ways to organize a glass recycling program in your community." Underscore the fact that a topic like "Ways

to organize a glass recycling program in your community" is an appropriate topic for a research paper because it is focused and of manageable size.

7. *Activity.* Working with the total class, ask volunteers to cite one of the items from Reproduction Page 87 that they either circled or checked. Then have the entire class suggest ways to narrow that topic until it is manageable.

8. *Activity.* Assign students at random to small groups and have them cite one topic they chose from Reproduction Page 87. Then have the group brainstorm all the possible subtopics that could be the focus of a research paper.

9. *Activity.* If students need more practice and instruction in limiting a topic for a paper, utilize the teacher presentations and activities dealing with this topic in Chapter 4.

10. *Activity.* Have each student choose one idea he or she found interesting or intriguing in Activities 4 and 5 and narrow it down to one aspect that is limited enough to be discussed in a single paper. When all students have finished writing, have them compare results, checking to make sure all topics have been sufficiently narrowed.

11. *Teacher Presentation.* Since a research paper generally attempts to persuade the reader to accept some point of view (although some papers may be simply informative), students should be encouraged to formulate a thesis statement—one single declarative sentence that states the writer's point of view on the topic. For example, "Unless drastic steps are taken, automobile pollution will become an extremely serious problem." Point out that a statement such as this is somewhat arguable (that is, not everyone would agree to it), whereas a statement such as "Grass is green" is not likely to arouse much debate.

12. *Activity.* Have students choose several ideas that interest them from Activities 4 and 5 and narrow them to manageable size. Then have them formulate a thesis statement for a research paper on that topic. When they have finished, assign them to small groups to share and compare their results.

13. *Teacher Presentation.* Suggest that students jot down all they already know about a topic they have chosen for a research paper before they begin systematic research. Doing this will save them work in looking for information they already have and will give them ideas about what information they need to collect.

14. *Activity.* Have students choose one or more thesis statements that they formulated for Activity 12 and list everything they already know that could be used to support it. Then have them make another list of the things that they think they might need to find out in order to support or explain their thesis sentence.

Topic III: Gathering Information

1. *Teacher Presentation.* Point out to students that from this point on in the process of collecting information for their papers, the material they find will belong to other people. The students are only borrowing or using it to help them prove a point. Therefore, the proper (and legal) thing to do is to give credit to all sources of information. This is done through context notes, footnotes for quotations and paraphrases, and bibliography entries, which will be explained in more detail later.

Also suggest ways that students can go about finding information that will be useful in writing their papers. If they have mastered the earlier section on use of the library, they will need little more than some reminders; otherwise, they may need explicit guidelines.

a. List all authors, titles and subjects suggested by your topic. Look these up in the card catalog and list the call number, author, and title of each book on the topic listed in the catalog.

b. Using the Dewey Decimal outline, find shelf location(s) of books on your topic. Use the index of all books in this section to locate material on your topic. Ask the librarian if there are similar books on reserve which you should look at.

c. Is there a possibility that there are pamphlets or newspaper articles on your topic in the vertical file?

d. Look up your topic in at least two encyclopedias. Use the index.

e. Look up your topic in the *Readers' Guide* and list all magazine material on cards.

f. Use any other reference books that might have material related to your topic.

g. Don't overlook the current issues of magazines and newspapers that will not have been listed in the *Readers' Guide* and other references.

h. Are there sources other than the library that you should consult? Can you secure information from interviews, for example, or from public records?

2. *Teacher Presentation.* Explain to students that as they search for and find information related to this topic, they need to do more than just read the material they find. They must record it for future use in writing the paper, since they cannot rely on memory alone to store all the details they will be reading. Keeping records, then, is an important part of research. Two kinds of records are particularly necessary: 1) notes of the ideas they have located that may be worth including in the paper, and 2) information about the sources of these ideas. Both types of records are best kept on 3x5 or 4x6 index cards so that students can rearrange their order when planning and writing their papers.

3. *Teacher Presentation.* Reproduce Reproduction Page 88 and distribute to students—or, preferably, make a transparency and project it, using the overhead projector. Point out that the paragraph at the top is part of a magazine article found on page 57 of the publication. The two cards have been used to record details from this passage that the researcher may wish to incorporate later into his or her paper. Emphasize that every note card should include the following (and point out each on the sample cards):

a. A heading indicating the subject of the notes. Only one subject (piece of information) should be written on a card. Use a different card for each new idea, even if it appears in the same article. Stress that the researcher does *not* attempt to put all notes about one article on a single card!

b. The page number of the article where the passage appeared.

c. A number in the upper right-hand corner indicating which source the idea came from. Thus all note cards from a given source would be designated with the same number. (This number will also appear on the bibliography card on which all the information about the source appears—more about that later.)

    d. Either a quotation, indicated by quotation marks, or a paraphrase of an idea (written in their own words) from the article, indicated by parentheses. Point out to students that the first sample note card contains a direct quotation from the article; the second contains a paraphrase.

4. *Activity.* Reproduce and distribute Reproduction Page 88. Have students assume they are writing a paper on automobile pollution, with the thesis statement, "Unless drastic measures are taken, automobile pollution will become an extremely serious problem." Have them imagine that the passages on the left side of the worksheet are taken from page 57 of a magazine article on automobile pollution, which they have found in the library. This is the third source of information they have used. Have students fill in the "cards" on the right-hand side with either direct quotations or paraphrases of the passages on the left. Remind them of the information that every note card should include (Teacher Presentation 3 above). Have students work individually. When everyone has finished, call on volunteers to tell the class how they filled out the cards. Answers will vary, of course. The class should try to determine whether each volunteer has filled out the cards correctly.

5. *Activity.* Distribute to each student a copy of a magazine. Tell students to choose an article that they are at least somewhat interested in. Give students several index cards apiece or have them draw facsimiles on their own paper. Have them record on the cards ideas from the article they have read, imagining that the article is a relevant source of information on the topic with which their paper is concerned. When they have finished, have students meet in small groups. Each student will select one of his or her cards to submit to the group for checking. The groups should consider the following questions in evaluating the cards:

    a. Has the researcher indicated the subject of the information at the top of the card?

    b. Does the card indicate what page the information appears on?

    c. Does the card indicate whether the information is a quote from the article or an idea expressed in the researcher's own words?

    d. Does the card indicate which source the information comes from? (Each student can use an imaginary number.)

6. *Teacher Presentation.* Explain to the class that it is essential that a researcher keep careful records of the source of each piece of information so that he or she can give credit to the source. Using someone else's ideas or words without giving credit is known as "plagiarism," an act that is both unethical and illegal. Therefore, every time the researcher makes notes of an idea or quotation from a source, he or she should indicate where it was obtained. To avoid having to write down the same information (title, author, and so forth) over and over when the same source is used for several ideas, the researcher can fill out a single card for each source, and each note card can carry a number that matches the number of the bibliography card.

    Duplicate and distribute to students Reproduction Page 90. Read through it with them and suggest they keep the handout to refer to in future activities that require them to fill out bibliography cards.

7. *Activity.* Distribute to students at least five index cards apiece or have them draw five facsimiles on their own paper. Write the following list on the board or project it for the class to see and have students fill out a bibliography card for each item, following the instruction on Reproduction Page 90.

   a. Article entitled "The Last Oil Well" by Will Hineline. *Time* magazine, January 21, 1965, pages 17-18.

   b. Book entitled *No Air to Breathe* by Sidney Frayberg. Published by Rayce Books, Princeton, New Jersey, copyright 1972.

   c. Encyclopedia Americana, volume 16, pages 446-48, subject is pollution, copyright 1967, Americana Company, Chicago, Illinois.

   d. Interview with Jake Scott, Newark City Council, Newark, New Jersey, April 18, 1974. Scott is opposed to any governmental regulation of automobile manufacturing, even if it helps to control pollution.

   e. A *Miami Dispatch* newspaper article entitled "Gasoline Shortage Cuts Tourism," by Ray Randall, May 5, 1975. The article appeared on page 1 of Section A, since Miami depends so heavily on tourism to maintain its economy.

   When all students have finished, draw sample cards on the board and fill them in correctly. Suggest that students determine whether their cards match those you have drawn on the board.

8. *Activity.* Duplicate and distribute Reproduction Page 91. Assign students at random to groups of three and have them fill out seven index cards (distributed by you or drawn by the students), using the information from the worksheet.

9. *Activity.* Have students choose any topic that interests them and locate in the library or elsewhere at least two books, three magazine articles, and one encyclopedia entry on the topic. For each, require them to fill out a bibliography card following the instructions given in previous activities. Either collect these for checking yourself or have students exchange with a partner for checking.

10. *Activity.* It is possible to give students practice in compiling information and making note cards and bibliography cards without having them go to the library to secure the information first-hand. The "casebook" is a commercially produced collection of articles on a single topic, from which students can draw information for use in writing a research paper on some aspect of that topic. Most casebooks are prepared for use in college composition classes and are thus too advanced for most high school students. An alternative, according to Edward Deluzain in an article in *On Righting Writing,* is to compile one's own case folders, manila folders containing newspaper and magazine articles on a particular topic. In compiling a set of these folders, he suggests that the teacher give each person in the class the task of choosing a topic and finding copies of articles that relate to it. The teacher could supplement the articles located by students. The folders could be kept on file in the classroom, and students could be assigned to choose the one that interests them most, to formulate a thesis statement related to the topic, and to compile information using only the sources in the folder. This approach, although not a substitute for students' actually visiting the library, is a way to give the class additional practice in gathering

information if the library is too crowded or if other conditions restrict students' free use of the library.

11. *Activity.* If you anticipate having students write a complete research paper as part of the learning experience for this unit (and you undoubtedly will), there are at least two different ways to make the assignment. One is to have them choose a topic and collect information about it after completing the Learning Experiences for Topics I, II, and III but before beginning the Learning Experiences for Topic IV. Thus they would be able to put into practice what they have learned immediately after completing the activities. The second approach is to complete the Learning Experiences for Topic IV before beginning work on a research paper on a topic of one's own. There are merits to either approach, and you will have to decide which is best suited to your class.

Topic IV: Organizing and Writing the Paper

1. *Teacher Presentation.* Refer the students to the steps for writing a research report on Reproduction Page 86. If they have successfully completed the activities for the preceding topics, they will have mastered the first five steps. Now we deal with the final steps: taking the raw material assembled through research, organizing it into a logical form, and writing a paper that conveys the information clearly and persuasively. The first concern is to examine all the ideas that have been collected and sort them into categories—with related ideas together. Since only one piece of information has been written on each note card, it is a fairly easy task to spread out the cards on the floor or on a table and begin to sort them.

2. *Activity.* Duplicate and distribute Reproduction Page 92 to the class and have students complete it, working individually. Then have them meet in small groups and compare answers. (Answers are provided in Appendix B.)

3. *Activity.* Reproduce and distribute the note cards that appear on Reproduction Page 93. Have students arrange them in a logical order to support the thesis statement "Unless some drastic measures are taken, automobile pollution will become an extremely serious problem." Have them work either individually or in small groups, numbering the cards in the order they feel is most effective. Then discuss with the total class the approaches that various groups took.

4. *Teacher Presentation.* In preparing students to write complete research papers, give them specific instructions on the proper form for footnotes and bibliography. Since most teachers have their own preferences, we have not attempted to specify one particular form here. Consult the resources section at the end of this chapter for suggestions on finding further information.

5. *Activity.* Using Reproduction Page 91, have students write footnotes in proper form for each item in the paper they are preparing and compile a bibliography in proper form.

6. *Activity.* Assign students to write a research paper of a length appropriate for the age and ability level of your class. Have them submit to you for checking (or evalu-

ation) each of the following as they are completed. This requirement will ensure that, if a student has not done one step of the process correctly, the error will be caught before he or she goes on to the next step.

a. The subject of the paper. This should be the "narrowed down" topic, not the general topic.

b. The thesis statement for the paper—a declarative sentence that indicates the writer's opinion or point of view toward the topic.

c. Note cards and bibliography cards for all information collected for the paper.

d. An outline or rough draft of the paper.

e. The final paper.

You might wish to have each student choose a partner to give each step a preliminary check before it is turned in to you. This will give the student a "last chance" for improving the work before submitting it.

ASSESSING ACHIEVEMENT OF OBJECTIVES

On-Going Evaluation

The extent to which students have mastered the individual skills covered under each topic above can be measured by having them submit for grading those experiences marked "Evaluation" or those marked "Activity" that appear near the end of each section. Almost any of the activities suggested in each section could also be submitted for grading.

Final Evaluation

For an overall evaluation of students' abilities to write research papers, the most logical procedure, of course, is to assign a research paper. Before students begin work, explain what criteria you will measure the paper against in grading it. You will probably wish to include the following among your criteria:

1. Has the writer chosen a topic that is narrow enough to be explained or supported in detail in a single essay?

2. Has the writer researched the topic thoroughly, using a variety of sources rather than just one or two?

3. Has the writer organized the information logically?

4. Has the writer been meticulous in giving credit for ideas that are not his or her own and in indicating all direct quotations?

5. Has the writer followed a consistent style in footnotes and bibliography?

RESOURCES FOR TEACHING THE RESEARCH PAPER

Below is a selected list of resources useful for teaching researching and writing a paper. Addresses of publishers can be found in Appendix A.

Audio-Visual Materials

Constructing Reports by Ruth G. Strickland. Encyclopedia Britannica Educational Corp. Six filmstrips dealing with "Digging for Facts," "Selecting a Theme," "Building Reports," "Painting with Words," "Finishing Reports," and "Using Reports." Suitable for junior high school only.

How to Write Reports. Eye-Gate. Six filmstrips with three records or cassettes. Explains footnotes, bibliographies, writing and presenting information, and the differences between writing a paper and a book report. Clear, direct, and easy to understand.

How to Write a Term Paper. Filmstrip House. Part of a series entitled *Conquering Composition.* The set on the term paper includes four filmstrips, four LP records or cassettes, and four scripts. Presents the true experience of how three students approached their writing assignments. Explains library research, resources and references, note taking, organizing and writing, and preparing the final draft. Thorough and interesting. Appropriate for all students.

Using Reference Materials More Efficiently. Applause Productions. Four filmstrips giving detailed instructions in locating reference materials and using them in essays, compositions, and reports. Explains the use of the dictionary, periodicals, biographies, sources of quotations, encyclopedias, almanacs, and other references.

Writing a Research Paper. The Reading Lab, Inc. One filmstrip, one cassette, and one copy of each of two guides. This complete teaching package provides instruction in library research, note taking, documentation, and writing the paper. Interesting, clear, and informative.

Print Materials

The Basic Guide to Research Sources by Robert O'Brien and Joanne Soderman. New American Library. This reference book gives descriptions and ratings of general and subject-area reference books and instructions on where to look for what one needs. It also includes tips on efficient use of the library.

The Freshman Writer by Michele F. Cooper. Barnes and Noble. A guide to writing first-year college papers. Deals specifically with length, style, subject matter, choosing a topic, library skills, determining a thesis, composing an outline, writing the paper, editing, and preparing the final draft, footnoting, and typing. Helpful diagrams and samples. Suitable for average and advanced students.

Guide to Writing Term Papers by Albert A. Theriault, Jr. Amsco School Publications. Provides instruction in planning, topic selection, outlining, library tools, reference materials, bibliographic documentation, quoting, and writing. Sample term paper provided. Valuable visual aids and models throughout.

How to Do Research by Linda Bennett and Barbara Feldstein. Learnco, Incorporated. A skills kit that introduces students to library resources. Contains twenty-seven self-directed learning activities. Skills are reinforced through a variety of activities ranging from crossword puzzles to library scavenger hunts for numbers and names.

How to Use the Readers' Guide to Periodical Literature and Other Indexes. H. W. Wilson Company, 950 University Avenue, Bronx, NY 10452. A helpful guide designed to teach students to use important resources. Includes practice exercises as well as explanatory material. Skills-oriented. A set of up to fifty copies is free; additional copies may be purchased at two cents each.

How to Write Reports, Papers, Theses, Articles by John P. Riebel. Arco Publishing Company. An informative guide to writing effective, technically correct papers. Practical and clear.

How to Write Themes and Term Papers by Barbara Lenmark Ellis. Barron's Educational Series, Inc. Contains a section on the research paper.

The Hutchinson Guide to Writing Research Papers by Helene D. Hutchinson. Glencoe Press. A comprehensive work. Examines choice of topic, range of scope, resources, research steps, and library skills. Valuable diagrams, summary charts, indices, and annotated bibliographies are included. A rather complex work most suitable for advanced students or for teacher reference.

Lessons in Report Writing by Alex Pirie. Learnco, Incorporated. Presents elementary skills of research for middle school and junior high school students. Skills on outlining, note taking, researching, writing the report, and preparing a bibliography.

A Manual for Writers of Term Papers, Theses, and Dissertations by Kate L. Turabian. The University of Chicago Press. Discusses the parts of the paper, documentation, spelling, punctuation, abbreviations, numbering footnotes, and typing the paper. Focuses on specifics; general step by step information is not given. Suitable only for advanced students or for teacher reference.

Multicultural Spoken Here: Discovering America's People through Language Arts and Library Skills by Josephine Chase and Linda Parth. Goodyear Publishing Co. A unique and exciting teacher's guide that teaches library skills through content related to various U.S. ethnic groups. Although designed for elementary school, materials would be appropriate for slower junior high school students. The guide includes lesson plans and tear sheets to use as posters or for reproduction.

Murder, Mischief and Mayhem: A Process for Creative Research Papers by W. Keith Kraus. National Council of Teachers of English. Describes an exciting approach to the research paper, using old newspaper accounts, primarily of murder cases. Includes ten examples of student papers based on this approach. Presents exercises to familiarize students with newspaper research and suggestions for helping students organize research and write the papers. An annotated list of topics is included.

Preparing the Research Paper by Philips G. Davies and Samuel J. Rogal. Educators Publishing Service. Includes sections on topic selection and scope, preparation, taking notes, and planning and documenting. A sample research paper is presented. Valuable visual aids and diagrams.

Preparing the Research Paper by Lorraine F. Dangle and Alice H. Haussman. CEBCO/Standard Publishing. Concise instructions on correct bibliographic form, note taking, direct quotations, footnotes, title page, and preparing and writing the final paper. Also includes a self-evaluating checklist. A good choice for the average student.

The Process of Writing: Building to the Research Paper. The Center for Learning. Uses discovery approaches to motivate writing the research paper and to teach skills of reading, thinking, writing, and organizing. The kit includes a teacher's guide and student handouts for duplication. Part I introduces library skills; part II teaches research skills in a limited context; and part III immerses students in the actual paper.

Research: An Introduction by Robert Ross. Barnes and Noble. Contains a thorough guide from initial planning to final copy—researching, planning, gathering, and organizing. Includes forms for documenting notes and writing bibliographic entries. Useful for more advanced students.

Researching and Reporting by Robert and Mary Lou Burch. Xerox Educational Publications. Probably the best single book for the average student in grades seven through twelve, particularly considering its low cost. The first section is written in short-story format; three students and a beleaguered teacher select a topic, decide upon sources, forage through the library, and put the paper together. The second section includes explanations, activities, diagrams, and checklists to guide the student in preparing his or her own paper. A free teacher's guide includes three worksheets that can be reproduced and distributed to students. Highly recommended.

The Research Paper Guide edited by Anthony G. Sherman. Pendulum Press, Inc. A guide to effective, precise writing. Chapters focus on topics and outlines, research resources, rough draft, revisions, documentation, bibliography, and footnotes. Sample paper included plus valuable writer's checklist.

Research Paper Project. New York State English Council. A series of worksheets for use in the senior high school. Can be used as a source for explanations to the class, even if you do not choose to reproduce the worksheets and distribute them to students.

Research Papers: A Guided Writing Experience for Senior High School Students, 2d ed. rev., by Richard Corbin and Jonathan Corbin. National Council of Teachers of English. A handy booklet for grades eleven and twelve outlining and explaining all steps of the research paper process. Clearly defined objectives and checklists guide the process.

Search: An Interaction Unit Introducing Library Skills. Interact. A complete teaching unit on library skills, emphasizing student involvement and interaction. Students work together on learning objectives in the areas of understanding the library's contents, using a book, and using the *Readers' Guide*.

Searching Writing by Ken Macrorie. Hayden Book Co. Inc. Macrorie describes this book as a contextbook, not a textbook, "an account of a search into the nature of searching." Demonstrates, with examples, how a person develops the initiative, self-discipline, and rigor necessary to carry out a sustained piece of research and offers a series of invitations to the reader to carry out his or her own research.

The Skills of Research by Norman L. Haider. Silver Burdett Company. Contains sections on narrowing the topic, uses of the card catalog and the *Reader's Guide* and other sources of information, note taking, and organizing material. A sample research paper is provided. Fine for the average student.

Ten Steps in Writing the Research Paper by Roberta H. Markham. Barron's Educational Series, Inc. Reduces the complications normally associated with writing research papers to ten easy-to-follow steps. Systematic and succinct. Suitable for average and advanced students.

Thinking for Writing by Dorothy U. Seyler and M. Noel Sipple. Science Research Associates. A text that combines instruction and practice in composition skills, critical analysis, persuasive writing, and the research process with a collection of readings.

Writing a Research Paper by Robert R. Putter. Globe Book Company. An easy-to-read guide to preparing a research paper, complete with bibliography and footnotes. A guide to standard usage deals with common writing problems.

Writing a Research Paper, Manuscript Form and Documentation by Eliot D. Allen and Ethel B. Colbrunn. The Reading Lab, Inc. Explains choice of topic, using the library, note taking, outlining, writing, pagination, margins, quoting, footnotes, and bibliographies. Sample pages and models provided.

Writing and Researching Term Papers and Reports by Eugene H. Ehrlich and Daniel Murphy. Bantam Books. Explains the use of reference books, procedures for note taking, outlining, writing, editing, and documenting. Annotated sample research paper and comprehensive bibliography of reference books provided.

About Writing Reports. Channing L. Bete Company. Visually interesting but somewhat superficial guide to selecting a topic, researching, using the library, compiling a bibliography, organizing ideas, outlining, note taking, quoting, and paraphrasing. Easy-to-follow examples.

Writing Term Papers and Reports by George Shelton Hubbell. Barnes and Noble. Excellent systematic instruction in choice of subject, reading and note taking, organization of materials, outlining, writing, documenting, and revising. Sample term paper provided. Valuable models and examples throughout. Ideal handbook for advanced students.

6

Teaching Students to Revise

Most good writing proceeds in three stages: prewriting (planning), writing (producing a rough draft), and revision (making improvements and correcting errors). Unfortunately, many times the first two stages are given proper emphasis, but the last is neglected. All too often students dash off a rough draft of a writing assignment and then, with no particular plan for proofreading or revision, correct a gross error or two and simply copy the whole composition over in a neater, more legible form and hand it in, feeling they have done their best.

The truth is that they seldom approach doing their best work. Revision is a skill that can contribute almost as much to the finished product as does the first rough writing. To get full benefit from this revision process, student writers should know what kinds of weaknesses to look for in their rough drafts, know how to spot and correct errors in spelling, punctuation, and usage, and know what stylistic problems are likely to plague their writing and how to correct them.

OBJECTIVES

As a result of the learning experiences in this chapter, students should be able to:

1. Identify and correct misspelled words in their own compositions.

2. Identify and correct ineffective punctuation in their own compositions.

3. Identify nonstandard usages of English in their own compositions and change them to standard usages.

4. Identify poor organization in their own compositions and improve it.

5. Identify poor development in their own compositions and improve it.

6. Eliminate clichés that appear in their own writing.

7. Eliminate any unnecessary words and phrases so as to make their writing as concise as possible.

LEARNING EXPERIENCES

Topic I: Using a Guide to Revision

1. *Teacher Presentation.* Prepare a revision guide or proofreading checklist by choosing those sections or items from the following guide which you consider most appropriate for your students. For younger students you may wish to limit the material to paragraphs and to include such basic items as "Have I indented the first line of the paragraph? Have I kept my margins straight?" You may wish to add a short line at the beginning of each item so that students can check off each point after examining their work and correcting any mistakes they find. Reproduce and distribute to students copies of the checklist and require them to use it as a guide whenever preparing a writing assignment.

A Complete Guide to Revision

I. *Expository Writing*

   A. Organization

   1. Do I introduce my subject or thesis idea clearly and precisely so the reader will know exactly what the essay is to be about?

   2. Do I divide my thesis into its logical parts (its factors), and do I then arrange these parts into a logical order (such as sequential, chronological, or climactic)?

   3. Do I state each of these parts in a topic sentence that is then developed by at least one paragraph?

   4. Do I have an introductory paragraph and a conclusion?

   5. Are there transitions where necessary throughout the essay so the reader will have no trouble following the organization?

   B. Development

   1. Is the topic sentence of each paragraph developed in adequate detail? Is every general statement made more specific by detailed statements?

   2. Does each paragraph develop only one topic idea? Are there irrelevant details in any paragraph? Do I get off the subject?

   3. Do the details in each paragraph follow a logical order, or do they simply appear in random order? Could the order of sentences be improved?

   4. Do the sentences in each paragraph flow smoothly one to the next? Do I help the reader by use of connectors and other transitional devices? Do I combine clauses and use subordination to make my sentences smooth and coherent?

   C. Style

   1. Do I know the exact meaning of every word I have used?

   2. Have I used any slang or nonstandard language?

   3. Have I used the most precise, direct words? Have I said exactly what I mean?

   4. Do I vary my sentence constructions to avoid dull, mechanical writing?

   5. Have I eliminated all clichés and stale metaphorical language?

II. *Mechanics for All Writing*

   A. Spelling. Is every word spelled correctly?

   B. Punctuation.

      1. Is every comma used for a valid reason?

      2. Are there places where I need a comma and have not put one in?

      3. Does every sentence end with a period, exclamation point, or question mark?

      4. Does every sentence begin with a capital letter?

      5. Are all quotations properly punctuated?

      6. Do I ever join two complete sentences with a comma?

      7. Is every colon, semicolon, and dash I used justified?

   C. Grammar and Syntax

      1. Does every sentence have a subject and a predicate?

      2. Does each subject agree in number with its predicate?

      3. Is every verb in the proper form and tense?

      4. Does every pronoun have an antecedent?

      5. Is every pronoun the proper number, gender, and case?

      6. Are my modifiers properly placed so it is obvious what or who is being modified? Have I left some modifiers dangling, with no subject identified?

      7. Does every sentence convey a clear meaning?

2. *Activity.* Have the class, using the proofreading checklist you have prepared, identify ways the student writer could improve the essay on Reproduction Page 94. The activity could be conducted with the total class or you could have students work individually, checking the essay against the revision guide and marking weaknesses that should be corrected. They could then share with the total class what they discovered. Students could also work in small groups of three to five pupils each, using the checklist to discover weaknesses in the essay.

3. *Activity.* Without indicating the name of the author, of course, reproduce one or more compositions written by students in your class. Then follow the instructions for Activity 2.

4. *Activity.* When papers are due to be handed in by your students, use class time to work through your revision guide. Have students read their papers several times, each time checking a different item in the checklist. When students have checked all of one category of skills—punctuation, for instance—they should write the word "punctuation" at the end of the paper and put their initials beside it to show they have done so. They should follow this procedure through the entire checklist.

    If you do not wish to take class time for such revision (particularly as some students may need more time for rewriting after such a thorough and enforced proofreading), you may wish to reproduce a large supply of your revision checklist so that you can give a copy to each student whenever a major assignment is due, with the instruction that every item on the list be checked by the student as they use the guide to proofread and revise the paper. Students could attach the guide to the paper when turning it in.

A GUIDEBOOK FOR TEACHING COMPOSITION

Topic II: Correcting Errors in Mechanics

1. *Teacher Presentation.* Give to students the two lists of words that are often misspelled on Reproduction Page 95 and 96. Go over the lists with the class, discussing the types of spelling errors that frequently creep into student writing. Then assign students to study the lists as homework.

2. *Activity.* Play the spelling game contained on Reproduction Pages 94-100. The game is designed to help students spot spelling errors and thus improve their proofreading skills. The heart of the game is a series of sentences, some of which contain no spelling errors, though most contain errors in the words listed on Reproduction Pages 95 and 96. The object is for students to find the errors by carefully reading the sentence in much the same way that people proofread their own writing. Thus what appears to be a "game" is really serious practice in identifying and correcting spelling errors. After discovering an error, students must give the correct answer and explain and support the correction. This is to insure that any given answer is not just a lucky guess. Also, by explaining the correction, students educate their peers and reinforce their own understanding of the correct answer.

    The game can be used in several ways. Two come to mind at once. First, by preparing the materials for one game set, the teacher has an activity for use by four or five students while the rest of the class works on another activity. These could be students who have finished other work and are ready for a change of pace, or they could be students who need extra work on spelling. Second, if the teacher prepares six to eight sets of materials, the entire class, divided into small groups, can play the game so all can gain proficiency in spotting spelling errors.

    The following are instructions for preparing the materials for one game set:

    a. Photocopy the 178 sentences that appear on Reproduction Page 97. Cut out each sentence from the photocopy and, using cellophane tape, mount it on a 3" x 5" index card. Shuffle the cards so they are not in any specific order.

    b. Photocopy the game board that appears on Reproduction Page 98 and mount it on a 8½" x 11" piece of cardboard. Then cover it with clear contact paper or have it laminated.

    c. Make one copy of the sheet of instructions for students (Reproduction Page 99) and the answer key (Reproduction Page 100).

    d. Obtain small buttons or coins for use as markers, one for each player.

    e. Put all components of the game in a large plastic Zip-Lock bag.

    The instructions provided on Reproduction Page 99 set up the game in a competitive fashion. Players are pitted against one another, racing against one another to reach the end. If you prefer not to encourage competition within the small groups, entire groups could be pitted against one another, or all members of a small group could work together in a race against the clock to see whether they can move a single marker to the end before, say, twenty minutes has elapsed.

3. *Activity.* Give students Reproduction Page 101. It contains a large number of misspelled words—in most cases misspellings of the same words that appear on Reproduction Pages 95 and 96. Have students identify and correct all the spelling errors they can find. Here are several ways the activity can be organized:

a. Have students work individually identifying and correcting the errors. Give a prize or other recognition to the first student who finds all the errors. (Deduct one point for every correct word the student mistakenly corrects.)

b. Assign students to small groups and let them work together to find and correct the errors. Require them to come to complete agreement on any changes that are made (that is, the majority cannot railroad through a decision against the protests of the minority). If you wish, you could have groups compete to see which group finds all the errors first.

c. Lead the total class through the activity together, letting volunteers suggest which words need to be changed.

(All the spelling errors on Reproduction Page 101 are identified in Appendix B.)

4. *Evaluation.* Use the sentences from the spelling game (see Reproduction Page 97) to construct a quiz in which students must locate and correct misspelled words.

5. *Teacher Presentation.* Give students copies of Reproduction Page 102. Point out to students that this guide summarizes the basic principles of punctuation and that these rules will be the basis of all punctuation activities that follow. You may wish to go over the sheet with the class, providing additional explanation and examples.

6. *Activity.* Assign students to groups of three or four students each and have them play the punctuation game contained on Reproduction Pages 103-105. The game is built around forty sentences, thirty-four of which contain one or more errors in punctuation. The purpose is for students to identify and correct the punctuation errors and thus improve their proofreading skills.

The student draws two kinds of cards—those on which are printed the sentences described above and smaller cards bearing marks of punctuation. The object is to correctly match punctuation cards with sentence cards that require punctuation. After a player matches a sentence with the necessary punctuation card, the cards are discarded. Play continues until one player manages to discard all the cards in his or her hand and thus is the winner.

Since players must show the other players their cards before they attempt to discard them and allow them to determine whether the sentence is correctly punctuated, everyone gets frequent practice proofreading for punctuation.

The following are instructions for preparing one set of materials for every three or four students in the class:

a. Photocopy the forty sentences provided on Reproduction Page 103. Cut out each sentence and mount it on a 3" x 5" index card, using rubber cement or transparent tape. Shuffle the sentence cards so they are not in any specific order.

b. Cut thirty-seven 3" x 5" index cards in half so that from each you have created two smaller cards measuring 2½" x 3". On each of the smaller cards draw a large mark of punctuation and below it write the name of that mark of punctuation. Make the following numbers of cards:

   ten periods

   twenty commas

   five question marks

eight sets of quotation marks

fifteen semicolons

ten exclamation points

five underlines

   c. Reproduce the instructions for playing the game (Reproduction Page 104) and the answer key (Reproduction Page 105).

   d. Obtain small buttons or coins for use as markers, one for each player.

   e. Insert all materials for a single game set into a large Zip-Lock bag to keep the components from getting lost.

The game can be used by a small group of students who have special difficulties with punctuation or need extra practice or by students who finish other activities before the rest of the class. By making six to eight sets, you can have the class divide into small groups and all play the game at the same time.

7. *Activity.* Give students the paragraph on Reproduction Page 106, which contains a large number of punctuation mistakes. Have them identify and correct all punctuation errors they can find. If you wish to give the total class guided practice in proofreading for punctuation, you could project the paragraph, using the opaque or overhead projector, and call on volunteers to point out errors. Make sure to require students to explain *why* they think a correction is necessary.

8. *Activity.* If you have not done so already, make sure that all students have a copy of Reproduction Page 102 so they can review the rules for inserting commas. Then pass out copies of Reproduction Page 107 and assign students to insert commas where needed and to put the number of the rule above the comma. If students need additional practice with commas, duplicate paragraphs from current magazines with the commas omitted. (Answers for Reproduction Page 107 are given in Appendix B.)

9. *Activity.* Make additional punctuation proofreading exercises for students by typing an essay on a spirit duplicating master, omitting all the marks of punctuation, and having students add them where needed.

10. *Evaluation.* Use the items from the punctuation game (Reproduction Page 103) to construct a quiz in which students must locate and correct punctuation errors.

11. *Teacher Presentation.* Review with the class the more common errors in usage and syntax—including subject-verb agreement, pronoun-antecedent agreement, the uses and degrees of adjectives and adverbs, parallel construction, double negatives, nonstandard idiomatic expressions, and the tenses of the following verbs: freeze, break, speak, swim, sing, shake, forecast, spring, take, go, open, and give. Several instructional sessions on usage and syntax may be necessary for a thorough review. Students will also find it helpful to read the explanations that appear in textbooks, such as those suggested in the resources section at the end of this chapter.

12. *Activity.* Have students play the usage game contained on Reproduction Pages 108–110. This game, played in small groups of three to five students, is identical to the spelling game (Reproduction Pages 97–100) except it gives students practice in identifying and correcting errors in grammatical usage and syntax rather than spelling. It requires students to inspect sentences that may or may not contain

errors. A player who correctly identifies the errors and explains them to the rest of the group is allowed to move his or her marker forward on the board. To prepare a set of materials for the game, photocopy the sentences on Reproduction Page 108. Cut them out and mount each on a 3" x 5" index card. The same board as used for the spelling game (Reproduction Page 98) can be used here. Instructions for playing the usage game are found on Reproduction Page 109. Review the directions in Activity 2, Topic II, for preparing the materials and organizing the class to play the game. The answer key for the usage game appears on Reproduction Page 110.

13. *Activity.* Give students Reproduction Page 111, which contains "The Grammar Witch." The Reproduction Page contains a large number of errors in usage and syntax as well as a few in spelling and punctuation (for purposes of review). Have students identify and correct all the errors they can find. Here are several ways to organize the activity:

   a. Have students work individually identifying and correcting the errors. Give recognition to the first student who finds all the errors. Deduct one point for every correct word the student mistakenly corrects.

   b. Assign students to small groups and let them work together to find and correct the errors.

   c. Use the worksheet for a total class lesson. Give each student a copy and lead the class through it.

   (A corrected version of Reproduction Page 111 appears in Appendix B.)

14. *Evaluation.* Construct a quiz using items from the usage game (Reproduction Page 108).

Topic III. Language That Gets in the Way

1. *Teacher Presentation.* All during elementary school, teachers encourage their students to develop more extensive vocabularies and to use more effective words in their writing. Most students progress in these skills in a satisfactory manner; however, a substantial number misinterpret these lessons and adopt the idea that good writers must use fancy, flowery language. These students prefer a long word to a short one, an uncommon one to a common one, a pretty one to a plain one.

    It is often difficult to persuade these students that simple, direct language is preferable. They believe they have been taught that wordy, metaphorical constructions are more admirable and somehow more exciting than straight talk.

    Explain to your class that styles of writing change as do styles in hair and clothes. Demonstrate this fact by passing out excerpts from writing created at different times in history or by reading several samples aloud. (Suggestions: Thackeray, Pepys, or Dickens as contrasted to Twain—the voice of Huck Finn!—Stephen Crane, Theodore Dreiser, or contemporary writers like James Farrell, Bernard Malamud or Ernest Hemingway.) Help your students see that writing has become simpler, more direct and, actually, easier to read and understand, as styles have changed through the years.

2. *Activity.* Give students copies of Reproduction Page 112, which lists words that have simpler, more common synonyms. Working with the class as a whole, help the

students select alternate words that you and they agree are simpler, more direct and precise, and, hence, more suitable for their writing. (Possible answers are given in Appendix B.)

3. *Activity.* On the other hand, students also must learn that underwriting is just as undesirable as overwriting. Reproduction Page 113 cites usages that are generally accepted in informal conversation but are much less acceptable in writing. Working with the total class or with students in small groups or individually, ask them to substitute for each slangy or substandard expression a word or phrase that states the same meaning but in a more acceptable way. (Suggested answers are given in Appendix B.) Then have students cite other examples of expressions that are a part of our spoken language but that are not appropriate in writing except when the author makes a deliberate attempt to convey nonstandard or colloquial usage.

4. *Activity.* Present to the class paragraph A on Reproduction Page 114, which is filled with pretentious, inflated diction. Ask students, working individually or in pairs, to remove the words that are inappropriate and replace them with more direct, precise words. When everyone has finished, have several revised paragraphs read aloud so that students can see how different or similar they are. Be sure to emphasize again how much more effective paragraphs are when they are written in simple, direct language that says precisely what it means.

5. *Activity.* Present to the class paragraph B on Reproduction Page 114, which contains many informal, nonstandard expressions not appropriate for written expression. Ask students, working individually or in pairs, to remove expressions they feel are out of place and to replace them with language more appropriate to writing. Remind them to make verb tenses consistent too. When everyone has finished, have several revised paragraphs read aloud so the students can see how different or similar they are. Be sure to emphasize that slang and nonstandard usage are not inherently "wrong" but merely inappropriate in formal writing situations such as most of the composition assignments students will encounter.

6. *Activity.* Have students take paragraphs they have previously written and revise them to remove flowery or pretentious diction and wordy constructions. Then have them exchange papers to see if they can detect the unsuitable language in each other's writing and replace it with everyday language.

7. *Activity.* Repeat Activity 6, except focus on slang and nonstandard usage.

8. *Activity.* Assign students at random to small groups of four or five and challenge each group to make a list of all the stale, overused metaphorical expressons they can think of. Remind them that a metaphor says one thing to mean another, as when we say "Red" to mean Communist or "creep" to mean someone unattractive to us. After they have worked for twenty or thirty minutes, have students compare their lists. The following is a list that you can use to "prime the pump" (a metaphor!), or to supplement the expressions the students cite. Remind your students that these are all overused, prefabricated expressions that they should avoid.

get it together	take it on the chin
hit it on the nose	stick to your guns
a lot going for him	stand up for what I believe

TEACHING STUDENTS TO REVISE

my hopes went down the drain	had a fit
uphill climb	lost her marbles
grain of salt	fell flat on his face
struck a sour note	tore through her speech
ran the show with an iron hand	make waves
I died laughing	rock the boat
no bed of roses	fall in line
went ape over her	take it easy
he cooled off toward her and gave her the gate	kill time
she got the axe	shake a leg
he's a real pile-driver	cut it out
took off like a shot	knock it off
in apple pie order	dress fit to kill
all broken up	a snail's pace
went to pieces	

9. *Activity.* Assign students at random to small groups of four or five and challenge each group to make a list of all the stale, overused similes they can think of. Remind them that a simile compares one thing to another, using "as" or "like." If the simile is familiar to the writer, very likely it is stale and should not be used. Here are some examples to get students started:

hard as a rock	hard as nails
dead as a doornail	quick as a wink
run like the wind	sing like a bird
slow as molasses in January	hot as a firecracker
ugly as a mud fence	rough as a cob
slept like a log	snore like a buzz saw
greedy as a pig	ate like a horse
happy as a lark	light as a feather
cursed like a sailor	

10. *Activity.* Give students the paragraphs on Reproduction Page 115, which are resplendent with clichés. Have students work in pairs or independently to remove all the clichés and, where suitable, replace them with fresh and original language.

11. *Activity.* Below is a list of clichés. Working with the class, take the items in the list one at a time. Name the first half of the cliché and see if someone in the class can call out the other half. If someone can, that is a sure sign that it is a cliché. For example, read "leaps and . . ." from the list. Pause for someone to supply the missing "bounds." If no one does, read the cliché to the class and go on to the next one.

Alternate approach: reproduce the list, with the second half of the clichés missing, and have students fill in the blanks working individually.

ups and (downs)	wedded (bliss)
flesh and (blood)	rude (awakening)
sink or (swim)	fresh as (a daisy)
tit for (tat)	regular as (clockwork)
sixes and (sevens)	snug as (a bug in a rug)
wrack and (ruin)	lost in (thought)
fits and (starts)	up in (arms)
rhyme or (reason)	cool as (a cucumber)
flesh and (blood)	pleased as (punch)
pride and (joy)	dead as (a doornail)
kith and (kin)	malice (aforethought)
nip and (tuck)	standing (offer)
leaps and (bounds)	sneaking (suspicion)
hale and (hearty)	square (shooter)
rough and (tumble)	likeable (chap)
hammer and (tongs)	depths of (despair)
fine and (dandy)	all wool and (a yard wide)
hard and (fast)	at cross (purposes)
straight and (narrow)	in dire (straits)
time and (tide)	ulterior (motives)
by and (large)	fiendish (glee)
wine, women and (song)	trusty (revolver)
morning, noon and (night)	watery (grave)
high, wide and (handsome)	vicious (circle)
free, white and (twenty-one)	faithful (retainer)
sadder and (wiser)	crying (shame)
humble (servant)	diamond in the (rough)
all due (modesty)	motley (throng; crew)
in the nick of (time)	humble (abode)
clear as (crystal) (a bell)	filthy (lucre)
quick as (a flash)	coin of (the realm)
good as (my word)	

Topic IV: Becoming Sensitive to Style

1. *Teacher Presentation.* Point out to students that the final question to ask themselves in revising a paper is "Does it create the effect that I want?" If the purpose is to write humor, is the paper funny? If the purpose is to explain something, is the explanation clear? If the purpose is to argue a point, is the argument convincing? If the purpose is to make the reader sad, is the discussion moving?

    Explain to students that the effect created by a piece of writing is the result of writing style. Ask students to define style as it relates to clothing. They should come up with something like "the way or manner that a person does something." Discuss some things that contribute to or destroy style in clothing. If you are a dramatic type, you may want to play around with contemporary styles—putting on currently popular accessories that are inappropriate or in wrong combinations and ask students to explain what is wrong with your dress. You can also ask students to explain the process a person goes through in creating a stylish outfit.

    Explain that style in writing is similar to style in clothing. Review the appropriate definitions that they gave for style earlier and show how they apply to writing. Point out that one can learn some things about style from following rules, but that to a great extent one has to be observant and notice how things fit together and recognize when they do not.

2. *Activity.* Explain to students that the first aspect of style one should consider is appropriateness to purpose. One needs to vary words and sentence structure according to the goals of the writing. Show students a large picture of an historical subject containing much action. The paintings of Diego Rivera or Thomas Hart Benson are ideal for this purpose. Ask students to write a pargraph about the picture to fulfill each of the following purposes:

    a. Explain what the picture is about to a three-year-old child.

    b. Describe the picture for a mail-order catalog that will sell prints for people to hang in their homes.

    c. Describe either the artistic technique or the historical significance of the painting, as though you were writing an essay for art or history class. (Don't worry if your facts are not accurate.)

    d. Ridicule the picture humorously in a letter to a friend who hates art.

    e. Tell a friend or relative who likes art why you like the picture and encourage him or her to go see it.

3. *Activity.* Show students a photograph or a picture of a person or a group of people that has much detail. Assign students to write a poem about the picture or a paragraph describing the picture, telling a story about a person in the picture, or discussing in poetry or prose the way the picture makes them feel. In other words, ask students to respond to the picture but give them much freedom with regard to the way they may write.

4. *Activity.* Divide students into groups of four and distribute copies of Reproduction Page 116. Ask students to share their paragraphs with the group so that each person in the group has a chance to read and evaluate them. Each person should fill in one column of the chart on Reproduction Page 116, for each paper, including his or her own work.

After all groups are finished, ask them to take a few minutes to compare their answers and then discuss the following questions with the whole class.

a. How similar were the papers? Did most people in your group have similar styles or different styles?

b. Did most people evaluate each paper in the same way or were there many disagreements? Note that individual preferences often influence responses to style more than to other aspects of writing.

c. Were you surprised at the way people evaluated your writing? Were you able to see the differences in style among other papers easily?

ASSESSING ACHIEVEMENT OF OBJECTIVES

To measure the extent to which students have mastered the skills taught in this unit, reproduce a student-written essay (or paragraph) that contains all the errors covered by the revision checklist you have prepared for your students. Give a copy to each student and have each identify and correct each weakness. Grade students in terms of their thoroughness in identifying weaknesses and the appropriateness of their corrections.

RESOURCES FOR TEACHING PROOFREADING AND REVISION

Below is a selected list of resources useful for teaching the skills of proofreading, editing, and revision. Addresses of publishers can be found in Appendix A.

Audio-Visual Materials

The Basics of Good Spelling. Applause Productions. One record or cassette. Provides instruction and learning aids designed to teach the correct spelling of 400 frequently misspelled words.

Brush up on Punctuation. Applause Productions. Four filmstrips examine in detail the uses of, and reasons for, various marks of punctuation. Script included. Appropriate for average and advanced students.

Capital Letters and How to Use Them, The Gentle Art of Punctuation, and *Getting Your Point Across* by George Shea. Educational Activities, Inc. Each set includes two filmstrips, two cassettes and six duplicating masters. Humorous illustrations teach basic rules, and follow-up comic strip stories for duplication reinforce learning.

Fearless Punctuation. Centron Films. A series of five movies designed for middle-school and junior high school students. The movies use unusual visual devices, humor, and strong visual reinforcement to teach basic punctuation rules.

Facts about Phrases, All about Clauses, and *Comma Sense.* Thomas Klise Company. Three filmstrips with record or cassette, sold separately, teach specific grammar and usage topics through lively cartoons.

Mechanics: Capitalization and *Mechanics: Punctuation.* Encyclopedia Britannica Corp. Two of seven parts of the Composition Skills series. Contains forty-six transparencies in a plastic case, practice pages, and duplicating masters. Special teaching-guide pages simplify teaching and planning and suggest ways to motivate and involve students.

Punctuation Problems. Filmstrip House. One title in the Conquering Composition series. Contains four full-color filmstrips, four LP record sides or cassettes, and four scripts. Examines end punctuation, the comma, the semicolon, parentheses, dash, colon, and quotation marks. Interesting, appealing format.

The Sense of a Sentence. RMI Educational Films, Inc. A filmstrip that deals with sentence structure and use. Explains what a sentence is and why it is a necessary component in writing. Visually attractive, contemporary illustrations.

Tracking Down Sentence Problems I and II. Applause Productions. Each set contains four filmstrips designed to help students improve their understanding of English. Both include practice exercises. The first set focuses on pronouns, agreement and awkward shifts. The second set focuses on sentence structure, fragments, run-ons, dangling modifiers, and wordiness. Scripts are included.

The Use of Pronouns. Applause Productions. Four filmstrips describing the use of personal pronouns and nouns, pronoun case, compound personal pronouns, reflexives, and inflexives.

The Use of Verbs. Applause Productions. Six filmstrips discussing in detail the use and misuse of tense; transitive, intransitive, linking, regular, and irregular verbs; dangling participles; and subject-verb agreement. Informative and helpful.

Printed Materials

The Art of Styling Sentences: Twenty Patterns to Success by Marie L. Wadell, Robert M. Esch, and Roberta R. Walker. Barron's Educational Series, Inc. Employs the principle of modeling (also called patterning) to teach correct sentence structure. Twenty sentence patterns are illustrated, explained, and presented for practice. Emphasis is on practical application of the rules. Also offers chapters on figurative language with excerpts from famous literary works illustrating the twenty sentence patterns. Notes to the instructor included. Appropriate for general classroom use or individual study. Most suitable for more advanced students.

Can/May, Caps, and Commas by Eric Broudy and A. M. Goldstein. Silver Burdett Company. Deals with both usage and mechanics. Includes a glossary of standard English usage and exercises that measure comprehension and improvement. Detailed examination of mechanics, capital letters, semicolons, and spelling with extensive final review section. Excellent, visually attractive, easy-to-follow format. Appropriate for average and advanced students.

Card Guide to English Grammar, Punctuation and Usage by Vincent F. Hopper. Barron's Educational Series, Inc. One four-page laminated card presents the fundamentals of grammar, usage, and punctuation. Offers definitions of parts of speech, sentence parts, and subject and verb agreement. Provides examples of correct and incorrect uses of ten different marks of punctuation. Extensive guide to correct usage listing commonly misused words. Card can be inserted into a two-, three-, or five-ring binder. Condensed, complete and clear. A handy reference for students.

Check That Punctuation! by Harold Braker. College Entrance Publications. Explains the uses of fourteen different marks of punctuation, including comma, semicolon, dash, and period. Provides helpful punctuation tests and a glossary of grammatical terms. Easy-to-follow format and instructive model and samples presented throughout. Appropriate for more advanced students.

Classroom Author's Kit by Gordon A. Russell, Jr. Curriculum Associates, Inc. A simulation game in which students play the roles of writers, literary agents, editors, and publishers. The game is a good review of punctuation, sentence structure, sensory writing, oral reading, writing for an audience, and writing directions.

Common Errors in English: And How to Avoid Them by Alexander M. Witherspoon. Littlefield, Adams, & Co. Contains substantial chapters on usage—general rules, colloquialisms and slang, grammatical relationships, and diction. Alphabetical list of frequently misused words and phrases points out correct usages. Includes a thorough chapter on spelling—rules, aids, special rules and exceptions, plurals, compound words, and rules related to suffixes and prefixes. Excellent list of the correct spelling of frequently misspelled words.

A Composition Handbook by William E. Merriss and David H. Griswold. Independent School Press. Deals with sentence errors (run-ons and fragments), necessary and superfluous commas, quotation marks, capitals, tense, agreement, case, diction, and style. Exercises and practice assignments included. Designed for grades seven through twelve. Appropriate for older students with learning difficulties.

A Concise Guide to Clear Writing, an excerpt from *Clear Writing* by Marilyn B. Gilbert. John Wiley & Sons, Inc. Contains a list of helpful, necessary transitional words and linking phrases plus words and phrases that point out contrasts, results, time relationships, and mood changes. Exceptional chart format increases comprehension and facilitates understanding. Appropriate for advanced students.

English Competence Handbook by Paul Kalkstein, Thomas J. Regan, and K. Kelly Wise. Independent School Press. Provides instruction in the four fundamental comma and spelling rules, usage, and diction. Helpful as a supplementary text. Appropriate for more advanced students.

Errors in English and Ways to Correct Them by Harry Shaw. Barnes and Noble. Excellent, thorough discussion of correct usage (includes definitions of hundreds of words frequently misused), correct sentence structure, spelling, punctuation, mechanics, grammar, and sentence diagramming. Outstanding explanations and examples. An extremely valuable handbook for average and advanced students.

Experiments in Effective Writing by Victor E. Gould. Harcourt Brace Jovanovich. Includes sections on syntax (the participle, gerund, infinitive, appositive, and working verb) and "Rhetoric of Productive Sentences" (the principles of direction of movement, texture, and levels of specificity). Also examines semantics as a factor related to style. For advanced students only.

Grammar Lives! by Ronald T. Shepherd and John MacDonald. McDougal, Littell & Co. Covers the parts of speech (definitions and correct uses), common usage problems, sentence structure and combination (common difficulties with compound sentences, fragments, and run-ons), and sentence and paragraph patterns. Visually attractive, easy-to-follow format. Helpful diagrams, models, and samples. Activities and exercises provided. Interesting and instructive. Appropriate for average and advanced students.

Grammar with a Purpose. The Center for Learning. A teacher's guide with student handouts for duplication encourages students to write their own guidebook of rules and memory devices after presenting inductive activities and reinforcing drills. Students are taught to choose words, word forms, phrases, and sentence structures that are appropriate to the language content.

Handbook of English: Reference and Study Guide —Punctuation by Joseph R. Orgel. Educators Publishing Service, Inc. The first volume in a series that covers all aspects of standard English. Discusses correct and incorrect uses of punctuation. Provides detailed analysis and explanation with practice exercises and achievement tests that measure improvement and serve as reinforcement to instruction. Designed for high school and college students.

Handbook of English: Reference and Study Guide —Spelling by Joseph R. Orgel. Educators Publishing Service, Inc. The second volume in a series that covers all aspects of standard English. Deals with prefixes, words, silent letters, pluralizations, homonyms, word derivations, and language development. Presents extensive word lists, exercises, and prescribed strategies for spelling improvement.

How to Achieve Competence in English: A Quick Reference Handbook by Eric W. Johnson. Bantam Books. An alphabetized handbook of basic English usage, grammar, and writing that can be effectively used from middle school through high school. Is also suitable for English-as-a-second-language courses.

Individualized English by J. N. Hook and William Evans. Follett Publishing Co. A kit including programmed exercise cards, diagnostic test, mastery test, card sleeves, answer sheets, and teacher's guide. Programmed exercises help students overcome problems in grammar, usage, sentence structure, style and punctuation. Set J is for junior high students; set H is for high school students.

1001 Pitfalls in English Grammar by Vincent F. Hopper. Barron's Educational Series, Inc. Analyzes the most common errors in technical English—spelling, grammar, word choice, and punctuation. Especially helpful to bilingual students learning English as a second language. Contains numerous examples and practice assignments designed to clarify important problematic areas. Appropriate for all students.

Practical English Handbook by Floyd C. Watkins, William B. Dillingham, and Edwin T. Martin. Houghton Mifflin Co. A comprehensive handbook examining tense, mood, agreement, usage, number, verb forms, punctuation, consistency (in six separate areas), case, mechanics, diction, style, and composition. Excellent examples and models provided. A fine resource for average and advanced students.

About Punctuation. Channing L. Bete Company. A brief, easy-to-understand guide to correct punctuation. Includes explanations and examples of the uses of the major marks of punctuation and their relationships to conjunctions, phrases, clauses, words in a series, and sentences. Excellent, simple and direct—covers every imaginable situation. Fine for all students, especially those with minor learning difficulties.

Reading, Writing, and Rating Stories by Carol Sager. Curriculum Associates, Inc. A kit of skills books introducing an editing and revising technique that middle-school students can readily apply to their own writing. The program helps students become aware of the quality of vocabulary, elaboration, organization, and structure in their writing.

Sentence Composing, 10, 11, and *12.* Don Killgallon. Hayden Book. Co., Inc. This three-volume series emphasizes sentence-manipulating techniques such as sentence scrambling, sentence imitating, sentence combining, and sentence expanding. Each book uses model sentences written by professional writers.

Sentence Improvement by Malcolm Moore. Houghton Mifflin Co. This non-graded workbook is flexible and easily adapted for total classroom study. Teaches the basic principles of sentence structure and then examines problems related to style and usage. Excellent examples enrich the discussion of sentence patterns, clauses, phrases, and parallel structures. Exercises included.

Skills and Drills. McDougal Littell & Co. Short ninety-six page worktexts on grammar, usage, vocabulary, capitalization, and sentence-improvement. Each lesson begins with a brief explanation, followed with examples, and concludes with exercises for reinforcement. An average of forty exercises per lesson.

Spellbound by Elsie T. Rak. Educators Publishing Service, Inc. Remedial worktext designed for junior and senior high school students reading far below grade level. Developmental emphasis with step-by-step progression from simple to complex spelling principles. Comprehensive oral and written exercises provide practice and kinesthetic reinforcement. Excellent for students with learning problems. Teacher's manual available.

Spelling Your Way to Success by Joseph Mersand and Francis Griffith. Barron's Educational Series, Inc. Provides systematic, incremental instruction toward independent spelling improvement. Teaches concrete skills and self-reliance; designed to discourage dictionary dependence. Includes lists of frequently misspelled words, exercises, and progress tests designed to measure improvement.

Spell it Right by Harry Shaw. Barnes and Noble. Six techniques for improving spelling are introduced and explained. A good individualized resource for the student with spelling problems.

The Student Writer's Guide by Eliot D. Allen and Ethel B. Colbrunn. Everett/Edwards, Inc. Thorough examination of agreement, usage, diction, case, tense, punctuation (including explanations and examples of twelve different marks of punctuation), mechanics, and manuscript form. Models and samples provided throughout. Exercises and assignments included. A combination text/workbook. May be used as a consumable product.

Systematic Spelling edited by Myron R. Williams and Carl M. Saspar. Educators Publishing Service, Inc. A brief, informative book presenting eight approaches to correct spelling: pronunciation, principles of letter combinations, plurals, prefixes and suffixes, derivation, association, compounds, and possessives. Includes a list of 600 commonly misspelled words along with suggestions on how to learn to spell them correctly. Exercises and practice assignments throughout. Designed for grades seven to twelve.

Style and Structure by David Rannin. Harcourt Brace Jovanovich. Teaches techniques of style through models from major writers, writing activities, analyses, and exercises.

The Teaching of English Usage by Robert C. Pooley. National Council of Teachers of English. A descriptive, situationally based approach to determining "correctness" in language usage. By teaching informal standard English, it avoids the rigidity of rules. Interesting approach. Designed for junior and senior high school students.

Teams, Games and Tournament. Language Arts 7-9 by David L. DeVries and associates. Argus Communications. An exciting grammar, usage, and spelling program that combines the benefits of peer tutoring and peer competition in a format almost guaranteed to motivate junior high or middle-school students.

Vitalized English by Mary Didas. CEBCO/Standard Publishing. Contains sections on usage, words frequently misspelled, and mechanical problems associated with grammar, case, tenses, phrases, and structure. Provides exercises and review assignments, copies of recent New York State Regents Examination questions in English, and practice sections for college entrance tests. Useful to the advanced student.

Write it Right! by Gail Kredenser. Barnes and Noble. Discusses diction, word consciousness, word effectiveness, expressive impact, dangling modifiers, idioms, grammatical difficulties, split construction, antecedents, and punctuation. Explanations provided in well-delineated outline framework along with examples. Clear and concise.

Writing Errors You Hate to Make and How to Avoid Them by Richard Uhlich. Xerox Educational Publications. Examination of sentence fragments and run-ons, clauses, compound subjects, pronoun agreement, problems with antecedents, inverted word order, and suggestions on how to correct all of these technical, mechanical mistakes. Excellent workbook format that allows students to respond to many of the exercises right in the book.

Writing Skills Practice Kit by Alix Pirie. Learnco, Incorporated. A kit of activity cards that teach capitalization and punctuation skills. Each section begins with a brief history of the punctuation mark explaining how its use developed.

Writing Handbook by Michael P. Kammer, S. J., and Charles W. Mulligan, S. J. Loyola University Press. A comprehensive handbook covering parts of speech, the sentence, syntax (subject and predicates, agreement, verb use, case, phrases, and clauses), spelling, and diagramming. Numerous examples, lists, models, and diagrams provided. Very thorough. Suitable for advanced students only.

APPENDIX A

Addresses of Producers of Resources

Addison Wesley Publishing Company
1 Jacob Way
Reading, Massachusetts 01867

Allyn and Bacon, Inc.
470 Atlantic Avenue
Boston, Massachusetts 02210

Amsco School Publications
315 Hudson Street
New York, New York 10013

Applause Productions
85 Longview Road
Port Washington, New York 11050

Arco Publishing Company
219 Park Avenue South
New York, New York 10003

Argus Communications
7440 Natchez Avenue
Niles, Illinois 60648

Bantam Books
666 Fifth Avenue
New York, New York 10019

Barnes and Noble
Division of Harper and Row, Publishers
10 East 53rd Street
New York, New York 10022

Barron's Educational Series
113 Crossways Park Drive
Woodbury, New York 11797

Channing L. Bete Company
45 Federal Street
Greenfield, Massachusetts 01301

Cambridge Book Company
488 Madison Avenue
New York, New York 10022

CEBCO/Standard Publishing
104 Fifth Avenue
New York, New York 10011

The Center for Learning
P.O. Box 910
Villa Maria, PA 16155

Center for the Humanities
Two Holland Avenue
White Plains, New York 10603

Centron Films
Box 687
Lawrence, Kansas 66044

Citation Press
906 Sylvan Avenue
Englewood Cliffs, New Jersey 07632

College Entrance Publications
104 Fifth Avenue
New York, New York 10011

CTB/McGraw-Hill
Del Monte Research Park
Monterey, California 93940

Curriculum Associates, Inc.
8 Henshaw Street
Woburn, Massachusetts 10801

Designs for English
351 Madison Street
Wisconsin Rapids, Wisconsin 54494

Dodd, Mead and Company
79 Madison Avenue
New York, New York 10016

Doubleday Multimedia
1371 Reynolds Avenue
P.O. Box 11607
Santa Ana, California 92702

Eaton Paper Company
Pittsfield, Massachusetts 01201

Educational Activities, Inc.
P.O. Box 392
Freeport, New York 11520

Educational Record Sales
157 Chambers Street
New York, New York 10007

Educational Research Associates
Box 767
Amherst, Massachusetts 01002

Educators Publishing Service
75 Moulton Street
Cambridge, Massachusetts 02138

Encyclopedia Britannica Educational Corp.
425 N. Michigan Avenue
Chicago, Illinois 60611

Everett/Edwards, Inc.
Post Office Box 1060
Deland, Florida 32720

Eye-Gate
146-01 Archer Avenue
Jamaica, New York 11435

Filmstrip House
6633 West Howard Street
Niles, Illinois 60648

Folkways Records
701 Seventh Avenue
New York, New York 10036

Follett Publishing Co.
1010 W. Washington Blvd.
Chicago, Illinois 60607

Frederick Muller, Ltd.
Victoria Works,
Edgware Road
London NW 2, 6 LE, England

Glencoe Press
8701 Wilshire Blvd.
Beverly Hills, California 90211

Globe Book Company
175 Fifth Avenue
New York, New York 10010

Goodyear Publishing Company
1640 Fifth Street
Santa Monica, California 90401

Greystone Films, Inc.
Box 303, Kingsbridge Station
Riverdale, New York 10463

Guidance Associates
757 Third Avenue
New York, New York 10017

Harcourt Brace Jovanovich
757 Third Avenue
New York, New York 10017

Hart Publishing Company
12 East 12th Street
New York, New York 10003

Hayden Book Co., Inc.
50 Essex Street
Rochelle Park, New Jersey 07662

D.C. Heath and Company
125 Spring Street
Lexington, Massachusetts 02173

Holt, Rinehart & Winston
383 Madison Avenue
New York, New York 10017

ADDRESSES OF PRODUCERS OF RESOURCES

Houghton Mifflin Co.
2 Park Street
Boston, Massachusetts 02107

Independent School Press
51 River Street
Wellesley Hills, Massachusetts 02181

Interact
P.O. Box 262
Lakeside, California 92040

Thomas Klise Company
P.O. Box 3418
Peoria, Illinois 61614

Laidlaw Brothers
Thatcher & Madison
River Forest, Illinois 60305

Learnco, Incorporated
Box L
Exeter, New Hampshire 03833

J. B. Lippincott Company
East Washington Square
Philadelphia, Pennsylvania 19105

Littlefield, Adams & Co.
81 Adams Drive
Totowa, New Jersey 07512

London Association for the Teaching of
    English
Blackie & Son, Ltd.
5 Fitzhardinge Street
London, W.I., England

Loyola University Press
3441 North Ashland Avenue
Chicago, Illinois 60657

McDougal, Littell & Co.
P.O. Box 1667
Evanston, Illinois 60204

Macmillan Publishing Co., Inc.
866 Third Avenue
New York, New York 10022

Mentor Book Company
1301 Avenue of the Americas
New York, New York 10019

National Council of Teachers of English
1111 Kenyon Road
Urbana, Illinois 61801

NEA Distribution Center
The Academic Building
Saw Mill Road
West Haven, Connecticut 06515

New American Library
1301 Avenue of the Americas
New York, New York 10019

New York State English Council
Alan Nelson, Executive Secretary
Union College Humanities Center
Schenectady, New York 12308

Oxford University Press
200 Madison Avenue
New York, New York 10016

Pendulum Press, Inc.
The Academic Building
Saw Mill Road
West Haven, Connecticut 06516

Prentice-Hall, Inc.
Educational Book Division
Englewood Cliffs, New Jersey 07632

Prentice-Hall Media
150 White Plains Road, Box 186
Tarrytown, New York 10591

Random House, Inc.
210 E. 50th Street
New York, New York 10022

The Reading Lab, Inc.
55 Day Street
South Norwalk, Connecticut 06854

RMI Educational Films, Inc.
701 Westport Road
Kansas City, Missouri 64111

Science Research Associates
155 N. Wacker Drive
Chicago, Illinois 60606

Silver Burdett Company
Morristown, New Jersey 07960

Teachers College Press
1234 Amsterdam Avenue
New York, New York 10027

Teachers & Writers Collaborative
490 Hudson Street
New York, New York 10014

The University of Chicago Press
5801 Ellis Avenue
Chicago, Illinois 60637

J. Weston Walch, Publisher
Portland, Maine 04104

Westwood Educational Productions
701 Westport Road
Kansas City, Missouri 64111

John Wiley & Sons, Inc.
605 3rd Avenue
New York, New York 10016

H. W. Wilson Co.
950 University Avenue
Bronx, New York 10452

Xerox Educational Publications
Education Center
1250 Fairwood Avenue
Columbus, Ohio 43216

APPENDIX B

Sample Answers

(for reproduction pages)

Reproduction Page 6: Good and Bad Topic Sentences

1. bad—two subjects
2. OK
3. OK
4. bad—too broad
5. bad—too broad
6. OK
7. bad—too broad
8. OK
9. bad—too broad
10. bad—too broad
11. bad—too broad
12. bad—too broad
13. bad—too broad
14. bad—too broad
15. OK
16. OK
17. bad—two topics
18. OK
19. OK
20. OK
21. bad—too broad
22. OK
23. bad—too broad
24. bad—too broad
25. OK
26. OK

Reproduction Page 7: Developing a Topic Sentence

1. the reasons
2. the many sites
3. the lakes
4. ways they are more mature
5. the problems
6. the breeds
7. past experiences
8. what it was the result of
9. their pranks
10. ways he knew
11. the lessons
12. the ways
13. steps in the process of carving the ham
14. reasons for her regret
15. description of the flowers

Reproduction Page 8: Means of Paragraph Development

A. facts
B. narrative
C. examples
D. facts
E. description
F. examples
G. description
H. narrative
I. explanation
J. explanation

Reproduction Page 9: Choosing a Method of Developing a Topic Sentence

1. examples
2. examples
3. explanation
4. facts or explanation
5. analysis
6. narrative
7. description
8. facts
9. analysis
10. examples
11. facts
12. explanation
13. narrative
14. description
15. facts
16. examples
17. examples
18. facts
19. explanation
20. examples
21. explanation
22. description
23. narrative
24. facts
25. description
26. narrative
27. explanation
28. facts
29. explanation

Reproduction Page 10: Planning a Paragraph Based on Details

A. *Unifying Theme:* dirty, busy road construction
   Eliminate: schoolhouse, garbage, birds, cows, and children
   Topic Sentence: We spent at least half of our tour driving through the dirt and excitement of major road construction
   Method of Development: description

B. *Unifying Theme:* vividness and excitement of tennis match
   Eliminate: dust, chefs, breeze, tournament take
   Topic Sentence: Excitement quivered in the brilliant summer air as the match progressed. *Or:* The tennis match was a scene of color and rising excitement.
   Method of Development: description

C. *Unifying Theme:* disintegration of a man
   Eliminate: morning paper, best sellers, voting, fishing, Yale
   Topic Sentence: As time went by, we watched him turn into someone very different from the George we had known.
   Method of Development: narrative

D. *Unifying Theme:* report of a rally, demonstration and riot
   Eliminate: fire at 93rd Street, I don't like.... if the demonstrators.... people should not flock...

SAMPLE ANSWERS 113

Topic Sentence: The rally honoring J. Singleton Flurry ended with arrests and injuries after a demonstration by his opponents turned into a riot.
Method of Development: facts

E. *Unifying Theme:* purpose and importance of kneading in making bread
Eliminate: staff of life, kneading is fun
Topic Sentence: Kneading is a very important part of bread making
Method of Development: explanation

F. *Unifying Theme:* artists, writers, musical composers with mental or physical illnesses
Eliminate: Caesar, Roosevelt, Monroe
Topic Sentence: Many of the world's most renowned artists, authors, and composers accomplished their great works in spite of the ravages of mental or physical illness
Method of Development: examples

Reproduction Page 11: Putting Details in Order

A. Best order is probably spatial as writer moves up walk to house.
B. Chronological order is probably best.
C. climactic order
D. climactic order

Reproduction Page 47: Restricting the Global Topic

1. Good health is essential to a happy life. Protein is the foundation of a healthful diet.
2. The Mississippi Valley provides a channel for Canadian polar air.
3. Television may well make war obsolete. Conscientious objection to war is on the rise in America.
4. Many American high school students choose a diet notably lacking in life-supporting nutrients. In America, bread is far from the staff of life.
5. Cars should be made to go no more than 75 miles per hour.
6. Drivers convicted of driving while inebriated should be given a prison sentence if convicted a second time.
7. Amateur sports offer an excellent outlet for a person's competitive impulses.
8. Many famous people wasted away from what we now know was tuberculosis. Every child should have finished an immunization program by the third or fourth grade.
9. A good father always has time to spend with his children. A child needs to know he is important to his parents.
10. Television commercials sell youth.
11. Children who grow up seeing actual battles on television will not have the romantic concept of war that their parents had in their youths. Hollywood sometimes makes war seem like lots of good, clean fun.
12. Instant foods taste good only to people who do not remember Grandma's cooking.
13. Voters are often negative toward spending tax money for programs to help the elderly.
14. California was the first state to pass a law requiring control of automobile exhaust pollution.
15. Electric appliances have made housecleaning an easier job.

Reproduction Page 48: Enlarging the Limited Topic

1. Children learn many important lessons about life and death from association with pets during their preschool and early school years.
2. Life has taught me that successful human relations depend on mutual thoughtfulness.
3. The lake and its wooded shoreline presented a scene of unsurpassed beauty.
4. I entered the old tenement building like a traveler embarking on a strange and perilous journey.
5. Play is the natural learning activity of young animals, including children.
6. Many of the species of animals threatened with extinction can be saved only through controlled and protected breeding programs.
7. Politics, it is said, is the art of the possible.
8. Friendship is an art.
9. Not all desserts are lacking in nutritional value.
10. Cancer is a disease that is a product of the way we live.
11. Athletics can teach a young person many lessons in character development.
12. Young people of our society are under strong pressure to achieve and to succeed at an early age.
13. The functions and influences of the American family are undergoing rapid and significant changes.
14. Children's patterns for winning love and approval are well established by the time they start school.
15. Schools should offer each student the freedom to grow in the direction of his or her own unique capacities and interests.

Reproduction Page 49: Determining Composition Size

1.	(b)	shelf of books	14.	(d)	chapter
2.	(f)	short essay	15.	(c)	book
3.	(c)	book	16.	(f)	short essay
4.	(a)	library	17.	(b)	shelf of books
5.	(d)	chapter	18.	(a)	library
6.	(e)	long essay	19.	(f)	short essay
7.	(c)	book	20.	(a)	library
8.	(g)	paragraph	21.	(b)	shelf of books
9.	(g)	paragraph	22.	(f)	short essay
10.	(d)	chapter, or	23.	(c)	book
	(c)	book	24.	(f)	short essay
11.	(f)	long essay	25.	(g)	paragraph
12.	(a)	library	26.	(g)	paragraph
13.	(g)	paragraph			

Reproduction Page 52: Developing a Thesis by Relating Two Subjects

Subject	Second Subject
loving families	crime
football	membership in society

SAMPLE ANSWERS

football	war
basketball	football
teen years	life decisions
apples	good health
grade chasing	good grades
good human relations	communication
loyalty	personal values
making own clothes	economy
vitamin C	getting colds
careful driving	courtesy
good manners	thoughtfulness
TV advertising	growing old

Reproduction Page 53: Constructing a Thesis by Relating One Subject to Another

1. What human beings can put together, a tornado can take apart.
2. It is a rare girl who can hold her own on a boys' basketball team.
3. Independent people seem to prefer cats as pets.
4. Some young men seem fearful of the new expectations concerning male roles being verbalized by leaders of the women's liberation movement.
5. Many teenagers habitually sleep far less than doctors recommend.
6. As unemployment increases, so does crime.
7. Life in modern society is not very conducive to peace of mind.
8. Europeans seem more disposed than Americans to utilize public transportation.
9. Spring is a perfect time to take a float trip on a gently flowing, scenic stream.

Reproduction Page 54: Determining the Subjects of Thesis Sentences

1. fertilizer—blue grass lawn
2. overcast day—good book
3. Wicker furniture—screened porch
4. Breakfast—nutritional needs
5. plants—endangered species
6. white bread—food value
7. hair—cultural differences
8. driver's license—ticket to freedom
9. kitchen—singing bird
10. cats—birds

Reproduction Page 55: Limiting the Sweeping Thesis

1. If a family is happy together.... As long as food and shelter are available.... If hard work can gain an adequate living.... If one lives in a beautiful setting....
2. Sometimes having all one wants is poor preparation for coping with adversity. Some people believe retaining their own wealth is more important than using it to help others. Some people believe that having great wealth makes them "better" than those who are poor.

3. Some politicians have less responsible fiscal policies than others. A few politicians who are corrupt make us mistrust all politicians.
4. For the accomplished surfer, the surf in Hawaii offers. . . .
5. For the invalid who still enjoys good eyesight and agile fingers. . . . For the handwork artist who wishes to create an heirloom.
6. Unless you prefer a less formal, clipped appearance. . . . Except for bluegrass that is dormant in July and August. . . .
7. Except for loud rock, which has damaged eardrums and raises blood pressure. . . .
8. One of the gravest problems. . . . The gravest economic problem. . . .
9. For most people. . . . For most American young people. . . .
10. Travel experience adds a great deal to one's education.
11. Cat lovers particularly love a frisky kitten. Most children. . . .
12. It is often useful to have a friend help you with. . . .
13. Some shy young people. . . . It is a rare young person who does not feel some nervousness when preparing to enter senior high school.
14. Some seniors. . . . Many seniors, involved with their own affairs, ignore. . . .
15. Some students. . . . some teachers. Students who are not superior achievers often find it . . . with teachers who are always impersonal and businesslike.

Reproduction Page 56: Finding Weaknesses in Thesis Statements

1. go around? romantic love? parental love? When a person is in love, the world seems more exciting and meaningful.
2. great? holiday? fun? For someone who wants to combine warm sun and sandy beaches with the excitement of a big city, Miami is a splendid place for a vacation.
3. free? worth living in? Life in a nation where civil liberties are protected by law is far better than life in a police state.
4. all? good? democracy? fight? liberty? If the United States is ever attacked by another nation, all citizens who appreciate our democratic government will work hard to defeat the enemy, in whatever ways are appropriate to their abilities.
5. patriotism? respond? in what way? needs? If we love our country, we will be willing to sacrifice some of our own comfort to help solve national problems.
6. lady? well bred? A girl should be courteous, dress neatly, and behave properly if she wants people to think well of her and her family.
7. the whole world? loves? Most people enjoy being around someone who is in love.
8. one? one? moving ahead? falling behind? A student who is not constantly learning more will soon fall behind his or her classmates.
9. get ahead? Most Americans are imbued with an old-fashioned ambition to make a lot of money.
10. all Americans? always? devoted? Many American farmers have undergone great hardships to keep their land.
11. Loyalty—to person or to principle? Loyalty to a friend or family is one of the noblest of human virtues.
12. a great portion? poverty? Approximately one-third of the world's people, according to some estimates, regularly does not get enough to eat.
13. every? beauty? Most people find it worthwhile to spend at least part of their energy trying to make their homes beautiful.

SAMPLE ANSWERS

14. much? major city? Professional football can attract visitors to any city large enough to support a successful team.
15. free? do battle? those? liberty? A country that wants to remain independent must be prepared to resist the enticements of other countries that offer them aid with strings attached.

Reproduction Page 57: Unifying the Thesis Sentence

1. *Sever or unify:* Because, all too often, the father is not an important figure in the ghetto family, juvenile delinquency is a serious urban problem.
2. OK.
3. *Unify:* Because recent political events have revealed the dishonesty of many politicians, a movement should be started to identify the good, honest politicians in America.
4. *Sever.*
5. *Sever.*
6. OK.
7. *Unify:* Although New York is the biggest city in the United States, San Francisco is the most cosmopolitan.
8. *Unify:* Cats are more independent than dogs. *Or:* Dogs are more eager to please than cats.
9. OK.
10. *Subordinate to a larger generalization:* The youth culture of the 1960s seemed to many adults to be a manifestation of all that was degraded. *Or combine:* Many of the people who saw the Beatles as a Communist menace were also sure that long hair was a mark of moral degradation.
11. *Divide into at least three subjects:*
    a. The beautiful colors of dawn reward the early riser.
    b. Poets of autumn have been inspired by the dramatic cloud formations and colors of sunset.
    c. Writers seem more likely to be night people than early risers.

Reproduction Page 58: Evaluating Thesis Sentences

1. no, personal preference
2. no, self-evident fact
3. no, imprecise and unrestricted
4. OK
5. no, personal preference
6. no, fact
7. OK
8. no, fact
9. OK
10. no, fact
11. no, fact
12. no, imprecise
13. OK
14. OK
15. no, imprecise and unrestricted
16. no, unrestricted

Reproduction Page 59: Dividing a Thesis Statement into its Parts

1. reasons why
2. real purpose behind our speaking
3. benefits derived

4. (a) beneficial consequences of wars—examples needed
   (b) peaceful means by which these same positive outcomes could have been achieved
5. (a) lessons a young person could learn
   (b) styles of living that would promote such learning
6. (a) behavior contrary to doctor's warning—smoking, etc.
   (b) behavior contrary to scientists' warning—DDT, etc.
   (c) behavior contrary to police's warning—hitchhiking, etc.
   (d) behavior contrary to safety experts' warnings—boating without life jacket, etc.
7. (a) free intercommunication enriches life
   (b) barriers exist to prevent intercommunication
   (c) how to overcome barriers
8. differences
9. ways in which it is horrifying

Reproduction Page 60: Determining Order of Thesis Parts

1. a. 5
   b. 1
   c. 4
   d. 2
   e. 3
2. a. 5
   b. 2
   c. 1
   d. 3
   e. 4
   f. 6
3. a. 3
   b. 6
   c. 2
   d. 4
   e. 1
   f. 5
4. a. 5
   b. 6
   c. 3
   d. 1
   e. 2
   f. 4
5. a. 6
   b. 3
   c. 5
   d. 7
   e. 1
   f. 4
   g. 2
6. a. 3
   b. 7
   c. 6
   d. 1
   e. 2
   f. 4
   g. 5
7. a. 2
   b. 6
   c. 5
   d. 4
   e. 3
   f. 1

Reproduction Page 64: Transition Devices

Part I:
1. (b) also
2. (a) another
3. (a) on the other hand
4. (a) as a result
5. (b) one form
6. (b) she still loves the outdoors, however
7. (a) however
8. (a) having managed to complete her English assignment for the week
9. (a) other, this
10. (a) however

Part II:
1. However, many American women will no longer accept this domination passively.
2. First I attacked. . . .

SAMPLE ANSWERS   119

   3. However, I had a deep....
   4. An equally difficult lesson for me....
   5. The tension on both sides was also increased by an incident....
   6. Equally important is that care be exercised in planning the guest list.

Reproduction Page 66: Identifying the Four Common Types of Introductions

Paragraph I.   contrast and outline
Paragraph II.   funnel
Paragraph III. anecdotal
Paragraph IV. funnel
Paragraph V.   outline
Paragraph VI. outline
Paragraph VII. anecdotal

Reproduction Page 68: Testing Funnel Introductions for Coherence

I. The generalization and thesis are opposite ideas.
II. Too large gaps in thought and change in direction.
III. Starts with friendship, changes direction in the middle, and ends with solitude, an entirely different subject.
IV. Introduction opens with discussion of ideas that do not in any way lead to the thesis statement.

Reproduction Page 71: Constructing Contrast Introductions

1. Assumption thesis contradicts: Ballet dancing looks effortless.
2. Assumption thesis contradicts: Receiving a compliment is always a pleasure welcomed by anyone.
3. Assumption thesis contradicts: Honesty is always the best policy.
4. Assumption thesis contradicts: You should always look before you leap.
5. Assumption thesis contradicts: Harry Truman, a rather uncultivated, uneducated specimen of the common man, accomplished very little.

Reproduction Page 92: Outlining Worksheet

1.   What I like about my hometown
    I. location
       A. near a large city
       B. on a river
       C. in the mountains
    II. facilities
       A. superior library
       B. park
       C. recreation center
       D. theaters

III. school
      A. well-trained teachers
      B. balanced curriculum
      C. modern classrooms
   IV. people
      A. friendly
      B. charitable

2. Kinds of dogs
   I. Sport dogs
      A. Setters
         1. Irish setter
         2. English setter
      B. Retrievers
         1. Golden retriever
         2. Labrador retriever
   II. House dogs
      A. Poodles
      B. Cocker spaniel
      C. Bull dog
   III. Working dogs
      A. As police dog
      B. As Seeing Eye dog
      C. As guard dogs
         1. Sheep dog
         2. German shepherd

Reproduction Page 101: Spelling Proofreading Exercise

    Recently I learned a very important lesson about <u>releiving</u> my own problems rather than expecting others to help me <u>bare</u> my troubles. I had been feeling pretty blue for some time. My dog, who had been with me <u>sinse</u> I was a little more <u>then</u> a baby, just <u>layed</u> down one evening, on the <u>bear</u> basement floor, and <u>dyed</u>. Of <u>coarse</u>, I <u>new</u> he had <u>lead</u> a good life, and he was <u>definately</u> not young, having lived six years, or about the same as <u>forty-two</u> years in the life of a <u>humane</u> being. Therefore, his death shouldn't have been considered a <u>tradgedy</u>. But it was, nonetheless, <u>a truely</u> sad <u>occassion</u>, and I couldn't seem to get over the <u>affect</u> of <u>loosing</u> such a good old faithful friend.

    One day it <u>occured</u> to me that I had not really <u>tryed</u> to do anything about <u>overcomming</u> the <u>indefinate sence</u> of loneliness that was making me feel depressed all the time, ever <u>sinse</u> my dog <u>dyed</u>. I hadn't <u>truely tryed</u> to <u>except</u> the fact that the death had <u>occured</u>, <u>weather</u> I <u>choose</u> to <u>reconize</u> it or not; and the time had come, I knew, when I must use good <u>sence</u> and move on into new <u>activitys</u>, <u>seperating</u> myself from the <u>passed</u>.

    I decided to follow the <u>principal</u> of replacement in training myself to a new and better attitude. I would replace the fun I <u>use</u> to have with Beau with other pleasures and <u>persuits</u>. (<u>Incidently</u>, this method is good <u>phsychology</u>, and I recommend it to anyone who has <u>alot</u> of problems <u>acheiving piece</u> of mind after <u>loosing</u> a pet.)

The first thing I did on the evening this idea finally <u>occured</u> to me was to check the <u>temparture</u> on the thermometer outside my window. Sure enough, it was a lovely warm 70 degrees, perfect gardening <u>whether</u>, and I knew I'd be <u>alright</u> planting flower seeds. I quickly <u>through</u> on my gardening <u>cloths</u> and went to the garage to get the tools I had <u>recieved</u> as a birthday gift. I also took <u>alot</u> of seeds I had <u>layed</u> away for the spring day when the <u>temperture</u> would be <u>alright</u> for planting.

Bearing these things with me to the back yard, I began to plant seeds along the <u>boundry</u> of our yard. I <u>choose</u> a place where the sun almost <u>allways</u> shone. I felt better at once, as soon as I began digging in the warm soil. Gardening has <u>allways</u> been a soothing <u>passtime</u> for me, and <u>immediatly</u> it began to divert my mind from poor Beau's death.

I did feel a little guilty about going ahead with the flower <u>graden</u> without waiting for my little brother, but I <u>beleive</u> the older child should have some <u>priveleges</u> that <u>definately</u> belong to him, so my <u>conscious</u> didn't hurt me <u>to</u> badly. My gardening soothed my spirit, and the whole experience <u>lead</u> me to a realization that life goes on, and one must move with it and not let any <u>tradegy</u>, <u>wether</u> major or <u>miner</u>, <u>effect</u> him <u>to</u> much.

Reproduction Page 106: Punctuation Proofreading Exercise

Painting is a multifaceted, versatile, and diverse field. There are many different, distinctive types of painting, such as naturalistic, nonrepresentational, geometric, biomorphic, symbolic, and literal, etc. Good artists always consider the possibilities open to them. They carefully decide how to communicate their feelings, what colors to use, what style, technique, and manner to employ. Competent, serious artists use their medium, explore its range and scope, and attempt to bring both their medium and their message into harmonious, lucid focus. It's the artist's job, according to many experts, to convey the message as expressively as possible. Many of the paintings that we laugh off and label simple, silly, and childish are really the products of enormous effort, tenacious, unending hard work, and limitless, creative decision. Don't be like one of my neighbors who said, "That painting is crooked, and any two-year-old could do better." Next time you view a painting, give it a fair chance; consider its message, its purpose, its expressiveness. Don't just decide on face value whether or not it's good.

Reproduction Page 107: Comma Exercise

My summer as a volunteer at Children's Hospital in Buffalo,[7] New York,[7] was a time when I learned to think about people besides myself,[4] developed a sense of responsibility,[4] and decided that I wanted a career working with children. Lucy,[10] who supervised my work in the playroom,[10] explained how important it was for me to come regularly,[4] be on time,[4] and take good care of equipment. Although I tried to be mature,[5] I sometimes goofed off,[9] but after a little boy almost got hurt because I was careless,[5] I became more careful. I soon forgot about my own interests and concerns and learned to concentrate on the children and what they wanted. I was sad when I had to leave,[9] but one little boy made me feel better. He said,[3] "You finish school so you can come back and work here all the time." You know,[6] I think I will.

Reproduction Page 111: **The Grammar Witch**

Once upon a time, a long time ago, in a green asbestos-shingled cottage by a deep, dark lake with monsters in its depth, there was a lady who was known as the grammar witch. The number of people who were lost in her grammar ovens was never known for sure, but it must have been high, according to the local gossip about whose family had lost its third member and whose family had lost its fourth, fifth, sixth, etc.

She was also one of those witches who didn't care about others' misusing grammar as long as they tried, tried, tried as hard as she. A lot of people don't feel that way; they think you're a social outcast whose need for grammar and usage lessons outweighs any good points that you might have. Either they or she is wrong; it's obvious, in their attitude.

Anyhow, this witch used to sit down by the lake as comfortable as she could be and watch for unwary victims whom she could entice into her grammar ovens. There were many weary travelers she caught on their way past her cottage, going home from work. She would lie in wait ten hours at a time; that's a long tiring time to sit in one place. As a matter of fact, ten hours is too long to do any one thing, it seems to me. However, remember, she was a witch, and they are not like the rest of us.

Well, she would lie there and wait and turn over in her mind all the grammar lessons she would teach to whomever she caught, no matter who they were. Agreement of verbs and subjects was her favorite lesson, and she would teach it to absolutely anyone; she wasn't particular. Businessmen, for instance along with a lot of employees, were her favorite victims. It was they who aroused in her a regular frenzy of teaching and inspired her to pedagogical extremes that were hers alone.

Be that as it may, since the victims she lured in and tried to teach were seldom fascinated by her efforts, she usually ended up in a violent, towering rage and popped them, screaming, writhing, and sobbing, into her ovens, which always had clouds of smoke pouring from their chimneys.

Now, that may sound cruel, inhuman, and atrocious to you, but if so, you're not thinking enough about how hard all this was on the poor, frustrated grammar witch. Think how she must have felt when those whom she was trying to teach just ignored her fine lessons, and acted as if they thought their lives would be perfectly happy without knowing grammar. Isn't that disgusting?

SAMPLE ANSWERS

One day in her ovens, a quite routine day, actually, ~~their~~ *there* was a businessman ~~who~~ *whom* she'd caught on his way home from work, a truck driver ~~who's~~ *whose* truck had ~~staled~~ *stalled* near her cottage, a high school student who had forgotten to do his homework, and three pastry cooks whom she felt convinced she could never educate to the joys of ~~grammer~~ *grammar*. Poor things. ~~There~~ *Their* attitude was not good. The others were less willing than the high school student, although they were, to tell the truth, somewhat smarter than ~~him~~ *he*. I would not like to be ~~him~~ *he*. Would you? Oh well.

Now, if ~~your~~ *you're* wondering why this short, unhappy story of the ~~grammer~~ *grammar* witch is, indeed, short, which is seldom the case of stories these days, let me remind you, dear students, that on another day, at another hour, you might well have another story to read, carefully trying to catch all errors in ~~grammer~~ *grammar*, and that other story will have spelling problems in it; thus this story—or another one like it—can't be to*o* long, isn't that right? Oh, well.

Reproduction Page 112: Eliminating Pretentious Language

1. desire—want
2. uttered—said
3. conveyed—carried
4. edifice—building
5. heavens—sky
6. pass away—die
7. veracity—truthfulness
8. poverty stricken—poor
9. loquacious—talkative
10. solar body—sun
11. heavenly body—star
12. gentleman—man
13. consumed—burned or ate depending on meaning
14. prevaricate—lie
15. inception—beginning
16. initiate—start or begin
17. inebriated—drunk
18. astronomical—high
19. consequently—therefore
20. fraught with peril—dangerous
21. non-motile—immovable
22. illuminate—light
23. truncated—cut off
24. disseminate—spread

25. give pleasure to—please
26. human frailty—weakness or fault
27. hirsute—hairy
28. elucidate—clarify
29. predicated—based
30. circumvent—avoid
31. unfortunate culmination—bad end
32. arrive at a determination—decide
33. to occupy a position of prominence—to be prominent
34. to rectify a misapprehension—to correct a misunderstanding
35. predilection for laborious effort—a love of hard work

Reproduction Page 113: Avoiding Inappropriate Informal Language

1. snuck—sneaked
2. all shook up—all shaken up or disturbed
3. I could care less—I do not care
4. kid—child
5. guy—man or boy
6. phony—false
7. ripped off—stolen
8. rap—discuss
9. they fell out—they quarreled
10. had a fit—became upset
11. told her off—criticized her frankly
12. had a ball—had a good time
13. out of this world—marvelous
14. broke up—ended the relationship
15. he's crazy—he's wrong
16. took the rap—took the blame
17. a jerk—someone I don't like
18. laid it on the line—spoke frankly
19. guts—courage
20. nuts—madly mistaken
21. screwball—an eccentric person
22. he bugged me—he irritated me
23. knock it off—stop doing that
24. get lost—go away
25. they took off—they left
26. it was neat—it was very satisfactory
27. it was real good—really good
28. out of his mind—very much mistaken
29. up against it—facing serious obstacles
30. she was carrying on—expressing her feelings loudly
31. to have a fun time—an enjoyable time

32. cops—police
33. he faked it—he pretended to know what he was doing
34. she knocked their eyes out—she impressed them with her beauty
35. he hit the skids—everything went wrong for him
36. I dig him—I understand and approve of him

APPENDIX C

Reproduction Pages

The pages that follow have been provided to facilitate the reproduction of exercises and other materials needed for activities suggested in the preceding pages. Each page is perforated to make removal from this book easy. Once removed, the page can be used in any of three ways:

1. *For projection with an opaque projector.* No further preparation is necessary if the page is to be used with an opaque projector. The page may simply be inserted in the projector for viewing by the whole class.

2. *For projection with an overhead projector.* The Reproduction Page must be converted into a transparency for use with an overhead projector. To produce the transparency, overlay the Reproduction Page with a blank transparency and run both through a copying machine.

3. *For duplication with a spirit duplicator.* A master can be made from the Reproduction Page by overlaying it with a special heat-sensitive spirit master and running both through a copying machine. The spirit master can then be used to reproduce 50–100 copies on paper.

Please note that all material appearing on Reproduction Pages (as well as all other material in this book) is protected under the Copyright Law of the United States of America. Allyn and Bacon, Inc. grants to readers the right to make multiple copies of Reproduction Pages for nonprofit educational use only. All other rights are reserved.

REPRODUCTION PAGE 1

NARRATIVE

INSTRUCTIONS. Make a list of all of the ideas that Katie has in the narrative below.

Katie chewed on her pencil as she started her English exercise. She glanced across the room at Paul. He was working quickly. He surely seemed to be smart. She gazed at Paul for a moment, looking at his curly blond hair, his rugged, handsome features, and his blue Future Farmers of America jacket. She wondered what he was really like. Like the other farm kids, he had gone to a rural elementary school and now he rode home on the bus right after school every day. The farm kids and the town kids never seemed to get together. Katie wondered how she could get to know him. She wondered if living on a farm was still like the description in her fifth grade textbooks. It really seemed strange that the town and rural areas were so close, but so far apart.

Katie was brought back to attention as the teacher directed the class to take out their literature books and turn to the story, "The Lottery." The story puzzled her. It was about a community that had a cruel custom of stoning one of its members chosen at random. Did people really do things like that? Was the story supposed to be symbolic? If so, what did it mean? She wondered what she would do if she were trapped in a situation where everyone else was being cruel. It reminded her a little of a time when she had been sitting in the cafeteria with Anne and Dana, and Kara, a new girl in school, had come up to them. Anne had winked at Dana and started making fun of Kara behind her back. Katie had felt bad, but she didn't know what to do.

The bell rang, and Katie gathered up her books. Tina pushed past her, knocking her books out of her hands and not even stopping. Katie muttered angrily under her breath. Tina surely was acting hateful lately. Katie wondered if something was wrong. Tina used to be much more pleasant. Maybe she and her parents were fighting again.

Katie was certainly glad her mother was so understanding and sometimes questioned where her mother got her patience. It must be hard working all day and raising two daughters. Even when she must have been exhausted, her mother seemed to love life. "Will I grow up like her?" Katie wondered.

Copyright © 1982 by Allyn and Bacon, Inc. Reproduction of this material is restricted to use with *A Guidebook for Teaching Composition*, 2nd Edition, by Gene Stanford and Marie Smith.

REPRODUCTION PAGE 2

QUESTIONS TO HELP YOU GET IDEAS

1. WHO. Who is the story or picture about? What can you tell about the person or people?

2. WHAT. What is happening? List all ideas you have about the events.

3. WHEN. When did this take place? Does the time matter? Could it happen today?

4. WHERE. Where did it take place? Does the place matter? Could it happen here?

5. WHY. Why did it happen? Do you know why it happened? If not, can you guess?

Copyright © 1982 by Allyn and Bacon, Inc. Reproduction of this material is restricted to use with *A Guidebook for Teaching Composition*, 2nd Edition, by Gene Stanford and Marie Smith.

REPRODUCTION PAGE 3

PROBLEM-SOLVING STRATEGY

Step I: Recognize the problem. The problem may be assigned by your teacher. If not, you can recognize a problem when you sense something that bothers you or that seems strange or difficult to understand. For instance, you can see that an author keeps repeating a certain descriptive phrase throughout an entire book and you wonder why, or you read that an Indian tribe made a 2,000-mile journey across the country to a new home and you cannot imagine what would cause them to undertake such a terrible journey.

Step II: Define the problem. Put the problem into your own words.

Step III: Identify the unknowns. Make a list of all of the things you need to know in order to solve the problem or answer your question.

Step IV: Collect information. Find all of the information that you decided in Step III you needed to know.

Step V: Allow the problem to incubate. After you have done the first four steps, if possible, put the problem aside for a few days or hours so you can come back with a fresh perspective.

Step VI: Think of a trial solution (hypothesis). Your hypothesis should be your answer to the problem. It will probably become the thesis statement of your essay.

Step VII: Test your trial solution. Before you begin writing with your hypothesis as the thesis, check it against all the evidence that you have.

Copyright © 1982 by Allyn and Bacon, Inc. Reproduction of this material is restricted to use with *A Guidebook for Teaching Composition,* 2nd Edition, by Gene Stanford and Marie Smith.

REPRODUCTION PAGE 4

USING THE PROBLEM-SOLVING STRATEGY

Step I: Recognize the problem.

The problem was assigned by the social studies teacher. It is: "Write an essay about the most important functions of the American family."

Step II: Define the problem.

In my own words, "What are the most important things that the American family does for people?"

Step III: Identify the unknowns (things you need to know).

1. What people does the family do things for?
2. What does the family do for each of those people?
3. How can I judge which of these things are most important?

Step IV: Collect information (answers to questions from Step III).

1. What people does the family do things for?
   a. children
   b. parents
   c. grandparents and other relatives
   d. neighbors
   e. society as a whole

2. What things does the family do for each of these people?
   a. children—gives them the essentials of life, that is, food, clothes, shelter; teaches them rules for society; makes them feel cared about; gives them an identity.
   b. parents—gives them a sense of belonging; makes them feel cared about and useful.
   c. grandparents and other relative—gives them someone they can call on for help; gives them someone who cares about them.
   d. neighbors—can't think of any.
   e. society as a whole—organizes people; teaches children social values and takes care of people's needs.

3. How can I judge which of these things are most important?
   a. Is the family essential for its members to stay alive?
   b. Does it contribute to a person's mental and emotional health?

Copyright © 1982 by Allyn and Bacon, Inc. Reproduction of this material is restricted to use with *A Guidebook for Teaching Composition,* 2nd Edition, by Gene Stanford and Marie Smith.

REPRODUCTION PAGE 4 — USING THE PROBLEM-SOLVING MODEL

Step V: Allow the problem to incubate.

Step VI: Think of a trial solution.

> In Step IV, the main ideas seemed to be:
> - Providing children with essentials for life and help to older people and relatives
> - Giving children, parents, and grandparents a sense of belonging and of being cared about.
>
> *Hypothesis:* The most important functions of the family are to provide the necessities of life for people who are unable to care for themselves and to give everyone a sense of belonging and being cared about.

Step VII: Test your trial solution.

> In looking over ideas from Step IV, I cannot find any other ideas this important. I think the trial solution will do.

Copyright © 1982 by Allyn and Bacon, Inc. Reproduction of this material is restricted to use with *A Guidebook for Teaching Composition,* 2nd Edition, by Gene Stanford and Marie Smith.

SAMPLE TOPIC SENTENCES

We never got along well after that.

Household plants add much to the charm of any house.

A cat's diet should not be varied from day to day.

A brisk walk after dinner can have a number of beneficial effects.

Some girls wear so much make-up that it detracts from their charm instead of enhancing it.

Putting too much effort into getting high grades can prevent one from profiting fully from an education.

I would rather take an examination than write a paper as a means of being graded.

Physical education classes are a source of embarrassment to many students.

The average student—one who makes mostly C's—is spared many problems in school.

The room had been thoroughly ransacked.

Her locker looked like the nest of a pack rat.

The mailman on our route had good cause to fear dogs.

Many students truly enjoy going to school.

There are many satisfactions to be gained from making bread.

Students in the 1980s seem more apathetic toward social issues than they were in the 1960s.

The bee is, indeed, a busy insect.

Green beans are easy to grow.

Only humankind does not order its days by the sun.

Lawn mowing need not be a boring task.

Breakfast is my favorite meal.

A good banana split is a work of art.

It was my fault more than his that we did not remain friends.

A boy can learn much from owning a dog.

I was never able to learn in her class.

It was a day made for kites.

I began to think the hour would never end.

She seemed to delight in making me feel foolish.

Copyright © 1982 by Allyn and Bacon, Inc. Reproduction of this material is restricted to use with *A Guidebook for Teaching Composition*, 2nd Edition, by Gene Stanford and Marie Smith.

REPRODUCTION PAGE 5 — SAMPLE TOPIC SENTENCES

Their names suited their personalities.

Many students feel that they should use fancy language when they write.

For the invalid, particularly, food should look attractive as well as be nutritious.

Even the experienced pilot needs to return to flying school periodically.

Wood furniture will soon be priced out of the market for all but the rich.

It is easier to learn from a teacher one likes.

Some lessons are harder to learn than others.

The students resented having to go outside to smoke.

I never could believe the principal was my pal, even though my spelling teacher said he was.

Of course, short hair does have its advantages.

Fences are not always barriers between people.

Schoolrooms are usually drab and uninteresting looking places, at least those in high school.

One cannot stay well informed just by reading one newspaper.

All too often people will treat their best friends as they would not treat their worst enemies.

Good manners have never been near the top of my list of most significant human values.

It turned out to be a terrible day for me.

She seemed to enjoy being miserable.

His term paper was a real work of art.

There, perched on my window sill, was an insect that looked just like a miniature tyrannosaurus rex.

In many ways he was different from the rest of the fellows in our crowd.

Most of us would have a hard time tracing the origin of our personal beliefs.

I somehow felt especially at ease in her class.

Most of us find it easier to tolerate faults in ourselves than in others.

Copyright © 1982 by Allyn and Bacon, Inc. Reproduction of this material is restricted to use with *A Guidebook for Teaching Composition*, 2nd Edition, by Gene Stanford and Marie Smith.

REPRODUCTION PAGE 6

GOOD AND BAD TOPIC SENTENCES

Instructions: Some of the topic sentences below are specific enough to be developed in detail in one paragraph. Others are too broad and general. Still others have two or more topics in one sentence and are therefore poor topic sentences. Indicate after each sentence whether it is <u>OK</u> or whether it is <u>bad—too broad</u> or <u>bad—two or more topics.</u>

1. Both dogs and cats have some habits that make them difficult to keep as pets in a small apartment.
2. Dachshunds make fine watch dogs.
3. Drinking eight glasses of water a day promotes good health.
4. The earth's oceans may already be irreversibly polluted.
5. There are many reasons why scientists consider it a mathematical certainty that human life exists somewhere in the universe.
6. Cockroaches are equipped to survive us all.
7. Politics have fallen into disrepute in our society.
8. It is not difficult to paint a house.
9. World War II, unlike World War I, did not result in disastrous social dislocations in Germany.
10. Revisionist historians are giving us a much different view of the American Revolution from the one most of us gained in elementary school.
11. A satisfactory definition of the term "pollution" must reach into many areas of our lives and environment.
12. Weather, we are told, has significant effects on emotional balance and social behavior.
13. The science of weather prediction has existed as long as there have been herdsmen and food gatherers.
14. Psychological maturity is demonstrated by a giving, sharing, producing orientation to life.
15. Stonehenge can be described as a huge calendar.
16. The rehabilitation of America's major cities will require a massive infusion of tax money.
17. Three of the players on our school's 1955 football team went on to illustrious careers as professional players, and two of these individuals later became successful politicians.
18. Our float trip ended in an adventure we had not foreseen and which we were ill equipped to handle.

Copyright © 1982 by Allyn and Bacon, Inc. Reproduction of this material is restricted to use with *A Guidebook for Teaching Composition*, 2nd Edition, by Gene Stanford and Marie Smith.

REPRODUCTION PAGE 6   GOOD AND BAD TOPIC SENTENCES

19. The secret of a successful camping trip lies in the preparations made before leaving home.

20. Parenthood is not as easy a task as many young people would argue.

21. Adolescence is not so much a time as a function.

22. Students often complain about a class's being boring without realizing that they themselves may share the responsibility for a class's failure to come alive.

23. Youngsters' patterns of behavior are established well before they enter school.

24. Many famous Americans have come from disturbed and unhappy families.

25. A walk over a western prairie at dawn reveals a richness of life forms and activities that rivals an awakening city.

26. The river, like a person, shows itself in ever-changing activities and moods.

Copyright © 1982 by Allyn and Bacon, Inc. Reproduction of this material is restricted to use with *A Guidebook for Teaching Composition*, 2nd Edition, by Gene Stanford and Marie Smith.

REPRODUCTION PAGE 7

DEVELOPING A TOPIC SENTENCE

INSTRUCTIONS: Describe the developmental parts of a paragraph to be written about each of the following topic sentences.

1. I simply can't stand frogs.

2. There are many historical sites near Philadelphia.

3. The United States has some of the world's largest lakes.

4. In many ways, seniors are more mature than freshmen.

5. My loyalty to her caused me a number of problems.

6. Many breeds of tropical fish are suitable for a communal tank.

7. His fear of dogs is deeply rooted in past experiences.

8. His unexpected appearance at the party was not a result of his loyalty to her.

9. Their pranks almost destroyed the class.

10. The coach knew how to pull the team together as a unit.

11. We taught one another important lessons about camping.

12. There are many ways to trim a Christmas tree.

13. It is easy to carve a ham.

14. She wished she had never given that speech.

15. His flower garden was a showplace.

Copyright © 1982 by Allyn and Bacon, Inc. Reproduction of this material is restricted to use with *A Guidebook for Teaching Composition*, 2nd Edition, by Gene Stanford and Marie Smith.

REPRODUCTION PAGE 8

MEANS OF PARAGRAPH DEVELOPMENT

INSTRUCTIONS: Indicate the method of developing each paragraph in the space following it. Choose from these main methods of paragraph development: explanation, facts, description, narrative, or examples.

A. It had never been a large high school as compared to many city high schools, and now it was shrinking. At its peak, the student body had never numbered more than 1500, and by 1975, when the World War II "baby boom" had almost expended itself, the entering freshman class was 200 students smaller than the freshman class of just five years before. In September 1974, the faculty numbered 113, and already there were signs of professional staff reduction. Three retiring teachers were not replaced, and the foreign language department, for one, lost one teacher who was not replaced. Both part-time assistant coaches went elsewhere. It was obviously a shrinking faculty. Specialists such as counselors, reading experts and teachers trained in working with students with learning disabilities numbered considerably fewer in 1975 than in 1970, and hardly a department did not suffer the loss of nonprofessional aides and clerks. The number of principals went from four to three in 1975, and the staff of librarians was reduced from four to two. The facilities did not change; the school looked as large as ever, but the truth was that in many important ways the school was becoming smaller. _____

_____

B. By the time Winston was three years old, he had already used up three of his nine lives. When he was almost a year old, he was hit by a car and badly shaken up. We found him lying on the back doorstep, eyes closed and obviously in a state of shock. He was breathing shallowly but cried out strongly when we picked him up to carry him into the house. He must have been badly bruised, for he hardly moved for several days and cried whenever anyone inadvertently touched him carelessly. In time Winston did recover, a sadder and wiser cat who never went near the street again. His next near miss was a virus infection in the following October. Antibiotics made him well by Christmas, in time for him to be shot in the leg and stomach by a young man trying out his new Christmas present, a .22 rifle. This trauma was Winston's worst and it took all of Dr. Benedict's devotion and skill to pull him through. He had wire stitches in his stomach and wore a splint for weeks, clumping around the house sounding like Old Pew, the peg-legged sailor in *Treasure Island*. In three months or so Winston was as good as new, and he seems to be looking forward to his six remaining lives. _____

C. Some television commercials demonstrate such questionable values with regard to human behavior that one wonders just what lessons children are learning as they sit transfixed before the screen. Perhaps, from one famous commercial, they are learning that it is perfectly all right to overeat and overdrink because a foaming tablet in a glass of water will take care of all harmful consequences. Or they may be watching a version of the oft-taught lesson that in order to be happy one must be loved by everyone and the way to be universally lovable is to use the best smelling mouth washes, deodorants, and tooth pastes. For an even more telling example of pernicious teaching, the boys may be gleaning wisdom from a series of commercials that teach them that the way to manhood is through good masculine violence and group camaraderie with plenty of full-bodied beer thrown in. With TV broadcasting such lessons for many hours a day, one wonders if parental teaching stands much of a chance. _____

_____

Copyright © 1982 by Allyn and Bacon, Inc. Reproduction of this material is restricted to use with *A Guidebook for Teaching Composition*, 2nd Edition, by Gene Stanford and Marie Smith.

MEANS OF PARAGRAPH DEVELOPMENT							REPRODUCTION PAGE 8

D. Off-campus activities have become much more of an integral part of our high school. In 1976 there were no activities away from the high school that were approved for students. All students were expected to be in class or in one of the approved building areas from 8:15 A.M. to 2:45 P.M. No exceptions to this rule were allowed. In 1977, however, the school established a special program on an experimental basis. Fifty students, this first year, were permitted to attend school for a minimum of three hours and work at a job in the community for at least three more hours daily. A teacher was hired to meet with these students as a class at the high school and supervise their job experiences by maintaining a close contact with their employers. This program was so successful in meeting the needs of some students that by 1980, three hundred youngsters were enrolled in the work-study schedule and two additional teachers had been hired to work with students and their employers. There is now an almost equal number of students spending all day in school and working as volunteers and trainees at various community support agencies for a portion of each day. This program is called Community Involvement, and it is available only to seniors as an enrichment experience. It seems a far cry from the school that was confined to one building and offered only six classes a day. _____

E. The noises of the storm surrounded us. The rolls of thunder never ceased, sometimes deep and roaring and sometimes dimly growling as if from a great distance. Periodically, sharp and dramatic crashes of thunder shook the house, warning of nearby lightning and sending the dog whining under the sofa for safety. The gutters soon overflowed, and great streams of water splashed noisily down the front windows, while in the rear of the house an avalanche of water from the roof spurted from a downspout obstructed by leaves and splattered with great force on the patio stones. We were surrounded by rivers, it seemed, and through it all the heavy spray driven by wind sounded like bullets pelting against the roof and walls. The house creaked and quivered, feeling the strength of the gale, but it was a strong, well-constructed house, and inside it we felt, if not a sense of quiet, at least an absence of fear. _____

F. Some books read in childhood are truly unforgettable. Some of the characters, the places, and the adventures experienced with so much excitement when one is quite young, stay in one's mind as long as memory lasts. Such a character is Long John Silver in Robert Louis Stevenson's *Treasure Island.* Who, once acquainted with this wily old pirate, could ever forget him as he stomps along the decks of his ship, as quick on his crutch as other men with two good legs? As for Heidi, the little girl who lived in the Swiss Alps, who, having once roamed those upland meadows with her, could ever forget her as she drove her goats to pasture or milked them at the end of the day? She remains forever a child in memory. Childhood's memories of *The Song of Roland* and the friendship between Roland and Oliver are untarnished by any later historical knowledge, and the Knights of the Round Table still ride, in a golden haze of vague romantic memories, King Arthur at their head, with Lancelot, ever faithful, at his right hand. Who would give up these perfect childhood memories? _____

Copyright © 1982 by Allyn and Bacon, Inc. Reproduction of this material is restricted to use with *A Guidebook for Teaching Composition,* 2nd Edition, by Gene Stanford and Marie Smith.

REPRODUCTION PAGE 8   MEANS OF PARAGRAPH DEVELOPMENT

G. Whenever I looked at him, I thought of Uriah Heep, the groveling, obsequious, sly character in *David Copperfield*. This was unfair of me, because I knew nothing about him to justify the comparison, but there was something about the way he used his eyes, small and set deep in folds of flesh, that made me distrust his every word and deed. He darted little looks at me, and at others as well, when he thought we were not watching him, and when caught in the act, he winked and smiled and rubbed his hands for all the world like old Uriah. He never looked anyone full in the face, never held his gaze locked with one's own, but looked sidelong or raised his eyes furtively from seeming to peer at something else beyond or beside the one he really wished to observe. Even after a year's experience of him, I would have been hard put to say what color his eyes were, lurking under the scraggly, sandy brows. I thought perhaps they had no color of their own, but like him, would take on whatever shade would seem to fit the moment's need. _____

H. Roger and Steve sallied forth to try out the white water of the upper St. Francis River for all the world like experienced canoers who knew what they were doing. Both were powerful swimmers and intelligent, athletic young men whose bodies were well trained and adequate for any reasonable challenge. Both had been canoeing for a year or two and had encountered no challenge to shake their confidence. They decided that they would challenge the St. Francis, one of Missouri's heftier stretches of white water, and find out what real canoeing is all about. They would, of course, take every sensible precaution. Four days later, when they brought home their dented and misshapen canoe, they knew what could go wrong. _____

I. Transplanting seedlings need not be a traumatic experience for either the seedlings or the beginning gardener. Small plants, like small children, are remarkably hardy and resilient and capable of withstanding all sorts of shocks to their systems. A very few simple procedures will help your plants come through transplanting successfully. You should only transplant your seedlings when it is cloudy or overcast or after the sun has set. Too much heat is hard for them to take when they are already undergoing strain. Strain is considerably reduced, also, if you take up each plant in a trowel full of its own soil and set it down in a hole big enough to receive a cup or so of water and all the soil you have kept pressed around the plant's roots. When you have pressed the plant firmly into place and given it another watering, your job is done. You need not fret if the plant looks a little spindly and droopy; next morning, after a quiet night's rest in its new spot, your plant will look healthier and sturdier than ever. _____

J. Sometimes the student who talks and argues endlessly in class discussions learns less than the student who sits quietly, saying little or even nothing, but listening to the contributions of others. The talkative student may simply feel a need to defend his or her viewpoints against all other views, regardless of whether he or she has previously done much study in arriving at these beliefs. Or the student may feel that speaking with seeming authority will cause everyone to regard him or her as intelligent and well informed. Such a person may have an unconscious need to seem superior to others, a need that expresses itself in verbal contentiousness and a refusal to respect the views of others. Whatever the reasons for that talkativeness, it is apparent that the person cannot be thinking all the time he or she is talking, and it may be that the more thoughtful, silent student is actually engaging in a more productive activity. Since he or she is not continually producing output during the discussion, the quieter student may well be receiving valuable input or at least be gaining insight into various viewpoints, while the constant talker and arguer will remain merely defensive of his or her own. _____

_____

Copyright © 1982 by Allyn and Bacon, Inc. Reproduction of this material is restricted to use with *A Guidebook for Teaching Composition*, 2nd Edition, by Gene Stanford and Marie Smith.

REPRODUCTION PAGE 9

CHOOSING A METHOD OF DEVELOPING A TOPIC SENTENCE

INSTRUCTIONS: In the space provided after each topic sentence, write the best method of development for that paragraph: analysis, explanation, facts, description, narrative, examples.

1. A number of students in the audience could have taught that particular lesson as well as the teacher. _____
2. American cars are often named after animals or birds. _____
3. Every football lineman has his particular duties. _____
4. Even in warm weather, mountain climbers have been known to die of a too sudden drop in body temperature. _____
5. There are three separate political groups in the United States. _____
6. From the beginning, that vacation was more work than play. _____
7. The halls were uniformly drab and dingy. _____
8. The beagle has become a favorite of dog fanciers and outsells all other dogs in the United States. _____
9. Students in our school seem to fall into four categories. _____
10. There are still many government figures whose names are not tainted by scandal or hint of corruption. _____
11. By the end of the season, the team had set five local records and three state records in various styles of swimming. _____
12. One should never wax a car without giving it a thorough washing first. _____
13. One night the haunted house had visitors who were not ghosts. _____
14. The bleachers were a kaleidoscope of shifting colors. _____
15. The Gateway Arch in St. Louis, Missouri, is an architectural and technical marvel. _____
16. On a few occasions a president's wife has seemed to gain more respect and admiration than the president himself. _____
17. Many a famous beauty has found that her physical attributes have won her more misery than joy. _____

Copyright © 1982 by Allyn and Bacon, Inc. Reproduction of this material is restricted to use with *A Guidebook for Teaching Composition*, 2nd Edition, by Gene Stanford and Marie Smith.

REPRODUCTION PAGE 9 CHOOSING A METHOD OF DEVELOPING A TOPIC SENTENCE

18. His records for passes completed and yards gained on the ground exceeded those of all but two former players at his school. _____

19. Class discussion is an effective way for students to share knowledge and experience and thus to learn from one another. _____

20. Great athletes, unfortunately, have not always proved to be great gentlemen. _____

21. Much of the space in a vegetable garden can be planted at least twice during the growing season. _____

22. Long John Silver resides in the memory of all who have read *Treasure Island*. _____

23. I remember very well the day a tornado struck our school. _____

24. Tourism is Hawaii's most profitable business. _____

25. Their Christmas tree looked as if it had been trimmed by an interior decorator rather than the family themselves. _____

26. My first blind date was an exercise in embarrassment and helplessness. _____

27. Lights play an important part in any theatrical production. _____

28. The dance was a great financial success in spite of high expenses. _____

29. It is a mistake to exclude students from curriculum planning. _____

Copyright © 1982 by Allyn and Bacon, Inc. Reproduction of this material is restricted to use with *A Guidebook for Teaching Composition*, 2nd Edition, by Gene Stanford and Marie Smith.

REPRODUCTION PAGE 10

PLANNING A PARAGRAPH BASED ON DETAILS

INSTRUCTIONS: Find a unifying principle or theme in each list of details and write it in the space provided. Then formulate a topic sentence covering as many of the given details as possible. Write the topic sentence for each list of details in the space provided. Then draw a line through the details that do not fit your topic sentence and indicate in the blank which method of development would be most appropriate for your topic sentence.

A. frequent dusty detours
   signs and arrows redirecting traffic
   a red schoolhouse on a hill
   heavy equipment at work
   great piles of gravel
   garbage in a ditch
   cement mixers
   clouds of dust hovering over earth-moving machines
   birds flying overhead
   cows grazing peacefully in nearby fields
   workmen in colorful hard hats
   huge steam shovels gulping broken cement
   school children waiting for a bus

   Unifying Theme: _____

   Topic Sentence: _____

   _____

   _____

   Method of Development: _____

B. bleachers full of colorfully dressed spectators
   dust rising from parking fields nearby
   the plunk of hard-hit balls on the clay
   applause after a long volley
   chefs busy at work in the clubhouse kitchen
   ball chasers scurrying out of the way
   swaying shade trees on the golf course
   spontaneous groan from crowd at missed lob
   tournament brought in $93,471.32
   crisp calls of line judges
   brilliance of white tennis costumes in the sun
   rising tension at each crucial point
   borders of scarlet geraniums edging the spectators' area

Copyright © 1982 by Allyn and Bacon, Inc. Reproduction of this material is restricted to use with *A Guidebook for Teaching Composition*, 2nd Edition, by Gene Stanford and Marie Smith.

REPRODUCTION PAGE 10 — PLANNING A PARAGRAPH BASED ON DETAILS

Unifying Theme: _____

Topic Sentence: _____

_____

_____

Method of Development: _____

C. he was so harsh with his son that he left home
his eating habits became irregular
he carried on a continuous argument with his daughter over her dress
he read the morning paper
one day he told his boss that he disapproved of his methods of management
he began drinking early in the day
he quit attending church
he read only best sellers
he picked arguments with his long-suffering wife
he refused to see his doctor or his psychiatrist
he voted in all elections, as usual
he was cruel to the dog, and even kicked him in the ribs one day
he withdrew from lodge activities
he had always enjoyed fishing
he was a Yale graduate

Unifying Theme: _____

Topic Sentence: _____

_____

_____

Method of Development: _____

D. the Flurry rally was scheduled for 2:00 p.m., March 3, 1923
four thousand people gathered at the site
seventy-nine people were arrested
there was a fire at 93rd Street
fourteen people were hospitalized
traffic was stalled for a six-block area around the scene
the speaker was to have been J. Singleton Flurry
all but four of those arrested were released
two persons were kept in the hospital overnight
I don't like J. Singleton Flurry
if the demonstrators had stayed out of the way, maybe the police could have done a better job
the demonstrators opposing Flurry marched in the streets
people should not flock to the scene of a riot
the speaker's stand was demolished
fire hoses finally dispersed the last of the crowd

Copyright © 1982 by Allyn and Bacon, Inc. Reproduction of this material is restricted to use with *A Guidebook for Teaching Composition*, 2nd Edition, by Gene Stanford and Marie Smith.

PLANNING A PARAGRAPH BASED ON DETAILS   REPRODUCTION PAGE 10

Unifying Theme: _____

Topic Sentence: _____

_____

_____

Method of Development: _____

E. it will not rise adequately without kneading
   the dough will be lumpy
   the final product will be heavy and dense
   bread is the staff of life
   yeast needs to be worked into every particle of the dough
   kneading works air into the dough, guaranteeing lightness
   kneading provides even texture
   kneading spreads yeast evenly so when it ferments, it will cause tiny bubbles of carbon dioxide to filter throughout the dough
   kneading is fun
   carbon dioxide bubbles stretch gluten in flour, thus leavening the bread

   Unifying Theme: _____

   Topic Sentence: _____

   _____

   _____

   Method of Development: _____

F. Gauguin did some of his most sensational work when he was wasting away with disease
   Toulouse-Lautrec was badly crippled as a result of a riding accident in his youth
   Virginia Woolf suffered from precarious mental health and spent time in mental hospitals
   Beethoven suffered from progressive deafness that finally became complete
   Julius Caesar was an epileptic
   John Milton lost his eyesight years before he wrote *Paradise Lost*
   Franklin D. Roosevelt lost the use of his legs as a result of an attack of polio
   Van Gogh continued to paint even when he was committed to an asylum
   Sylvia Plath had periodic depressions that finally drove her to suicide
   Marilyn Monroe had a tragic life

   Unifying Theme: _____

   Topic Sentence: _____

   _____

   _____

   Method of Development: _____

Copyright © 1982 by Allyn and Bacon, Inc. Reproduction of this material is restricted to use with *A Guidebook for Teaching Composition,* 2nd Edition, by Gene Stanford and Marie Smith.

REPRODUCTION PAGE 11

PUTTING DETAILS IN ORDER

INSTRUCTIONS: Read each topic sentence and the list of details that support it. Decide what type of order might be the best for the details and number them in order.

A. *Topic Sentence:*   The lawn was a disgraceful mess.
   Details: weeds among flowers
   pile of dead branches to one side
   an old automobile chassis beside the porch
   instead of grass there were weeds and bare, worn places
   bushes unpruned
   cement on front walk broken and crumbling
   fence sagging on left side of yard
   fence broken entirely on right side

B. *Topic Sentence:*   The conference went on all day.
   Details: opening speech at 9:00 *a.m.*
   lunch at 12:00 noon
   preconference breakfast at 7:30 *a.m.*
   workshops at 2:00 *p.m.* and 4:00 *p.m.*
   cocktail hour at 6:30 *p.m.*
   seminar at 10:30 *a.m.*

C. *Topic Sentence:*   The teacher persuaded her to stay in the class.
   Details: he felt she would learn a lot
   he told her it would get more interesting
   he thought she would enjoy the new people coming in
   he would flunk her if she dropped out
   he reminded her that she would lose half a credit if she dropped out

D. *Topic Sentence:*   She decided not to try for early graduation.
   Details: would have to go to summer school
   none of her friends were graduating early
   her father opposed her graduating early
   she felt she was not yet ready for college
   there were still some courses at the high school she wanted to take

Copyright © 1982 by Allyn and Bacon, Inc. Reproduction of this material is restricted to use with *A Guidebook for Teaching Composition*, 2nd Edition, by Gene Stanford and Marie Smith.

REPRODUCTION PAGE 12

IMPROVING THE ORDER OF DETAILS

INSTRUCTIONS: Read the paragraphs below. In the space provided after each, indicate a better method of ordering the details and then number the details accordingly.

A. When you are baking a cake, it is important to double-check the ingredients as you put each one in. Being wrong with just one tablespoon of salt can mean an inedible cake rather than one of which you may be proud. Your first task is to read the recipe thoroughly and make sure you have all ingredients on hand. The orderly habit of putting everything away after you have used it is also a good one to cultivate. Mix the ingredients in the order and in the manner instructed by your recipe. Be sure to turn your oven to the proper setting at the very beginning so that by the time your batter is prepared, the oven is properly preheated. It is wise, also, to prepare your pan at the beginning, to avoid having to stop and do so at the last minute. If you follow your recipe carefully, there is no reason you cannot succeed every time you bake a cake.

B. The history of the school was a chronicle of constant expansion and construction. An entire new wing of classrooms was added when the school was only five years old. The original building was finished in 1958 and had only nineteen classrooms. Completed in 1963, the new wing added six more classrooms as well as additional library space. The original library seated only fifty-eight students. The gymnasium was doubled in size by construction undertaken in 1971, making it possible for the girls to have their own facilities; and in 1972, the pool, which had been part of the construction plan of 1968, was completed after two years of work. The original library and gymnasium had been planned and built to allow for ease of enlargement. Plans for their expansion had been presented even prior to the 1968 addition, but unfortunately the district voted against such an improvement at that time. The school board was pleased that the district approved the new gymnasium and pool as well as the new wing.

C. Some students felt that there had been any number of occasions when the administration might have closed down the smoking lounge before the event that finally caused them to take action. For instance, there was a week early in the school year when freshmen who had come from the two different junior high schools began expressing animosity for one another, and several fist fights broke out when the faculty supervisor was not watching. Even worse, perhaps, was the time in January when a group of so called "jocks" harassed a group of chorus students and a real free-for-all broke out before order was restored. Fortunately, or so the student smokers felt, the girl who was paralyzed after being shoved down a flight of stairs outside the lounge was withdrawn from

Copyright © 1982 by Allyn and Bacon, Inc. Reproduction of this material is restricted to use with *A Guidebook for Teaching Composition,* 2nd Edition, by Gene Stanford and Marie Smith.

REPRODUCTION PAGE 12 — PUTTING DETAILS IN ORDER

school by her parents, and the administration failed to connect her injury with the smoking lounge. Trash was scattered all over the area by student groups expressing displeasure with various actions by the principal, and the student committee charged with emptying ashtrays and policing the lounge quietly disbanded early in the year. Another example of student misuse of the lounge could be seen in the graffiti of all degrees of obscenity that defaced the walls.

D. Mrs. Burnell's yard showed the hours she spent each week caring for it. The flower border that stretched across the entire lot at the head of the house was a triumph of the illustrious gardener. Not a weed could be seen among the rows and clumps of yellow daisies and dahlias, multicolored pansies and cosmos, and flaming poppies. Just as vivid were the clumps of scarlet salvia by the sidewalk leading to the front door. On either side of the white cement walk, near the doorstep, were neatly clipped beds of English ivy. The picket fence, which ran entirely around the property, also supported occasional tendrils of ivy as well as one scarlet climber, which rose to the right of the front gate. Other roses appeared occasionally down the left side of the yard, which itself looked like a lovingly protected putting green with hardly a blade of grass standing out from its fellows. No crabgrass was tolerated here, and no dandelion ever profaned the perfect expanse of velvet green.

E. When I was eight years old, my family moved to a house very different from any home I had known before. When I was two, we had lived in an old farmhouse with a large yard and huge elm trees shading the area where I played. That had been a wonderful place for a child to play. I had a fine play place later, too, when I was seven and had a suburban bungalow with an enclosed yard and garden. It was from this bungalow that my father moved us—my mother, brother and me—to a townhouse in downtown Buffalo. Here there were no lawns, only sidewalks and streets and asphalt parking areas. I missed having a place to play. Even when we had lived in Chicago, during my first years at school, we were near a park so that I didn't mind not having a yard. But in Buffalo we were far from any park, and my brother and I were not allowed to go far from home by ourselves. My mother solved our problem, finally, by converting the unused room on the third floor of our house into a play room, and here my brother and I spent many happy hours during the three years we stayed in Buffalo.

Copyright © 1982 by Allyn and Bacon, Inc. Reproduction of this material is restricted to use with *A Guidebook for Teaching Composition*, 2nd Edition, by Gene Stanford and Marie Smith.

REPRODUCTION PAGE 13

IDENTIFYING CONNECTORS

INSTRUCTIONS: Circle all the connecting devices you can identify in the following paragraph.

The reason for the Philadelphia Eagles' success in the National Football League was new General Manager and Coach Joe Kuharick. Virtually all of the Eagles' weaknesses were filled either by his trades or by his signing of draft choices. For instance, Kuharick saw that the initial need was for a pile-driving fullback to complement the break-away running of his speedy halfback, Tim Brown. Hence Earl Groe was acquired from the Green Bay Packers. However, trading was not Kuharick's only accomplishment. He also had the knack of switching players from position to position in order to produce a diversified offense and an aggressive defense. For example, when his star halfback Tim Brown was injured, rookie Jack Concannon was placed in his halfback position. This was an especially interesting maneuver since the use of Concannon, who was a star quarterback at Boston College, gave him not only an excellent running threat but also a continual passing threat. Likewise, on defense, players were shuttled in and out, especially at the linebacker position. In this instance Maxie Baugh and Dave Lloyd were alternated constantly, depending on whether the situation called for the quarterback to be rushed or not. Although these accomplishments were great, there was another thing that Kuharick did which was even greater. Because of the Eagles' last place finish each of the past two years, there was much dissension on the Eagles' team. Even the ownership changed hands. Kuharick instilled a new spirit into the team. Now the Eagles were playing to win, as a team, and each individual was not just out for himself. Joe Kuharick did a remarkable job in making a successful team out of one that was struggling in last place just one short year ago.

Joe Finkelstein
(12th grade student)

Copyright © 1982 by Allyn and Bacon, Inc. Reproduction of this material is restricted to use with *A Guidebook for Teaching Composition*, 2nd Edition, by Gene Stanford and Marie Smith.

REPRODUCTION PAGE 14

SUPPLYING CONNECTORS

INSTRUCTIONS: The following paragraph lacks coherence because the writer did not use connectors where necessary. Insert the needed connectors in the paragraph.

The continued success of the Red Legs gave rise to several unexpected and not wholly desirable consequences. The team as a whole began to show signs of overconfidence. Their play on the field became just a little sloppy. Their activities off the field began to include certain lapses of training discipline. There were instances of rudeness toward fans who wanted autographs. Four players became loud and boisterous on an airplane flight. They were actually put off the plane at the next scheduled landing. The team's playing became less sloppy after the manager imposed a few stiff penalties. He made it clear that the mark of a true champion lay in the ability to handle success as well as failure. He made it clear that any player who behaved in a rude or overbearing manner would be suspended. The team settled down. The players began to behave more acceptably both on and off the field.

Copyright © 1982 by Allyn and Bacon, Inc. Reproduction of this material is restricted to use with *A Guidebook for Teaching Composition*, 2nd Edition, by Gene Stanford and Marie Smith.

CONNECTORS SUPPLIED

The continued success of the Red Legs gave rise to several unexpected and not wholly desirable consequences. *For one thing*, the team as a whole began to show signs of overconfidence and, *as a result*, their play on the field became just a little sloppy. Their activities off the field *also* began to include certain lapses of training discipline. There were instances of rudeness toward fans who wanted autographs, *and* four players became so loud and boisterous on an airplane flight *that* they were ejected from the plane at the next scheduled landing. *However*, the team's playing became less sloppy after the manager imposed a few stiff penalties. He *also* made it clear that any player who behaved in a rude or overbearing manner would be suspended. *After that*, the team settled down, *and* the players began to behave more acceptably both on and off the field.

Copyright © 1982 by Allyn and Bacon, Inc. Reproduction of this material is restricted to use with *A Guidebook for Teaching Composition*, 2nd Edition, by Gene Stanford and Marie Smith.

REPRODUCTION PAGE 16

IMPROVING COHERENCE THROUGH CONSISTENT SUBJECTS

INSTRUCTIONS: Rewrite the following paragraph, making it more coherent by using the same grammatical subject for all or most of the sentences.

A. Advance planning is half the secret of a good party. A wise hostess will want to examine her guest list and plan the sort of party those particular guests will most enjoy. Some people like a nonalcoholic punch, while others will feel cheated unless the refreshments include alcoholic beverages of some kind. Food is also a matter the hostess should consider carefully ahead of time. Dieters will not appreciate an array of creamy, high-calorie goodies, but neither will the happy eaters enjoy munching carrot sticks and celery. The food, in short, will need to be planned to fit all the guests. Entertainment is also a matter concerning which guests might have a wide range of preferences. Young people tend to want loud rock music, while quiet semi-classical or show music is usually more pleasing to adults. Pencil and paper games delight some guests, particularly adults, but dancing or quiet conversation is the choice of others. All these questions **must** be solved ahead of time if you are to be sure of a successful party.

Copyright © 1982 by Allyn and Bacon, Inc. Reproduction of this material is restricted to use with *A Guidebook for Teaching Composition*, 2nd Edition, by Gene Stanford and Marie Smith.

SAMPLE REVISION OF PARAGRAPH A

B. The experienced hostess knows that advance planning is half the secret of a good party. She will want to study her guest list and plan the sort of party those particular guests will most enjoy. She will want to know ahead of time which of her guests might prefer a nonalcoholic punch and which would feel cheated if she did not serve some kind of alcoholic beverage. If she is planning to serve refreshments, the hostess will carefully consider what foods will be most suitable for her dieting guests and at the same time plan something a bit more palatable than carrot sticks and celery for those guests who eat heartily regardless of calories. The skilled party giver is also aware that guests may well have a wide range of preferences in entertainment. If her guests are all young, she may choose loud rock music for dancing or listening, but if entertaining adults, she may prepare a program of show records or light classical music. She will be prepared for the possibility that some guests might enjoy cards or pen and pencil games as well as the likelihood that others would enjoy simply conversing or, perhaps, dancing. She will, in short, be thoroughly prepared to give a very successful party.

Copyright © 1982 by Allyn and Bacon, Inc. Reproduction of this material is restricted to use with *A Guidebook for Teaching Composition,* 2nd Edition, by Gene Stanford and Marie Smith.

REPRODUCTION PAGE 18

IMPROVING COHERENCE THROUGH ADHERING TO THE SUBJECT

INSTRUCTIONS: Rewrite the following paragraph, making it more coherent by adhering to the (grammatical) subject introduced in the topic sentence.

C. The police officers who patrol the northeast district of the city must cope with problems more numerous and complex than those of any other section of the inner city. The population density is the highest in the city, even though the district itself is the smallest in terms of city blocks. The nineteen eight-story buildings in the Jefferson Street high-rise housing project partially account for the large number of people living in such a restricted ground area. The narrow streets, shallow building lots, and almost hidden alleyways and inner courtyards are so densely crowded with old tenement buildings, multifamily houses, shacks, and sheds that fleeing criminals easily find a haven. Traffic in heroin and cocaine is heavy in the northeast district, and many known criminals live in the area. Glittering pastel Cadillacs are often seen parked amid the litter of the filthy streets, and at any time of day or night the painted street girls may be seen sallying forth to make their way to the more prosperous areas to the south. Known underworld characters live and work next door to pimps and numbers racketeers in this most multiracial and ecumenical of neighborhoods. Most of the churches that once served the community have boarded up their broken windows and moved to the suburbs, and the school survives only with the help of armed guards. Yet, amid all this social refuse live many helpless, frightened citizens who need and value the help of the police.

Copyright © 1982 by Allyn and Bacon, Inc. Reproduction of this material is restricted to use with *A Guidebook for Teaching Composition,* 2nd Edition, by Gene Stanford and Marie Smith.

SAMPLE REVISION OF PARAGRAPH C

D. The police officers who patrol the northeast district of the city must cope with problems more numerous and complex than those of any other section of the inner city. They must cope with a population density that is the highest in the city, even though the district itself is the smallest in terms of city blocks. In the center of their patrol area are the nineteen eight-story buildings of the Jefferson Street high-rise housing project, which partially accounts for the large number of people living in such a restricted area. In other parts of the district the police are forced to find their way through a warren of narrow streets, shallow building lots, and almost hidden alleyways and inner courtyards so densely crowded with old tenement buildings, multifamily houses, shacks, and sheds that the fleeing criminal can easily find a haven the police cannot penetrate. Here, also, the police are faced with the city's heaviest traffic in heroin and cocaine, and they must maintain surveillance over the many known criminals who live in the area. They observe with frustration the glittering pastel Cadillacs parked amid the litter of the filthy streets and watch the painted street girls sally forth at all hours of the day and night to take their wares to the more prosperous areas to the south. They try to keep order on the streets where known underworld characters live and work next door to pimps and numbers racketeers and where they receive little help from any other source. They have watched church organizations that once served the community board up their broken windows and move away, and they give what help they can to the armed guards who patrol the school. Yet, amid all this social refuse live many helpless, frightened citizens who need and value the help of the police.

Copyright © 1982 by Allyn and Bacon, Inc. Reproduction of this material is restricted to use with *A Guidebook for Teaching Composition*, 2nd Edition, by Gene Stanford and Marie Smith.

REPRODUCTION PAGE 20

IMPROVING COHERENCE THROUGH ADHERING TO THE SUBJECT

INSTRUCTIONS: Rewrite the following paragraph, making it more coherent by adhering to the same grammatical subject throughout.

E. Anyone who spends much time in the smoking lounge is well aware of the disadvantages of its present outdoor location. Rainy weather makes a joke out of the word "lounge," and snow makes having a cigarette an exercise in frostbite. Winter weather is not very pleasant when one is outdoors without a coat, and carrying a coat from class to class is tiresome to say the least. Tardiness becomes a serious problem when there are only five minutes between classes. Running through the halls between classes is frowned upon, but it is impossible to get to class on time after a stop at the smoking lounge without running. Teachers are not always sympathetic when a student straggles in after attendance is half taken. Administrators are so suspicious of what goes on in the smoking area that many smokers feel nervous whenever they see a principal in the hall. The situation is really far from ideal.

Copyright © 1982 by Allyn and Bacon, Inc. Reproduction of this material is restricted to use with *A Guidebook for Teaching Composition,* 2nd Edition, by Gene Stanford and Marie Smith.

REVISION OF PARAGRAPH E

F. Students who spend much time in the smoking lounge are well aware of the disadvantages of the present arrangement. They know that rainy weather makes a joke out of the word "lounge" and that snow makes having a cigarette an exercise in frostbite. They have faced the choice, in winter weather, of freezing outdoors without a coat or of carrying a coat around all day, which is tiresome, to say the least. They have faced the problem of tardiness, which is almost inevitable when there are only five minutes between classes and the smoking area is located far away from many classrooms. Student smokers have been reprimanded for running through the halls, something they have to do because they have found it almost impossible to get to class on time, after a stop at the smoking lounge without running. They report that teachers are not very sympathetic when they arrive in class after attendance is half taken and that they get nervous whenever a principal comes down the hall because administrators are so suspicious of what goes on in the smoking area. The situation is really far from ideal.

Copyright © 1982 by Allyn and Bacon, Inc. Reproduction of this material is restricted to use with *A Guidebook for Teaching Composition*, 2nd Edition, by Gene Stanford and Marie Smith.

REPRODUCTION PAGE 22

IMPROVING COHERENCE THROUGH ELIMINATING PASSIVE VOICE

INSTRUCTIONS: The paragraph below is incoherent because there are a number of verbs in the passive voice. Rewrite the paragraph, putting all or most verbs in the active form and providing a subject for each verb.

A. As our car was driven through the gate, it was swung shut behind us, and our car was driven on. As we approached the next gate, it also was opened at our command. Our car was eyed with suspicion, but no stones were thrown, and no epithets were shouted that could be heard in the car. We had been promised that the way would be cleared for us, and it must be acknowledged that the pledge was meticulously honored.

Copyright © 1982 by Allyn and Bacon, Inc. Reproduction of this material is restricted to use with *A Guidebook for Teaching Composition*, 2nd Edition, by Gene Stanford and Marie Smith.

SAMPLE REVISION OF PARAGRAPH A

B. As Pedro drove our car through the gate, the keeper pulled it shut behind us, and we drove on down the road. Soon we saw another gate ahead, but in spite of some trepidation, we were able to pass through immediately upon showing our official pass to the guard. We saw groups of sullen peasants eyeing us with suspicion but we had received a pledge that the road to the border would be clear for us, and that pledge was meticulously honored.

Copyright © 1982 by Allyn and Bacon, Inc. Reproduction of this material is restricted to use with *A Guidebook for Teaching Composition*, 2nd Edition, by Gene Stanford and Marie Smith.

REPRODUCTION PAGE 24

ELIMINATING PASSIVE VOICE

INSTRUCTIONS: The paragraph below is incoherent because there are many verbs in the passive voice. Rewrite the paragraph, changing all or most verbs to active voice as needed to improve coherence.

C. A garden should be planned very carefully before a single seed is planted. Plans must be made not only for all the space that is available but also for all the time provided by your growing season. Each vegetable must be selected not only because it is enjoyed by your family and recommended by nutritionists but also because the time taken in growing from seed to table is not out of proportion to the number of vegetables that can be produced by each plant. For instance, zucchini squash takes only forty-five days from seed to table, and once the first squash appears, if every succeeding one is picked before it reaches a length of eight or so inches, more squash will be produced steadily until the vines are killed by frost. It can be seen, therefore, that the space occupied by each zucchini plant is utilized productively. A similar extended productivity can be expected from tomatoes, green peppers, Swiss chard, and broccoli, and these vegetables are, hence, prized by home gardeners. On the other hand, root vegetables such as carrots, parsnips or radishes, produce only one vegetable for every seed and should be planted only when the gardener knows they are well liked by the family.

Copyright © 1982 by Allyn and Bacon, Inc. Reproduction of this material is restricted to use with *A Guidebook for Teaching Composition*, 2nd Edition, by Gene Stanford and Marie Smith.

SAMPLE REVISION OF PARAGRAPH C

D. Home gardeners should plan their gardens carefully before they plant a single seed. They must plan not only for the space available to them but also for the time the growing season provides. They should select each vegetable they will grow not only because their families like it and because it has nutritional value but also because the time it will take in growing from seed to ripeness is not out of proportion to the number of vegetables each plant will produce. For instance, gardeners should know that zucchini squash takes only forty-five days from seed to ripeness and that once they pick the first squash, the plant will continue to produce right up to frost, as long as they pick each squash before it exceeds approximately eight inches in length. Thus, they will utilize space productively by planting zucchini. They should know that they can expect a similar kind of extended productivity from tomatoes, green peppers, Swiss chard and broccoli, but that root vegetables, such as radishes, carrots, and parsnips, produce only one vegetable for each seed. They will want to be sure their families are fond of such one-shot vegetables before they devote a great deal of limited garden space to them.

Copyright © 1982 by Allyn and Bacon, Inc. Reproduction of this material is restricted to use with *A Guidebook for Teaching Composition,* 2nd Edition, by Gene Stanford and Marie Smith.

REPRODUCTION PAGE 26

ESTABLISHING A CONSISTENT POINT OF VIEW

INSTRUCTIONS: The paragraph below is incoherent because of many errors in point of view. The writer did not choose the person and number of the subject and stick to them faithfully throughout. Rewrite the paragraph, improving coherence by making the point of view consistent.

A. Students often dislike a teacher because they do not understand him or her. It is not uncommon, for instance, for a student to make a negative judgment of a teacher and consequently have a bad experience in their class as a result of a simple cultural difference to which, in all fairness, no blame should be attached. We tend to judge teachers by standards more stringent than those one applies to himself and, as a result, to put up artificial barriers that prevent a pleasant and productive relationship from developing between yourself and the teacher. The student is the one who loses in such a situation, and sometimes our loss is a great one, indeed. You will do well to remind yourself that teachers—in addition to being teachers—are husbands, fathers (wives and mothers), wage earners, bill payers, voters, gardeners, and a host of other things. And we will profit from learning to regard them in the context of their total personhood.

Copyright © 1982 by Allyn and Bacon, Inc. Reproduction of this material is restricted to use with *A Guidebook for Teaching Composition,* 2nd Edition, by Gene Stanford and Marie Smith.

REPRODUCTION PAGE 27

SAMPLE REVISION OF PARAGRAPH A

B. Students often dislike a teacher because they do not understand him or her. It is not uncommon, for instance, for students to make a negative judgment of a teacher and, consequently, to have a bad experience in his or her class as a result of a simple cultural difference to which, in all fairness, no blame should be attached. Students tend to judge teachers by standards more stringent than those by which they judge themselves and, as a result, to put up artificial barriers that prevent pleasant and productive relationships from developing between themselves and certain teachers. Students are the ones who lose in such situations, and sometimes their loss is a great one, indeed. They would do well to remind themselves that teachers—in addition to being teachers—are also husbands and fathers (wives and mothers), wage earners, bill payers, voters, gardeners, and a host of other things. And students will profit from learning to regard them in the context of their total personhood.

Copyright © 1982 by Allyn and Bacon, Inc. Reproduction of this material is restricted to use with *A Guidebook for Teaching Composition,* 2nd Edition, by Gene Stanford and Marie Smith.

REPRODUCTION PAGE 28

IMPROVING COHERENCE THROUGH POINT OF VIEW

INSTRUCTIONS: The paragraph below lacks coherence because of frequent shifts in point of view. Rewrite the paragraph, making the point of view consistent.

C. I have observed that careful young drivers strongly resent the endless criticism heaped on the youthful driver in general. They feel, and rightly so, that there is every kind of young driver, just as there are all degrees of skill among older drivers, and it is unfair to tar all with the same brush. The young fellow of nineteen who has never had so much as a parking ticket should not be unthinkingly lumped with the relatively small number of careless speed demons who create unfavorable statistics with regard to the youthful driver. One can understand their feelings.

Copyright © 1982 by Allyn and Bacon, Inc. Reproduction of this material is restricted to use with *A Guidebook for Teaching Composition*, 2nd Edition, by Gene Stanford and Marie Smith.

SAMPLE REVISION OF PARAGRAPH C

D. I have observed that careful young drivers strongly resent the endless criticism heaped on youthful drivers in general. They feel, and rightly so, that there are all kinds of young drivers just as there are all degrees of skill among older drivers, and it is unfair to tar all with the same brush. They believe that young fellows of nineteen who have never had so much as a parking ticket do not deserve to be lumped with the careless speed demons who create unfavorable statistics for their age group. I can understand their feelings.

Copyright © 1982 by Allyn and Bacon, Inc. Reproduction of this material is restricted to use with *A Guidebook for Teaching Composition*, 2nd Edition, by Gene Stanford and Marie Smith.

REPRODUCTION PAGE 30

ELIMINATING INCONSISTENT VERB TENSES

INSTRUCTIONS: Rewrite the paragraph below, improving the coherence by correcting the inconsistencies in verb tense.

A. The children poured onto the beach from the landing boat in a confused and noisy stream. Struggling to find their way to safety and fearful that the boat will pull away before they are safely ashore, they push and shove against those in the front ranks, heedless of the additional danger this creates. John, who was sitting in the stern of the craft before it reached the shore, was one of the last children to disembark. He looks around, frantically searching for his little sister, Susan, whom he last saw on the dock before they were placed aboard the big ship. Where was she?

Copyright © 1982 by Allyn and Bacon, Inc. Reproduction of this material is restricted to use with *A Guidebook for Teaching Composition,* 2nd Edition, by Gene Stanford and Marie Smith.

SAMPLE REVISION OF PARAGRAPH A

B. The children poured onto the beach from the landing boat in a confused and noisy stream. Struggling to find their way to safety and fearful that the boat would pull away before they were safely ashore, they pushed and shoved against those in the front ranks, heedless of the additional danger this created. John, who had been sitting in the stern of the craft before it reached the shore, was one of the last children to disembark. He looked around, frantically searching for his little sister, Susan, whom he had last seen on the dock before they were placed aboard the big ship. Where was she?

Copyright © 1982 by Allyn and Bacon, Inc. Reproduction of this material is restricted to use with *A Guidebook for Teaching Composition*, 2nd Edition, by Gene Stanford and Marie Smith.

REPRODUCTION PAGE 32

IMPROVING COHERENCE THROUGH VERB-TENSE CONSISTENCY

INSTRUCTIONS: Improve the coherence of the following paragraph by rewriting it, correcting any inconsistencies in verb tense.

C. The basement looked as if everything that had ever come into it was still there, stacked in random layers through which one moves at one's own risk. Beside the entrance door, on the left, is a leaning tower of crates, some containing whole sets of books that were obviously never even unpacked and some overflowing with an accumulation of daily newspapers whose dates, one can see, stretched far into the past. Nothing seems ever to be thrown out. From the ceiling beams, dimly discernible in the feeble light from my flashlight, hang various sizes of wheels and tires and other parts of what might once upon a time have been unicycles or bicycles. And stacked in unbelievable disorder throughout the whole area were crates, baskets, bins, and boxes holding heaven only knows what and interspersed with, leaning against, and falling upon such objects as statues, paintings, urns, ship models, rolled-up carpets, and, far to the back, in regal splendor, a gigantic cigar-store Indian who surveys the accumulated flotsam through unswerving and opaque eyes.

Copyright © 1982 by Allyn and Bacon, Inc. Reproduction of this material is restricted to use with *A Guidebook for Teaching Composition*, 2nd Edition, by Gene Stanford and Marie Smith.

SAMPLE REVISION OF PARAGRAPH C

D. The basement looked as if everything that had ever come into it was still there, stacked in random layers through which one moved at one's own risk. Beside the entrance door, on the left, was a leaning tower of crates, some containing whole sets of books that had obviously never even been unpacked and some overflowing with an accumulation of daily newspapers whose dates, one could see, stretched far into the past. Apparently nothing was ever thrown out. From the ceiling beams, dimly discernible in the feeble light from my flashlight, hung various sizes of wheels and tires and other parts of what might once have been unicycles or bicycles. And stacked in unbelievable disorder throughout the whole area were crates, baskets, bins, and boxes holding heaven only knew what and interspersed with, leaning against, and falling upon such objects as statues, paintings, urns, ship models, rolled-up carpets, and, far to the back, brooding in regal splendor, a gigantic cigar-store Indian who surveyed the accumulated flotsam through unswerving and opaque eyes.

Copyright © 1982 by Allyn and Bacon, Inc. Reproduction of this material is restricted to use with *A Guidebook for Teaching Composition*, 2nd Edition, by Gene Stanford and Marie Smith.

REPRODUCTION PAGE 34

IMPROVING COHERENCE THROUGH VERB-TENSE CONSISTENCY

INSTRUCTIONS: Improve the coherence in the following paragraph by rewriting it, making the verb tenses consistent.

E. The dog limped slowly along on the hot pavement. He seems to have one foot that hurts so badly he could not put any of his weight on it. His tail was tucked between his legs and his head was low, looking as if he is too tired to hold it up. There are long scratches along his sides, and one of his eyes was swollen shut. There was blood on one foot, which left bloody tracks on the pavement. We feel very sorry for him and want to take him home and take care of him. However, we know our parents do not believe in taking in stray animals; thus we sadly watched him limp away.

Copyright © 1982 by Allyn and Bacon, Inc. Reproduction of this material is restricted to use with *A Guidebook for Teaching Composition,* 2nd Edition, by Gene Stanford and Marie Smith.

REVISION OF PARAGRAPH E

F. The dog limped slowly along on the hot pavement. He seemed to have one foot hurt so badly he could not put any of his weight on it. His tail was tucked between his legs and his head was low, looking as if he was too tired to hold it up. There were long scratches along his sides, and one of his eyes was swollen shut. There was blood on one foot, which left bloody tracks on the pavement. We felt sorry for him and wanted to take him home and take care of him. However, we knew our parents did not believe in taking in stray animals; thus we sadly watched him limp away.

Copyright © 1982 by Allyn and Bacon, Inc. Reproduction of this material is restricted to use with *A Guidebook for Teaching Composition*, 2nd Edition, by Gene Stanford and Marie Smith.

REPRODUCTION PAGE 36

INCREASING COHERENCE THROUGH SUBORDINATION

INSTRUCTIONS: The paragraph below is incoherent because it contains nothing but a series of short, choppy sentences. Increase coherence by moving the simple sentences into compound or complex sentences.

A. I was in the valley. I could not see the old church building. I climbed up on a nearby outcropping of rock. It reached thirty feet above the valley floor. I could see much farther. I could see trees in a bend. I could see trees in a curving line. They were following the river's bend. I could see a hill on the other side of the river. On it I could see the old church building. The steeple caught the sun's last rays. It was white against the darkening evening sky.

Copyright © 1982 by Allyn and Bacon, Inc. Reproduction of this material is restricted to use with *A Guidebook for Teaching Composition,* 2nd Edition, by Gene Stanford and Marie Smith.

SAMPLE REVISION OF PARAGRAPH A

B. From where I was on the floor of the valley, I could not see the old church building. However, observing a nearby outcropping of rock that reached a height of almost thirty feet, I climbed to its top and discovered that I could see much farther. In the distance, a graceful line of trees followed the river's bend, and on the other side of the river, on a low hill, I could see the old church, its steeple a brilliant white in the sun's last rays against the darkening evening sky.

Copyright © 1982 by Allyn and Bacon, Inc. Reproduction of this material is restricted to use with *A Guidebook for Teaching Composition*, 2nd Edition, by Gene Stanford and Marie Smith.

REPRODUCTION PAGE 38

IMPROVING COHERENCE THROUGH SUBORDINATION

INSTRUCTIONS: Improve the incoherent paragraph below by combining sentences, making some ideas subordinate to others.

    He ran up the front steps. He burst through the door. The door slammed noisily against the wall. He did not stop to close the door. He raced through the rooms. He kept calling Peter's name. His voice was hoarse and frantic with fear. He wanted to find Peter. He was afraid of what he might find. He raced upstairs. He flung open doors to bedrooms and closets. He raced back downstairs. He went down into the basement. A noise, half scream, half groan, burst from him. I stood at the top of the steps. I was afraid to go down. I knew what he had found.

Copyright © 1982 by Allyn and Bacon, Inc. Reproduction of this material is restricted to use with *A Guidebook for Teaching Composition,* 2nd Edition, by Gene Stanford and Marie Smith.

REPRODUCTION PAGE 39

RECOGNIZING GAPS IN THOUGHT

INSTRUCTIONS: Read the following paragraphs, noting the glaring gaps in thought that the writer has left. How do these gaps make it difficult for you to understand the writer's meaning?

A. I have always said that "come the holocaust," I would want to be somewhere in the country with my mother. My mother was a country woman, born on a small farm in Missouri near the end of the nineteenth century. She had many skills her city daughters knew nothing of, and she possessed a rich fund of old-time lore. She knew how to do many things that would be important to survival. After all, she was poor all her life. She was accustomed to fending for herself and solving her own problems. When I was a child, there were few things she could not fix more skillfully than could my city-bred father.

B. The porch was a shambles. There had been a storm in our absence, and the neighbor's dog had gotten in through a broken window. Apparently there had been a strong wind which played havoc with potted plants and hanging flower baskets.

Copyright © 1982 by Allyn and Bacon, Inc. Reproduction of this material is restricted to use with *A Guidebook for Teaching Composition*, 2nd Edition, by Gene Stanford and Marie Smith.

REPRODUCTION PAGE 40

SAMPLE REVISION OF PARAGRAPHS A AND B

C. I have always said that "come the holocaust," when survival would be the only issue, I would want to be somewhere in the country with my mother. My mother was a country woman, born on a small farm in Missouri near the end of the nineteenth century. Like all farm women of that time, she had many skills her city daughters know nothing of, and she possessed a rich fund of old-time lore that could mean the difference between living or dying in a time when there would be no stores, doctors or hospitals, and little medicine. She knew how to find a spring, spear a fish, butcher and skin an animal, set a trap, make soap, and do many other things that would be important to survival. After all, she was poor all her childhood, and poverty forced her and her brothers and sisters to learn many lessons that her more affluent children never had the opportunity to learn. She was accustomed to fending for herself and solving her own problems, which is a kind of independence we city people often lose, finding it easier to call a plumber or an electrician. When I was a child, I remember, there were few things she could not fix more skillfully than could my city-bred father.

D. The porch was a shambles. There had been a storm in our absence, and the wind had blown in a window so that rainwater had drenched the rug and furniture, and the neighbor's dog had gotten in through a broken window and rooted through all the containers and left muddy tracks over everything. Apparently there had been a strong wind that played havoc with potted plants and hanging flower baskets. Broken planters lay in shattered pieces on the floor and potting soil formed a thick mud over all.

Copyright © 1982 by Allyn and Bacon, Inc. Reproduction of this material is restricted to use with *A Guidebook for Teaching Composition*, 2nd Edition, by Gene Stanford and Marie Smith.

REPRODUCTION PAGE 41

ELIMINATING GAPS IN THOUGHT

INSTRUCTIONS: Improve the following paragraphs by filling in the gaps in thought, thus improving the coherence of the paragraphs.

A. I always wanted to go to Harvard. I went to the University of New Mexico. My folks moved to Washington, D.C. I finished my degree at Harvard.

B. Eleanor found her schedule to be more demanding than she had anticipated during her two years of working full time and also attending night school to finish her nursing degree. During that time she was promoted to a supervisory position at the hospital. A shortage of critical care nurses often forced on her the responsibility of working an extra shift. The hospital more and more frequently sent her to other cities to attend medical workshops and symposia. Her husband, at the same time, was completing his Master of Arts degree. She often felt she was holding her real life in abeyance until she should have her degree.

Copyright © 1982 by Allyn and Bacon, Inc. Reproduction of this material is restricted to use with *A Guidebook for Teaching Composition*, 2nd Edition, by Gene Stanford and Marie Smith.

REPRODUCTION PAGE 42

SAMPLE REVISION OF PARAGRAPHS A AND B

C. When I was a child I always wanted to go to Harvard. My great-grandfather had gone there, and as a small child I heard many tales of Harvard life. My grandfather attended Harvard also and spoke often of his years there. He brought his family to New Mexico in the 1980s, and my father attended the University of New Mexico. Dreams of Harvard seemed out of the question when I was eighteen; thus I enrolled at the University of New Mexico also. However, because my folks moved to Washington, D.C. during my junior year, I was able to finish my degree at Harvard and thus fulfill my childhood dream.

B. Eleanor found her schedule to be more demanding than she had anticipated during her two years of working full time and also attending night school to finish her nursing degree. Had she continued to work simply as a staff nurse, she would, perhaps, have been able to manage without too much strain, but during that time she was promoted to a supervisory position at the hospital and, as a consequence, her responsibilities and her hours devoted to the hospital were greatly increased. One particular hardship stemmed from the shortage of critical care nurses at that time, which frequently required that she, as supervisor, work an extra shift in the Intensive Care Unit as well as perform all her usual supervisory duties. In addition, the hospital, evidently recognizing her increasing value as an employee, more and more frequently sent her to other cities to attend medical workshops and symposia. These absences not only made it difficult for her to keep her course work current, but also deprived her of time she would have liked to devote to her personal life. Her husband, during this same time, was completing his Master of Arts degree at a nearby college and was, himself, on such a busy schedule that Eleanor and he sometimes felt that they saw one another only in passing. Small wonder that she often felt she was holding her real life in abeyance until she would have her degree.

Copyright © 1982 by Allyn and Bacon, Inc. Reproduction of this material is restricted to use with *A Guidebook for Teaching Composition*, 2nd Edition, by Gene Stanford and Marie Smith.

FILLING GAPS WITH EXTENDER SENTENCES

INSTRUCTIONS: Observe that in paragraph A below the author's meaning is expressed almost entirely in general statements. Read paragraph B and underline the "extender sentences" that have been added. Observe how much more complete and coherent the paragraph is once the meaning of the general statements has been made more specific by the insertion of "extender sentences."

A. As Jules Henry commented in his book *Culture Against Man*, ours is an advertising culture in which we must learn that much of what purports to be truth is, instead, partial or total falsehood. Even the small child must learn that all that is advertised is not so. And unfortunately, everyone's youth is filled with more such disillusionments. Yet, in spite of constant disappointments, we retain some residue of faith. When we want to be slim, we buy the $8.95 book that promises to tell us how to reduce without inconvenience. We continue to try to believe even when it is no longer possible.

B. As Jules Henry commented in his book *Culture Against Man*, ours is an advertising culture in which we must learn that much of what purports to be truth is, instead, partial or total falsehood. Even the small child must learn that all that is advertised is not so. The "delicious," "candy-like" toothpaste that he badgered Mom to buy may well turn out to taste more like spearmint-flavored chalk. Unfortunately, everyone's youth is filled with such disillusionments. Why does the complexion cure not take away teenage blemishes as promised? Yet, in spite of constant disappointments, we retain some residue of faith. Surely, we think, "they" would not create that ad out of whole cloth. We try, over and over, to gain the blessings promised. We show faith and buy, even when we doubt. When we want to be slim, we buy the $8.95 book that promises to tell us how to reduce without inconvenience. We won't have to give up anything. And we are hurt and disappointed when we don't lose ten pounds a week as the "doctor" said we would. We continue to try to believe even when it is no longer possible. We are like the early saint who cried out in anguish, "I believe, I believe, O, help Thou my unbelief."

Copyright © 1982 by Allyn and Bacon, Inc. Reproduction of this material is restricted to use with *A Guidebook for Teaching Composition*, 2nd Edition, by Gene Stanford and Marie Smith.

REPRODUCTION PAGE 44

PROVIDING EXTENDER SENTENCES

INSTRUCTIONS. Improve the coherence of the paragraph below by inserting in the blanks sentences that further specify and extend the sentences they follow.

Different breeds of dogs have different qualities that endear them to their owners. _____ _____ _____ _____. The owners of Irish setters will rhapsodize at length about the aesthetic appeal of their aristocratic animal. _____ _____ _____ _____

On the other hand, dachshund owners seem to take particular pleasure in their little fellows' feisty personalities. _____ _____ _____ _____

Owners of big, powerful breeds, such as German shepherds or boxers, take particular pride in their dogs' strength and also in their loyalty. _____ _____ _____ _____

Dog owners, like the rest of us, differ in their tastes and needs, and it is fortunate that such diversity exists among the breeds of dogs.

Copyright © 1982 by Allyn and Bacon, Inc. Reproduction of this material is restricted to use with *A Guidebook for Teaching Composition,* 2nd Edition, by Gene Stanford and Marie Smith.

REPRODUCTION PAGE 45

PROVIDING EXTENDER SENTENCES

INSTRUCTIONS: Improve the coherence of the paragraph below by inserting in the blanks sentences that further specify and extend the sentences they follow.

E. Children who watch a great deal of TV may well become confused about what life is really like. If children watch policemen breaking into homes or offices without warrants, they will get a false impression as to what the police really do. _____

_____

_____

_____

Children might also gain from TV the idea that heavy drinking is part of everyone's life.

_____

_____

_____

TV must lead children to believe that no one ever stays home and goes to bed at a reasonable hour. _____

_____

_____

_____

Television's portrayal of marriage is surely poor preparation for marriage in real life.

_____

_____

_____

Wise parents make sure their children know the difference between TV life and real life.

Copyright © 1982 by Allyn and Bacon, Inc. Reproduction of this material is restricted to use with *A Guidebook for Teaching Composition,* 2nd Edition, by Gene Stanford and Marie Smith.

REPRODUCTION PAGE 46

Restricting A Subject

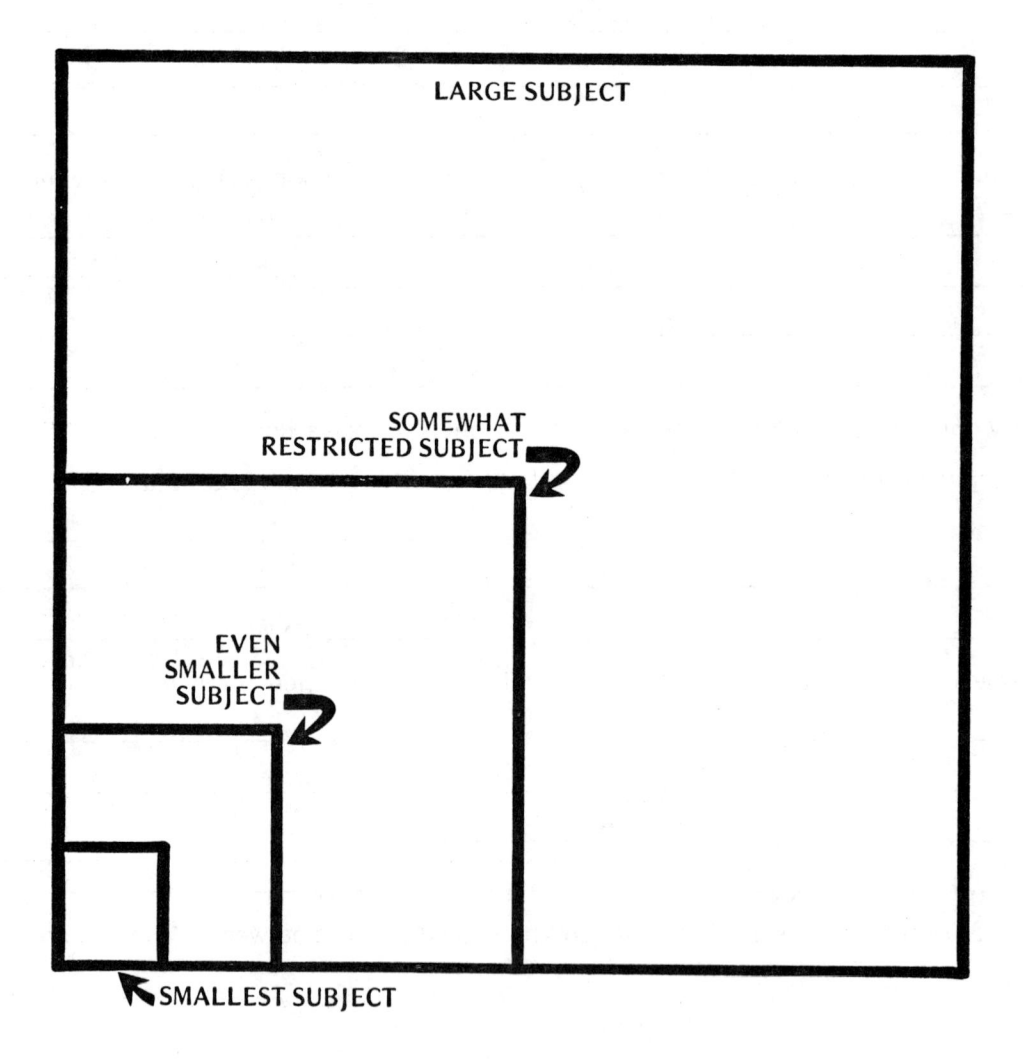

```
┌─────────────────────────────────────────┐
│              LARGE SUBJECT              │
│                                         │
│                                         │
│                                         │
│                    SOMEWHAT             │
│                 RESTRICTED SUBJECT ↘    │
│       ┌──────────────────────────┐      │
│       │                          │      │
│       │   EVEN                   │      │
│       │  SMALLER                 │      │
│       │  SUBJECT ↘               │      │
│       ┌──────────┐               │      │
│       │          │               │      │
│       │          │               │      │
│       ┌───┐      │               │      │
│       │   │      │               │      │
│       └───┴──────┴───────────────┴──────┘
│     ↖ SMALLEST SUBJECT
```

Copyright © 1982 by Allyn and Bacon, Inc. Reproduction of this material is restricted to use with *A Guidebook for Teaching Composition*, 2nd Edition, by Gene Stanford and Marie Smith.

REPRODUCTION PAGE 47

RESTRICTING THE GLOBAL TOPIC

INSTRUCTIONS: Limit the following ideas to a scope appropriate for a paper with only three or four developed paragraphs.

1. Health is important. _____
   _____

2. The topographies of the continents have pronounced effects on their weather patterns.
   _____

3. War, in the past, has been a reasonably effective means of settling international problems. _____

4. Malnutrition is found in all classes of people all over the world. _____
   _____

5. America is entering the postindustrial age. _____
   _____

6. Traffic deaths in the United States demonstrate the American urge for self-destruction.
   _____

7. It is possible for young people to take a conscious, significant part in assisting their own psychological growth. _____
   _____

Copyright © 1982 by Allyn and Bacon, Inc. Reproduction of this material is restricted to use with *A Guidebook for Teaching Composition*, 2nd Edition, by Gene Stanford and Marie Smith.

REPRODUCTION PAGE 47   RESTRICTING THE GLOBAL TOPIC

8. Modern medicine has performed miracles in conquering diseases that once were scourges of humanity. _____
_____

9. Great men have not always been successful fathers. _____
_____

10. In the United States, there is much more prestige to being youthful than to being old.
_____

11. In the history of wars is written the story of the human race's greatness and baseness.
_____

12. The "good old days" were not always so good. _____
_____

13. Many people act as if old age were something that could never happen to them. _____
_____

14. The automobile is one of the major causes of air pollution. _____
_____

15. Housecleaning was hard labor in the good old days. _____
_____

Copyright © 1982 by Allyn and Bacon, Inc. Reproduction of this material is restricted to use with *A Guidebook for Teaching Composition*, 2nd Edition, by Gene Stanford and Marie Smith.

REPRODUCTION PAGE 48

ENLARGING THE LIMITED TOPIC

INSTRUCTIONS: Enlarge the following ideas (which are limited enough to be topic sentences of paragraphs) to a scope appropriate for a paper of five to ten paragraphs.

1. A boy can learn much from owning a dog. _____
   _____

2. I lost a friendship by being thoughtless. _____
   _____

3. The water of the lake was a deep, dark blue. _____
   _____

4. I navigated the dark stairway cautiously. _____
   _____

5. The otter is the most playful of animals. _____
   _____

6. The whooping crane is one bird that apparently has been saved from extinction by timely conservation efforts. _____
   _____

7. The new member of Congress soon learns to give a little in order to get a little. _____
   _____

Copyright © 1982 by Allyn and Bacon, Inc. Reproduction of this material is restricted to use with *A Guidebook for Teaching Composition*, 2nd Edition, by Gene Stanford and Marie Smith.

REPRODUCTION PAGE 48   ENLARGING THE LIMITED TOPIC

8. One should never betray a friend's confidence. _____
   _____

9. Ice cream has a good deal of nutritive value, even if it is fattening. _____
   _____

10. Too much sun can cause skin cancer. _____
    _____

11. A football player learns self-discipline, cooperation, and dedication. _____
    _____

12. Young people are pushed to choose careers before they are halfway through high school. _____
    _____

13. Today, young people seem to learn their social values from their peers rather than from their families. _____
    _____

14. Some children in the early grades seem unduly eager to please their teachers. _____
    _____

15. When making assignments, a teacher encourages students' growth by offering as many options as possible. _____
    _____

Copyright © 1982 by Allyn and Bacon, Inc. Reproduction of this material is restricted to use with *A Guidebook for Teaching Composition*, 2nd Edition, by Gene Stanford and Marie Smith.

REPRODUCTION PAGE 49

DETERMINING COMPOSITION SIZE

INSTRUCTIONS: In the blank at the left of each subject, print the letter that corresponds to the size of composition it would take to develop that subject: (a) a library, (b) a shelf of books, (c) a book, (d) a chapter, (e) a five- to ten-paragraph essay, (f) a three-paragraph essay, and (g) one paragraph.

_____ 1. The apple is a remarkable fruit.
_____ 2. Drinking eight glasses of water a day is beneficial to health in a number of ways.
_____ 3. Achieving psychological maturity can also be called mastering the art of loving.
_____ 4. The history of the human race is revealed most truly in its art, architecture, literature, and music.
_____ 5. It does not matter if people are free so long as they think they are.
_____ 6. The fall of Rome has been so instructive to people of all subsequent generations that if it had not occurred, it would have been invented.
_____ 7. Suicide has a long and respected history in Japan.
_____ 8. Tomatoes should not be planted in the same spot two years in a row.
_____ 9. Dogs are more expensive to feed than cats.
_____ 10. We will cherish our old people only when society has changed so that people become loving and lovable.
_____ 11. There are still a number of prestigious careers for which a college education is not at all necessary.
_____ 12. Religion and humanity have coexisted from the beginning.
_____ 13. Fat people often lack self-esteem.
_____ 14. Obesity is a serious health problem in the United States.
_____ 15. It is possible to rear thin children and thus eradicate the problem of obesity.
_____ 16. Counting calories is the surest way for the nutrition-wise person to lose weight.
_____ 17. The functions and effects of cholesterol in the human blood comprise a complex and poorly understood subject.
_____ 18. We human beings have gained a great deal of knowledge about the workings of our bodies.
_____ 19. Obesity is hardly an asset to a happy social life.
_____ 20. The human soul has never been located, but it has been the subject of conjecture and study for thousands of years.
_____ 21. The early Christian church was indebted to many of the other so-called miracle religions for much of its form and substance.
_____ 22. "Progress" is a difficult term to define.
_____ 23. Modern art has developed in directions quite unrelated to the tastes and understandings of the public for whom it presumably was created.
_____ 24. The tiger in captivity can never be considered an entirely trustworthy animal.
_____ 25. Bear baiting, a popular spectacle in the London of Shakespeare's time, was a brutal sport.
_____ 26. The English bull dog was bred for bear baiting.

Copyright © 1982 by Allyn and Bacon, Inc. Reproduction of this material is restricted to use with *A Guidebook for Teaching Composition*, 2nd Edition, by Gene Stanford and Marie Smith.

REPRODUCTION PAGE 50

From Subject To Thesis

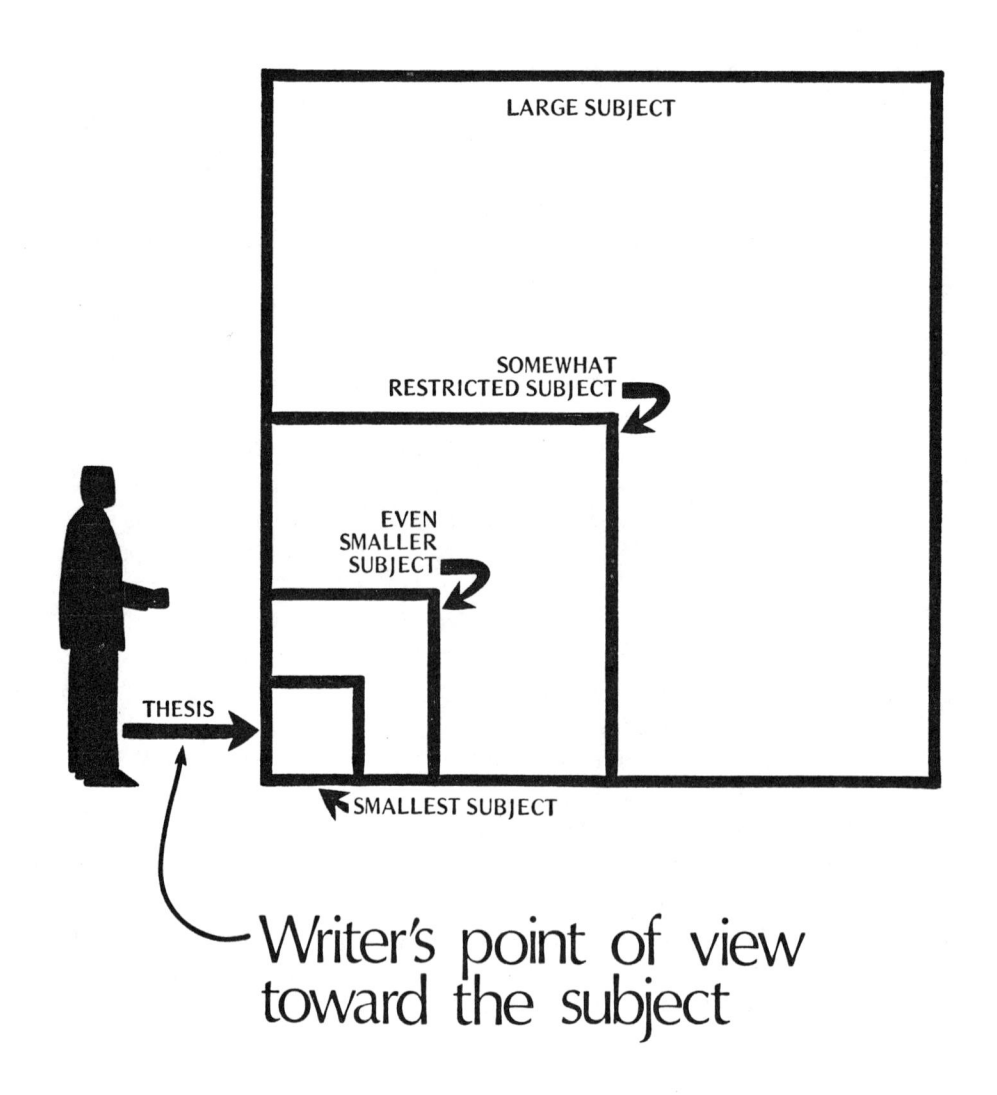

LARGE SUBJECT

SOMEWHAT RESTRICTED SUBJECT

EVEN SMALLER SUBJECT

THESIS

SMALLEST SUBJECT

Writer's point of view toward the subject

Copyright © 1982 by Allyn and Bacon, Inc. Reproduction of this material is restricted to use with *A Guidebook for Teaching Composition,* 2nd Edition, by Gene Stanford and Marie Smith.

188

REPRODUCTION PAGE 51

CONSTRUCTING A THESIS FROM A RESTRICTED SUBJECT

INSTRUCTIONS: The subjects below have already been restricted in size. For each, compose a thesis sentence that indicates a point of view toward that restricted subject.

winter in my community

deep sea fishing in Florida

my sophomore English class

experiences playing football in high school

learning to drive at school last year

thefts in the boys' locker room

snorkeling in clear water streams

The Cherokee Indians' trek to Oklahoma

Copyright © 1982 by Allyn and Bacon, Inc. Reproduction of this material is restricted to use with *A Guidebook for Teaching Composition*, 2nd Edition, by Gene Stanford and Marie Smith.

REPRODUCTION PAGE 51 **CONSTRUCTING A THESIS FROM A RESTRICTED SUBJECT**

being poor in the country rather than in the city

voting for the first time

making ones' own clothes

a raft trip at the bottom of the Grand Canyon

changes in rock music

high school dress codes

old people in poor health

quiet, shy students

living in a high crime area

Copyright © 1982 by Allyn and Bacon, Inc. Reproduction of this material is restricted to use with *A Guidebook for Teaching Composition*, 2nd Edition, by Gene Stanford and Marie Smith.

REPRODUCTION PAGE 52

DEVELOPING A THESIS BY RELATING TWO SUBJECTS

INSTRUCTIONS: An easy way to develop a thesis about a subject is to relate it to another subject. For example, the subject "loving families" can be related to the subject "crime" to produce the thesis "A loving family is a major preventive to crime." Using the following chart, name the second subject that has been related to the first subject to produce the thesis.

Subject	Thesis	Second Subject
loving families	A loving family is a major preventive to crime.	crime
football	Football teaches lessons of good citizenship and group awareness.	_____
football	Strategies of football are similar to military tactics.	_____
basketball	Basketball is more exciting than football for spectators.	_____
teen years	The teen years encompass some of the most important and consequential decisions a person will ever make.	_____
apples	An apple a day keeps the doctor away.	_____
grade chasing	Grade chasing is not always the best way to get good grades.	_____
good human relations	Good human relations always thrive on open and honest communication.	_____
loyalty	People owe their highest loyalty to their own personal values, not to any person who would ask them to go against them.	_____
making own clothes	People who can make their own clothes will usually have better clothes for less money.	_____
vitamin C	Taking high quantities of vitamin C can help one avoid the common cold.	_____
careful driving	Motorists owe their passengers the courtesy of careful driving.	_____
good manners	All courtesy and so-called "good manners" are based on simple thoughtfulness.	_____
TV advertising	TV advertising makes it clear that there is something terribly undesirable and unattractive about growing old.	_____

Copyright © 1982 by Allyn and Bacon, Inc. Reproduction of this material is restricted to use with *A Guidebook for Teaching Composition,* 2nd Edition, by Gene Stanford and Marie Smith.

REPRODUCTION PAGE 53

CONSTRUCTING A THESIS BY RELATING ONE SUBJECT TO ANOTHER

INSTRUCTIONS: Write a thesis that relates each of the following pairs of subjects

1. human beings—tornadoes _____

2. girls—basketball _____

3. cats—people _____

4. young men—women's liberation _____

5. sleep—teenagers _____

6. crime—unemployment _____

7. modern society—peace of mind _____

8. European public transit—Americans _____

9. spring—floating _____

Copyright © 1982 by Allyn and Bacon, Inc. Reproduction of this material is restricted to use with *A Guidebook for Teaching Composition*, 2nd Edition, by Gene Stanford and Marie Smith.

REPRODUCTION PAGE 54

DETERMINING THE SUBJECTS OF THESIS SENTENCES

INSTRUCTIONS: The following thesis sentences have been composed by joining two subjects. Identify the two subjects in each sentence by drawing a line under each.

1. Regular applications of fertilizer are necessary to the maintenance of a good bluegrass lawn.

2. A gray and overcast day is a fine time to settle down with a good book.

3. Wicker furniture, with its light and airy design, is suitable for decorating a screened porch.

4. Breakfast should provide one-fourth or more of one's nutritional needs for the day.

5. Many plants, as well as animals, are on the growing list of endangered species.

6. Much of the white bread we purchase at the market has little food value beyond calories.

7. During the 1960s, hair became a symbol of cultural differences.

8. To many young people, the driver's license looks like a veritable ticket to freedom.

9. Every kitchen should have a singing bird to keep the cook cheerful.

10. People who keep cats for pets but who also like birds should attach bells to the cats' collars.

Copyright © 1982 by Allyn and Bacon, Inc. Reproduction of this material is restricted to use with *A Guidebook for Teaching Composition*, 2nd Edition, by Gene Stanford and Marie Smith.

REPRODUCTION PAGE 55

LIMITING THE SWEEPING THESIS

INSTRUCTIONS: Limit and qualify the sweeping thesis sentences below, first, by asking questions such as: all? everyone? always? everywhere? and all kinds? and, second, by rewriting the sentences in view of your answers.

1. Poverty is not as bad as it is thought to be.

2. Being rich is destructive to human character.

3. All politicians are just looking for a chance to get their hands into our pockets.

4. Surfing in Hawaii is something everyone can enjoy.

5. Hooking rugs is an excellent hobby.

6. Lawns should be mowed at least once a week if they are to be kept in good condition.

7. Music, after all, never hurt anyone.

8. The gravest problem facing the United States today is inflation.

9. The ideal vacation includes sunshine, sports, a change of scenery and plenty of good food.

10. It is impossible to be well educated without some travel experience.

11. Everyone loves a frisky kitten.

12. It is a wonderful treat to have someone else do your work for you.

13. Young people enter senior high school with much fear and trepidation.

14. Seniors, in their arrogance, ignore the lowly underclassman.

15. Students find it hard to talk freely with teachers.

Copyright © 1982 by Allyn and Bacon, Inc. Reproduction of this material is restricted to use with *A Guidebook for Teaching Composition*, 2nd Edition, by Gene Stanford and Marie Smith.

REPRODUCTION PAGE 56

FINDING WEAKNESSES IN THESIS STATEMENTS

INSTRUCTIONS: The following thesis statements are imprecise and misleading. Identify the weaknesses in each thesis sentence. Look for: words that could be interpreted more than one way or unqualified terms about which the reader might have questions. Then rewrite each thesis to make it more precise.

EXAMPLE: Catcher in the Rye *is a dirty book and should be banned. (dirty? entirely banned? everywhere? to all people?)* Catcher in the Rye *includes language that offends some people, and a teacher who wishes to assign the book would be wise to determine the community's attitude toward the book before doing so.*

1. Love makes the world go around. _____

2. Miami is a great place to go for holiday fun. _____

3. The free parts of the world are the only parts worth living in. _____

4. All good citizens of a democracy will welcome a chance to fight for liberty. _____

5. Patriotism demands that we respond to our country's needs. _____

6. A girl must behave like a lady if she wishes to be thought well bred. _____

7. The whole world loves a lover. _____

Copyright © 1982 by Allyn and Bacon, Inc. Reproduction of this material is restricted to use with *A Guidebook for Teaching Composition*, 2nd Edition, by Gene Stanford and Marie Smith.

REPRODUCTION PAGE 56 FINDING WEAKNESSES IN THESIS STATEMENTS

8. If one is not moving ahead, one is falling behind. _____
_____
_____

9. Most Americans are imbued with an old fashioned ambition to get ahead. ____
_____
_____

10. Americans have always been devoted to the land. _____
_____
_____

11. Loyalty is one of the noblest of human virtues. _____
_____
_____

12. A great portion of the world's population lives in poverty. _____
_____
_____

13. Every individual should devote at least a portion of his or her life to the pursuit of beauty. _____
_____
_____

14. According to an old adage, "Neatness and system are heaven's first laws, and cleanliness is next to godliness." _____
_____
_____

15. Professional football can do much for any major city. _____
_____
_____

16. A country wishing to remain free must be prepared to do battle with those who would destroy its liberty. _____
_____
_____

Copyright © 1982 by Allyn and Bacon, Inc. Reproduction of this material is restricted to use with *A Guidebook for Teaching Composition,* 2nd Edition, by Gene Stanford and Marie Smith.

REPRODUCTION PAGE 57

MAKING SURE YOUR THESIS SENTENCE IS UNIFIED

INSTRUCTIONS: The following list of sentences contains both unified and ununified thesis sentences. Identify the unified ones and correct the ununified ones by severing them, unifying them by finding a relationship between the various parts, or subordinating both parts to a higher generalization large enough to include them both.

1. All too often the father is not an important figure in the inner-city family, and juvenile delinquency is a serious urban problem.

2. Like the extremes of poverty, an excess of wealth can be destructive to good human values.

3. Recent political events have revealed the dishonesty of many politicians, and a movement should be started to identify the good, honest politicians in America.

4. If you learn a few labor-saving devices, gardening need not be hard work, and it can also be profitable.

5. Cooking, like any creative work, is done best by those who enjoy it and who can afford to buy the best ingredients.

6. While Americans are accustomed to a diet whose foundation is meat, more of the world's inhabitants eat a diet based on cereals.

7. New York is the biggest city in the United States, and San Francisco is the most cosmopolitan.

8. Dogs are always eager to please, and cats are independent.

9. In Denmark the cultural differences between the generations seem even greater than in the United States.

10. There were people who saw the Beatles as a Communist menace and were sure that long hair was a mark of moral degradation.

11. People who get up early know that dawn shows beautiful colors unlike those of the sky at sunset, when dramatic cloud formations catch everyone's attention and inspire poets, who in these days more often see the sunset than the sunrise.

Copyright © 1982 by Allyn and Bacon, Inc. Reproduction of this material is restricted to use with *A Guidebook for Teaching Composition*, 2nd Edition, by Gene Stanford and Marie Smith.

REPRODUCTION PAGE 58

EVALUATING THESIS SENTENCES

INSTRUCTIONS: Determine whether or not the thesis sentences below meet the criteria for good thesis sentences outlined by your teacher. Circle the numbers of those that meet the criteria, and revise those that do not.

1. I love apple pie.

2. The word "feline" refers to cats.

3. It seems to be true, as George Orwell said, that "all animals are equal but some are more equal than others."

4. A child can learn the lesson of responsibility from owning a dog.

5. Swimming has always been my favorite sport.

6. Many people between the ages of eight and eighteen play baseball.

7. Baseball fascinates people as much by its possibilities for strategy as by its demonstration of athletic skills.

8. The trials of life tend to be overwhelming for many people.

9. A well-reared cat is an endlessly entertaining pet.

10. There are not as many kings and queens in the world today as there were one hundred years ago.

11. Physical education classes are included in almost all U.S. school curricula.

12. Football is an excellent sport.

13. There is a big difference between friendship and romance.

14. Young women today have an ever-widening range of career opportunities open to them.

15. Movies are fine entertainment.

16. Not only are boys and girls sharing gym classes and home economics classes, but the reallocation of educational funds and revision of traditional curricula are foreseen as consequences of the women's movement, and some educators are strongly opposed to the changes coming about.

Copyright © 1982 by Allyn and Bacon, Inc. Reproduction of this material is restricted to use with *A Guidebook for Teaching Composition,* 2nd Edition, by Gene Stanford and Marie Smith.

REPRODUCTION PAGE 59

DIVIDING A THESIS INTO ITS PARTS

INSTRUCTIONS: List the logical parts of each thesis sentence below. That is, list the aspects of the thesis that will have to be developed to cover the thesis entirely.

1. It is a mistake to have a smoking lounge in any public high school.

2. In our personal conversation we often use our own speaking for purposes other than to reveal ourselves or convey information.

3. Despite the absence of immediate victory, there are benefits derived from devoting oneself to a losing cause in which one sincerely believes.

4. It is difficult to identify any beneficial consequences of war that could not have been achieved by more peaceful means.

5. There are many lessons that young people could learn from old people if they lived with their elders.

6. Many Americans behave as if they considered themselves immune to the dire consequences of which they are warned by doctors, scientists, policemen, and safety experts.

7. Life becomes richer and more rewarding as we learn to break down the obstacles to free and open communication.

8. The history of the American Revolution as it is presented in high school is a far cry from the simple story of a battle for human liberty that most of us learned in grade school.

9. A civil war is one of the most horrifying of all human conflicts.

Copyright © 1982 by Allyn and Bacon, Inc. Reproduction of this material is restricted to use with *A Guidebook for Teaching Composition,* 2nd Edition, by Gene Stanford and Marie Smith.

REPRODUCTION PAGE 60

DETERMINING ORDER OF THESIS PARTS

INSTRUCTIONS: Read each of the thesis sentences and parts listed below and determine the proper order of the parts, numbering them.

1. *Thesis:* As a result of numerous disastrous experiences on blind dates, I am convinced that no right-minded young man should ever go on a date with a girl he does not already know.
   Parts: (numerous disastrous experiences)
   _____ a. Girl was so nervous she threw up in the car and cried all the way home.
   _____ b. Girl was 5'10" and made me feel like a pigmy.
   _____ c. Girl argued violently over everything I said, including the value of rock music, health food, politics, the sexual revolution, college education, communes, and my way of dressing.
   _____ d. Girl would not talk about anything.
   _____ e. Girl did not know anything about sports.

2. *Thesis:* Lionel Farber's life was a demonstration of how a criminal is created.
   Parts: (events in Farber's life)
   _____ a. His father, a convicted murderer, was executed.
   _____ b. His mother deserted the family when he was four.
   _____ c. He had a disfiguring birth mark on half his face.
   _____ d. He was brutalized by a neighborhood gang as a child.
   _____ e. He was unsuccessful in school.
   _____ f. His older brother, his model and a petty criminal, was his only friend and support.

3. *Thesis:* The new college freshman's first semester is a time when he or she is forced to make successful adjustments to many new demands.
   Parts: (new demands)
   _____ a. The freshman is forced to regulate his or her own life with no help.
   _____ b. Classes are harder, and teachers are more demanding.
   _____ c. The person is away from home and family, perhaps for the first time.
   _____ d. There is a roommate, a stranger the student must live with.
   _____ e. Unfamiliar environment is confusing.
   _____ f. He or she must choose companions and make friends.

Copyright © 1982 by Allyn and Bacon, Inc. Reproduction of this material is restricted to use with *A Guidebook for Teaching Composition*, 2nd Edition, by Gene Stanford and Marie Smith.

DETERMINING ORDER OF THESIS PARTS REPRODUCTION PAGE 60

4. *Thesis:* Persons who achieve renown in one field often show great talent or competence in others.
   Parts: (multitalented people)
   _____ a. Albert Schweitzer: medical missionary, expert on Bach and organs.
   _____ b. Albert Einstein: superb violinist, scientist.
   _____ c. Thomas Jefferson: inventor, statesman.
   _____ d. Eugene McCarthy: baseball player, poet, politician.
   _____ e. Winston Churchill: painter, statesman.
   _____ f. Ben Franklin: diplomat, printer, journalist, inventor.

5. *Thesis:* Careful study has suggested certain circumstances that predispose a marriage to failure.
   Parts: (causes of failure in marriage)
   _____ a. Deep devotion to different religions by pair.
   _____ b. Coming from home broken by divorce.
   _____ c. Wide divergence in cultural or educational backgrounds.
   _____ d. Emotional immaturity of one or both people.
   _____ e. Short acquaintance before marriage.
   _____ f. Insufficient financial means.
   _____ g. Parental disapproval.

6. *Thesis:* The least experienced person can, with advance preparation, give a successful dinner party.
   Parts: (steps in preparation)
   _____ a. Plan arrangement of the table the day before.
   _____ b. Choose menu you already know how to cook.
   _____ c. Plan dishes that don't require last-minute activities.
   _____ d. Polish silver well in advance.
   _____ e. Be sure table cloth and napkins are ironed the day before.
   _____ f. Plan in advance which serving dish will hold which item on the menu.
   _____ g. Choose records to provide congenial background music.

7. *Thesis:* A hospital is not the place to go for a rest.
   Parts: (unnerving elements of hospital life)
   _____ a. They wake you up to give you a sleeping pill.
   _____ b. After lunch, when you would like a nap, visiting hours begin.
   _____ c. Nurses and interns are constantly coming to see you.
   _____ d. You are being bathed constantly.
   _____ e. Someone is always taking blood tests.
   _____ f. Nurses wake you up at dawn.

Copyright © 1982 by Allyn and Bacon, Inc. Reproduction of this material is restricted to use with *A Guidebook for Teaching Composition*, 2nd Edition, by Gene Stanford and Marie Smith.

REPRODUCTION PAGE 61

DIVIDING AND ORDERING THE THESIS SENTENCE

INSTRUCTIONS: Divide the following thesis sentences into their parts. Then list the parts in logical order.

1. Good study habits go a long way toward producing good grades.

2. Some people seem to do everything they can to alienate others.

3. Violent crime seems to rise and fall with changes in the weather.

4. Even with the best intentions, many parents of adolescents alienate their children.

5. The high school principal must be an expert at more than teaching.

6. Student honor codes are rarely successful in high schools.

7. Disciplinary measures in school should be aimed at teaching and helping students, rather than punishing them.

8. Much dating in high school is an exercise in ego building rather than a matter of true friendship or love.

9. A long engagement period increases the likelihood of a successful marriage.

10. A good correspondent writes letters that are a pleasure to receive.

11. A particularly admirable kind of courage is the capacity to endure.

12. Academic knowledge and skills are by no means the only lessons one should strive to master in high school.

Copyright © 1982 by Allyn and Bacon, Inc. Reproduction of this material is restricted to use with *A Guidebook for Teaching Composition,* 2nd Edition, by Gene Stanford and Marie Smith.

REPRODUCTION PAGE 62

TEST: DIVIDING AND ORDERING THE THESIS

INSTRUCTIONS: Divide each of the thesis statements below into its logical parts and number the parts in a logical order.

1. The decision of what college to attend must be based on a number of considerations.

2. Our failures often teach us more than our successes.

3. The high school dropout has many problems that will plague his or her future.

4. The ways we are treating our environment today may well threaten the quality of life for our grandchildren.

5. Punishment is seldom the most effective technique for teaching young people guidelines for socially responsible behavior.

6. Secondary education in the United States is overdue for some major changes.

Copyright © 1982 by Allyn and Bacon, Inc. Reproduction of this material is restricted to use with *A Guidebook for Teaching Composition,* 2nd Edition, by Gene Stanford and Marie Smith.

REPRODUCTION PAGE 63

TRANSITION DEVICES

Following is a list of possible wordings for transitions:

1. It is evident, *then*, that the Gallic Wars proved Caesar's military genius.
2. *In spite of* these powerful arguments, there were still many dissenters.
3. Administrators, *however*, are not the only ones disturbed by this problem.
4. *Not only* must students solve these financial problems, *but* also they face new and difficult academic challenges.
5. *Having seen* how the early popes handled this problem, *let us* turn to the popes of later centuries and see whether they were as successful.
6. We will go *either* to the movies *or* to the game.
7. *Having considered* the Renaissance, *let us now* move on to the Baroque period.
8. We decided, *finally*, to cancel the meeting.
9. No discussion of literature would be complete without mentioning Shakespeare.
10. *Granting that this viewpoint has some validity*, we still question its overall viability.
11. *In view of this evidence, then*, why is it that so many people continue to smoke?
12. *Let us turn, now*, to some more positive issues.
13. *In concluding* this presentation of photography, let us discuss lighting.
14. Answers, *as we shall see*, are not easily formulated.
15. Hemingway is *not the only* author who deals with *this* theme.
16. *The third and last* example to be discussed involves the Supreme Court decision on euthanasia.
17. Let us consider, *on the other hand*, the benefits of vocational training.
18. The answers, *nevertheless*, remain to be seen.
19. Ice cream is fattening; yogurt, *conversely*, is low in calories.
20. We should mention, *in addition to the facts already presented*, that there were two witnesses.

Copyright © 1982 by Allyn and Bacon, Inc. Reproduction of this material is restricted to use with *A Guidebook for Teaching Composition*, 2nd Edition, by Gene Stanford and Marie Smith.

TRANSITION DEVICES: EVALUATION ACTIVITY

Part I Identifying Transitions

INSTRUCTIONS: In each group below you are given a sentence that you are to imagine is the last sentence in a paragraph and two sentences from which to choose the first sentence of the next paragraph. Circle the letter of the sentence in each group that provides the smoothest transition. Underline the transitional or connecting device.

1. A simple misunderstanding, then, can become a major stumbling block to communication between teenagers and parents.
    - (a) Embarrassment plays a considerable part in the lack of communication between generations.
    - (b) Embarrassment also plays a considerable part in this lack of communication between generations.

2. Reading a textbook assignment actively, therefore, is an excellent way to use your study time most effectively.
    - (a) Another effective study habit is that of asking the right questions as you read.
    - (b) You should learn to ask the right questions as you read.

3. Courses at the high school level are generally difficult, and students are often expected to work on their own.
    - (a) On the other hand, the junior high program is organized quite differently.
    - (b) The junior high program is organized quite differently.

4. In general, students who are interested in school take more active roles in school affairs than do apathetic students; they run for offices, work hard on committees, help to make plans and formulate ideas, and interact with administrators and teachers.
    - (a) As a result of this more active role, interested students develop faster socially.
    - (b) Interested students often develop faster socially than students who are not interested in school.

5. We are not surprised, therefore, to learn that almost all teenagers are deeply interested in increasing their skills in human relations.
    - (a) Most young people are willing to work hard at any task that seems to contribute to group cohesiveness.
    - (b) One form this interest takes is a willingness on the part of most young people to work hard at any task that seems to contribute to group cohesiveness.

6. As a result of this experience, she never again cared to get on a horse.
    - (a) She turned her attention to bird watching, a safe pastime for one who loves the outdoors.
    - (b) She still loved the outdoors, however, and soon settled on bird watching as an outdoor pastime somewhat safer than horseback riding.

Copyright © 1982 by Allyn and Bacon, Inc. Reproduction of this material is restricted to use with *A Guidebook for Teaching Composition,* 2nd Edition, by Gene Stanford and Marie Smith.

REPRODUCTION PAGE 64 — TRANSITION DEVICES: EVALUATION ACTIVITY

7. With these instructions, she was finally able to finish step three with no further difficulty.
   - (a) Step four, however, was another problem entirely.
   - (b) Step four presented a problem.

8. After a great deal of hard work, she was able to turn in the completed paper on Thursday.
   - (a) Having managed to complete her English assignment for the week, she next turned her attention to her overdue biology reports.
   - (b) She turned her attention to her overdue biology reports.

9. We can see, then, that this method is relatively simple and requires little technical training.
   - (a) There are three other methods of which, unfortunately, this cannot be said.
   - (b) There are three difficult methods that require lengthy technical training.

10. She was, in short, the most beautiful girl he had ever seen.
    - (a) However, it was not her physical beauty that drew him to her.
    - (b) He was not drawn to her because of her physical beauty.

Part II Writing Transitions

INSTRUCTIONS: In each group below you are given a sentence that you are to imagine is the last sentence in a paragraph and another sentence which is the first sentence in the next paragraph. Rewrite the second sentence to provide a better transition between the paragraphs.

1. Thus, the American woman accepted the domination of her husband for many years, apparently without question or regret.
   Many American women will no longer accept domination passively.

   Better opening sentence for the second paragraph: _____
   _____
   _____
   _____

2. The materials were assembled and I was ready to begin work immediately.
   I attacked the Spanish translation, which I dreaded the most.

   Better opening sentence for second paragraph: _____
   _____
   _____
   _____

Copyright © 1982 by Allyn and Bacon, Inc. Reproduction of this material is restricted to use with *A Guidebook for Teaching Composition*, 2nd Edition, by Gene Stanford and Marie Smith.

TRANSITION DEVICES: EVALUATION ACTIVITY

REPRODUCTION PAGE 64

3. In fact, I was so far behind I was afraid I would not be able to finish the course.

    I had a deep interest in the next course in the sequence, so I caught up and finished the course on time.

    Better opening sentence for the second paragraph: _____

    _____

    _____

    _____

4. Having learned this hard lesson, I was never again tempted to take something that did not belong to me.

    It was hard for me to learn the lesson that I should always tell the truth.

    Better opening sentence for the second paragraph: _____

    _____

    _____

    _____

5. This particular incident contributed to the mutual hostility that finally led to the outbreak of fighting.

    An incident that brought two soldiers into personal conflict increased the tension on both sides.

    Better opening sentence for the second paragraph: _____

    _____

    _____

    _____

6. If all these considerations are taken into account ahead of time, it is clear that the actual arranging of the buffet will present no problems on the day of the dinner.

    Care must always be exercised in planning the guest list.

    Better opening sentence for the second paragraph: _____

    _____

    _____

    _____

Copyright © 1982 by Allyn and Bacon, Inc. Reproduction of this material is restricted to use with *A Guidebook for Teaching Composition*, 2nd Edition, by Gene Stanford and Marie Smith.

REPRODUCTION PAGE 65

FOUR COMMON TYPES OF INTRODUCTIONS

1. An *anecdotal introduction* relates an incident that demonstrates or exemplifies the author's thesis. It is usually quite brief, points clearly and directly to the thesis, and culminates in a statement of the thesis. It captures the reader's interest both by its content and by its easy and informal style. This opening is more likely to be favored for articles written for popular consumption than for formal scholarly works. Here is an example of an anecdotal introduction:

   Thelma Gray and Lucy Taylor, both fifteen years old and known for their adventurous spirits, said goodbye to their mothers on a sunny morning in May, 1976, and set out for their bus stop at the corner. They were invited to a picnic and swimming party at a suburban park a few miles away. Clutching their bathing suits and bright beach towels, they hurried toward a fun-filled day with their friends. Thelma and Lucy, however, never reached that park and never saw their friends again. By nightfall their bodies had been found beside a seldom used road in an isolated area of the country near the park. Both had been bludgeoned to death. Police, reconstructing the young women's last day, determined that they were two more on a growing list of girls who had decided to hitchhike and who had paid the ultimate price for their decision. Chief of Police Erwin T. Miller had tears in his eyes as he announced the cause of the teenagers' deaths and pleaded with other girls to heed police warnings against hitchhiking. "People who accept rides with strangers," he said, "run the risk of losing their lives in the same tragic manner as these two poor girls."

2. The *outline introduction* includes a statement of the thesis along with the major parts to be covered in the essay. This introduction is not suitable for a brief essay but may be very helpful to introduce a long essay on a difficult and complex subject. In such cases it is often helpful for the reader to know in advance exactly what aspects of a subject the author plans to develop and in what order. Thus, the reader is equipped with a "road-map" through the essay. Here is an example of the outline introduction:

   The American Civil War is often described as the bloodiest and most tragic experience in the nation's history. The very nature of civil war, with family members divided by differing loyalties and friend estranged from friend, is, of course, sufficient reason to regard such a war with particular horror. However, a study of the toll in human suffering in the war between the North and South requires close examination of the specific aspects of the conflict. This present study will attempt to show that immediate battlefield losses, serious as they were, represented only a minor portion of the human suffering caused by the war. An examination of actual direct casualties (dead and injured) for

Copyright © 1982 by Allyn and Bacon, Inc. Reproduction of this material is restricted to use with *A Guidebook for Teaching Composition*, 2nd Edition, by Gene Stanford and Marie Smith.

FOUR COMMON TYPES OF INTRODUCTIONS

both North and South will comprise the opening section. Succeeding sections will examine in turn the prisoner of war camps of both the North and South with their grossly inadequate living facilities, diet and medical provisions; military hospitals and other medical establishments, with emphasis on the primitive nature of facilities and technology; and legal and historical records of cases in which individuals of one side or the other were accused of wreaking atrocities on helpless persons in their power. The final section will deal with sufferings of civilian populations in areas where the two armies fought, foraged, and scorched the earth. The miseries of the American Civil War, we shall see, fell on soldier and citizen alike.

3. The *contrast introduction* is especially appropriate when your thesis contradicts or modifies a commonly held belief or assumption. It begins with several sentences explaining the commonly held opinion and then presents the thesis as the opposite of this belief or assumption. Here is an example of the contrast introduction:

    Most people assume that learning to ski is not extremely difficult. They imagine the process consists of little more than strapping on two long boards, pushing off at the top of a hill, and gliding gracefully and effortlessly to the bottom. However, learning to ski is more difficult than these people realize and requires long hours of practice, extremely good physical condition, and a lot of determination.

4. The *funnel introduction* is very useful and common. The writer identifies the general subject area in the opening sentence, making some generalization aimed at arousing interest and, perhaps, establishing a common bond of awareness and knowledge with the reader. The author narrows the subject down step by step, sentence by sentence, to the specific aspect of the general subject and the specific viewpoint toward it that form the thesis. In other words, the funnel introduction begins with a very broad general idea and continues with ideas that are more and more specific, until it arrives at the thesis sentence—the most specific idea in the introduction. Since it becomes more and more narrow from top to bottom, this kind of introduction is given the label "funnel." Here is an example of the funnel introduction:

    The life of a teenager in modern America is not always pleasant. He or she is faced with a multitude of conflicts and problems, many of which seem almost impossible to overcome. Most of these problems center around school, which is not surprising considering that the teenager devotes an average of eight hours a day to school and school-related activities. One of the primary problems created by school is the intense pressure for good grades.

Copyright © 1982 by Allyn and Bacon, Inc. Reproduction of this material is restricted to use with *A Guidebook for Teaching Composition*, 2nd Edition, by Gene Stanford and Marie Smith.

REPRODUCTION PAGE 66

IDENTIFYING THE FOUR COMMON TYPES OF INTRODUCTIONS

INSTRUCTIONS: Determine which method was used—anecdotal, outline, contrast, or funnel—in constructing each of the following introductions. Identify each paragraph by writing its correct type in the space provided.

Introduction I

Since the human is the only one capable of reasoning, it would seem to follow that above all animals human beings would be able to plan and execute a regimen for living that would result in vigorous health and a harmonious, productive life. That this is far from the case is evident to the most casual observer. The lowliest of animals, unaided by anything remotely resembling human intelligence, manage more successfully than we do to eat what is good for them, sleep as much as their bodies require, and exercise enough to stay agile and remain through life a functional part of nature's harmonious whole. Human beings get low marks in all these achievements. Our sophisticated intellect, far from being an aid to promotion of health, spurs us to destructive behavior in terms of food, drink, sleep, exercise, work, and play. An examination of human behavior with regard to these lifelong activities might well persuade one that good health is better promoted by animal instinct than by an intricate and miraculous brain.

Introduction type _____

Introduction II

Friendship is an art that requires more than ordinary skill and commitment. It requires, in its highest form, knowledge of the mysteries of human motivation and a willingness to accept one's friends for what they really are instead of for their all too often imperfect external expressions of self. This kind of knowledge and this capacity for acceptance are not easily gained and are most often the consequences of long experience and practice. For young people, therefore, who are at the beginning of their practice of friendship, a simpler capacity must suffice. This can be found, I believe, in the deliberate development of the quality of loyalty. Of all the components that are important to a rich, long-lasting friendship, loyalty is the most essential.

Introduction type _____

Introduction III

I wanted, more than anything, to be invited to join a sorority when I entered high school. I was sure that to be left out of this magic circle of popular girls would mean the absolute end of my hopes for teenage happiness and social success. Imagine my excitement, therefore, when I received invitations to rush parties from three different clubs. And imagine the frenzy of preparations I entered into—the endless efforts to insure the acceptability of

Copyright © 1982 by Allyn and Bacon, Inc. Reproduction of this material is restricted to use with *A Guidebook for Teaching Composition*, 2nd Edition, by Gene Stanford and Marie Smith.

IDENTIFYING THE FOUR COMMON TYPES OF INTRODUCTIONS

my face, figure, hair, clothes, conversation, and table manners. I was to be whatever each club wanted me to be, perfect in all respects and equally pleasing to all. As it happens, I did join a sorority but not, it soon became apparent, because I was perfect in all respects. On the contrary, my making over began the day I joined. In time the magic circle became a restricting cage, and I longed to exercise my own standards and search for my own goals. Many a young girl, I suggest, learns as I did that the important task of becoming her best self is seldom served by unthinking efforts to become what others want her to be.

Introduction type _____

Introduction IV

From the beginning of history myths have abounded in which some magical elixir of youth or good health or long life has been hoped for, searched for, and, as some tales would have it, discovered and lost again. Such natural phenomena as geysers or sulphur springs have been thought to produce miraculously restorative waters, and people have traveled long distances to drink foul-tasting potions in the hopes of regaining health or retaining youthful vigor. Even today, we are not far removed from our grandparents' faith in the "tonic" sold by the traveling medicine show. We buy billions of dollars worth of highly advertised, medically questionable elixirs of one kind or another and at the same time undervalue and ignore the true fountain of life that pours out its gifts in almost endless supply all around us. Water, the most accessible of all drinks, is also the most essential to human health; and yet, it is a rare person, indeed, who drinks as much water as he or she should. Every adult, according to current medical knowledge, should drink at least eight full glasses of water a day for maximum support of health.

Introduction type _____

Introduction V

A successful wedding, even a relatively small one, is generally the result of careful planning. There are, in fact, so many considerations to be kept in mind that it is common for the bride-to-be to hire a bridal consultant. Many girls, however, cannot afford such a consultant or, even if they can, prefer to do their own planning. Such an independent young woman might find helpful the following brief but complete collection of traditional and innovative ideas for planning a wedding. Her entire delightful task is covered, beginning with ideas for announcement of the engagement and written invitations to the wedding and continuing through choices of wedding clothes; selection of attendants and conventions pertaining to their participation and the bride's obligations to them; choice of location, whether religious or social; decorations, including suggestions for color schemes, uses of flowers, candles, and other lighting; personal flowers for the bride as well as the two mothers, any grandmothers and the various attendants; options available as to the ceremony itself, including readings

Copyright © 1982 by Allyn and Bacon, Inc. Reproduction of this material is restricted to use with *A Guidebook for Teaching Composition*, 2nd Edition, by Gene Stanford and Marie Smith.

REPRODUCTION PAGE 66   IDENTIFYING THE FOUR COMMON TYPES OF INTRODUCTIONS

and music; and the reception following the ceremony, be it large or small. Armed with such complete and helpful advance information, the least experienced young woman can take pleasure in planning her own wedding.

Introduction type _____

Introduction VI

Choosing a puppy to be a family pet is a happy and exciting occasion, but one that requires serious advance consideration. Many circumstances relate to the making of the proper choice, and the consequences of ignoring any of them could be expensive, inconvenient, and disappointing. The prospective owners should make a careful study of the suitability of the pet to the environment it will be living in, both as a puppy and as a full-grown dog. They should learn about the dispositions and habits of the various breeds they are considering, with special concern, first, for the welfare of the children in the family and, second, for the feelings and safety of neighbors and others who might visit the house. They must be aware of the demands that proper care of their puppy will make on their time, energy, and funds; and they must be sure that their selection is compatible with their actual situation. Thus, informed and knowledgeable, the family should be ready to choose a pet that can add to the happiness of the household for many years.

Introduction type _____

Introduction VII

Great-grandmother Margaret, as she expected to be called, was my father's grandmother, and although she had lived with us as long as I could remember, my affection for her was tempered by a large measure of nervous respect. She was too distant and too dignified for me to feel entirely at ease in her company. When she disappeared from our house one night without any explanation, I took for granted that she would be back; and when she did not return, I began to wonder if others in the family might disappear also. I timidly questioned my mother, who assured me that no one else in the family would leave and that even great-grandmother Margaret had not really left but was still watching over us from up in Heaven. This failed to reassure me. For some weeks I felt as if a stern, ghostly eye were, indeed, watching me, and it was a long time before I was free of a vague feeling of anxiety. The memory of this experience leads me to believe that small children should be carefully prepared for the experience of a death in the family and that when a death actually occurs, they should receive careful and reassuring explanations.

Introduction type _____

Copyright © 1982 by Allyn and Bacon, Inc. Reproduction of this material is restricted to use with *A Guidebook for Teaching Composition*, 2nd Edition, by Gene Stanford and Marie Smith.

REPRODUCTION PAGE 67

CONSTRUCTING FUNNEL INTRODUCTIONS

INSTRUCTIONS: Imagine that in each pair of sentences below the generalization is the first sentence in an introductory paragraph and the thesis is the last sentence in that introduction. For each pair write a funnel introduction by connecting these two sentences with two or more other sentences that will lead the reader gradually from the large generalization to the more specific thesis sentence.

1. *Generalization:* If there is one truism in our society that receives almost universal acceptance, it is that experience is the best teacher.
   Thesis: Increasingly, we are putting our older people out to pasture and depriving ourselves of contributions they could be making.

2. *Generalization:* Puppy love is the rather condescending name adults give to the romantic feelings of very young people.
   Thesis: Parents should be aware that the feelings of young people involved in a first love affair may well be as intense as any they will ever experience.

3. *Generalization:* Nature is a great healer.
   Thesis: We must fight the constant efforts of powerful industrial forces to encroach on our great wilderness sanctuaries.

4. *Generalization:* No person will be truly educated without reading constantly for pleasure.
   Thesis: The best way for parents to be sure their child is a reader is to be readers themselves.

5. *Generalization:* Values are learned primarily in the home.
   Thesis: Parental example is the most powerful teacher of values.

6. *Generalization:* The first year away at college is both an adventure and a challenge.
   Thesis: The college freshman's first task is to learn to organize his or her time.

7. *Generalization:* Mother Nature is our best teacher.
   Thesis: People could improve their health if they would listen more attentively to the signals their bodies provide for them.

8. *Generalization:* The times are changing.
   Thesis: Within two decades some regulation on the manufacture and use of automobiles will be recognized as essential.

9. *Generalization:* Loneliness is the most painful of human emotions.
   Thesis: For emotional health an individual should engage in three different kinds of human relationships: intimate, casual, and nurturing.

10. *Generalization:* Many people feel a need to be different from others, to stand out from the crowd.
    Thesis: True individualism need not preclude a comfortable acceptance of most group styles, customs, and conventions.

Copyright © 1982 by Allyn and Bacon, Inc. Reproduction of this material is restricted to use with *A Guidebook for Teaching Composition,* 2nd Edition, by Gene Stanford and Marie Smith.

REPRODUCTION PAGE 68

TESTING FUNNEL INTRODUCTIONS FOR COHERENCE

INSTRUCTIONS: Test the following funnel introductions for coherence and consistent direction from the opening generalizations to the thesis sentence. (Check for large gaps in flow of ideas between sentences.)

I. Americans have always claimed to be devoted to quality education for all youngsters. Many school districts are currently caught in the fiscal squeeze, with costs rising rapidly and property taxes proving inadequate as a source of revenue. More and more parents claim that the schools are not doing a good job of preparing students to make their way in society. At the same time, educators suggest that parents are failing to do their part in influencing their children to behave acceptably in an educational setting. In view of such an impasse, it is not surprising that parents are often unwilling to vote for increased costs to themselves for their children's schooling. When class sizes get too large, quality education becomes impossible.

II. Young people are taking an increasing interest in planning their own education. Students feel that they know best what they should be studying and should, therefore, be allowed a dominant role in establishing course requirements. In theory one can hardly quarrel with this viewpoint, but in practice several considerations must be kept firmly in mind if such student participation is to be fruitful.

III. Some people seem to have a natural gift for friendship. They are thoughtful; they remember birthdays and other important occasions. They seem to have an unusual ability to sense the feelings of others and to avoid trespassing on the private moods of their friends. After all, one doesn't always want to be with others or reveal what one is feeling, even to a friend. Sometimes one simply wants to be alone. A person may not be upset or depressed but may just feel a need for solitude. Solitude is essential to us all in some degree, and everyone should try to spend some quiet time alone each day.

IV. Clothes make the man, or so the saying goes. But what do they make him, one might well ask. His necktie must make him uncomfortable and his suit jacket must make him hot, particularly if he wears it faithfully in summer time. His shirt collar and cuffs must make him feel stifled; his vest must make him feel padded; and his belt must make him feel like a package tied around the middle. The rebellion against such formal business dress as the right way, the only way to array oneself to face the world, is not surprising; in fact, to many it seems long overdue. More and more men are gaining the courage to flout traditional standards for masculine dress and are daring to wear comfortable and colorful clothes to even the most formal business occasions. They are also beginning to wear their hair at casual lengths that please their sons and dismay their barbers. Men have gradually become accustomed to hair styles that horrified them ten years ago. They would have been hard put to explain their horror in rational terms, but it was evident that their responses were to hair as a symbol rather than to hair as something real.

Copyright © 1982 by Allyn and Bacon, Inc. Reproduction of this material is restricted to use with *A Guidebook for Teaching Composition,* 2nd Edition, by Gene Stanford and Marie Smith.

REPRODUCTION PAGE 69

CONSTRUCTING ANECDOTAL INTRODUCTIONS

INSTRUCTIONS: Construct an anecdotal introductory paragraph for each of the thesis sentences given below. Be sure that you begin the introduction with the anecdote and lead into the thesis at the end. You may wish to change the wording of the thesis slightly to make it better fit your introduction.

1. The best camping trips are those that follow careful planning.

2. Tourists should remember that bears in state parks are not always as friendly as they seem.

3. What seems like a very small fib can have disastrous consequences.

4. There is no denying the fact that mothers often do know best.

5. A lesson worth learning is that sometimes a lesson cannot be taught; one must learn it for oneself.

6. Simple courtesy makes life more pleasant for everyone.

7. Parents should be aware that the example that they set speaks more loudly to their children than any words they say.

8. If parents will listen carefully, they will find that their children have much to teach them.

Copyright © 1982 by Allyn and Bacon, Inc. Reproduction of this material is restricted to use with *A Guidebook for Teaching Composition*, 2nd Edition, by Gene Stanford and Marie Smith.

REPRODUCTION PAGE 70

WRITING AN OUTLINE INTRODUCTION

INSTRUCTIONS: Write an introduction (outline type) for the following outline on the uses of airplanes in World Wars I and II.

Thesis: World War I provided only a glimpse of the contribution the airplane would make in such later wars as World War II.

I. Planes used for actual combat
   A. Fighter planes
      1. Numbers of planes, makes, etc.
         a. World War I
         b. World War II
      2. Missions accomplished and results
         a. World War I
         b. World War II
      3. Quality of aircraft as compared to enemy aircraft quality
         a. World War I
         b. World War II
      4. Assessment of value to war effort
         a. World War I
         b. World War II
   B. Bombers
      (same subdivisions as above)

II. Transport Planes
   A. Personnel transport
      1. Planes available
         a. World War I
         b. World War II
      2. Men carried, numbers, where, when, success
         a. World War I
         b. World War II
      3. Assessment of importance to war effort
         a. World War I
         b. World War II
   B. Transportation of equipment
      (same subdivisions as above)

Copyright © 1982 by Allyn and Bacon, Inc. Reproduction of this material is restricted to use with *A Guidebook for Teaching Composition*, 2nd Edition, by Gene Stanford and Marie Smith.

WRITING AN OUTLINE INTRODUCTION

III. Reconnaissance planes

    A. Long-range planes
       1. World War I
       2. World War II

    B. Combat-support planes
       1. World War I
       2. World War II

    C. Spy planes
       1. World War I
       2. World War II

IV. Aircraft industry in America

    A. World War I

    B. World War II

Copyright © 1982 by Allyn and Bacon, Inc. Reproduction of this material is restricted to use with *A Guidebook for Teaching Composition,* 2nd Edition, by Gene Stanford and Marie Smith.

REPRODUCTION PAGE 71

CONSTRUCTING CONTRAST INTRODUCTIONS

INSTRUCTIONS: For each of the thesis sentences below, construct an introductory paragraph of the contrast type by beginning the introductory paragraph with a popular misconception that the thesis contradicts.

1. Ballet dancing requires that performers be in top physical condition.

2. Accepting praise gracefully requires skill.

3. On many occasions, honesty is not the best policy.

4. If one is always cautious, one misses some of life's greatest joys.

5. Harry Truman was perhaps the most effective president of recent times.

Copyright © 1982 by Allyn and Bacon, Inc. Reproduction of this material is restricted to use with *A Guidebook for Teaching Composition,* 2nd Edition, by Gene Stanford and Marie Smith.

CONSTRUCTING AN INTRODUCTION

INSTRUCTIONS: Choose one of the thesis statements below and construct an effective introductory paragraph based on it.

1. One learns, as years go by, that there is always another day; there is always a new chapter beginning as the old one ends.

2. Young love is at least as serious and meaningful as the love of older persons.

3. One must develop his or her own ways of achieving peace of mind.

4. In the long run, your best friend is the one who is honest with you.

5. The development of missiles and rockets in both Russia and the United States rested on work done in Germany before and during World War II.

6. Both the South and North stand convicted of poor treatment of prisoners during the American Civil War.

7. The most significant war prizes of World War II were the minds of captured German scientists.

8. Where the white man went on his explorations, he took not only his culture and religion but also his diseases and weapons.

Copyright © 1982 by Allyn and Bacon, Inc. Reproduction of this material is restricted to use with *A Guidebook for Teaching Composition*, 2nd Edition, by Gene Stanford and Marie Smith.

REPRODUCTION PAGE 73

WRITING CONCLUSIONS

1. The conclusion can be a summary of the main points made in the essay—a reminder of the thesis and the arguments that the writer has used to support it. A summary conclusion is usually most suitable for long and complex essays—often those for which it is also helpful to provide the outline introduction.

2. The conclusion can be an "upside-down funnel." That is, it can begin with a restatement of the thesis and then enlarge the idea with statements that become more and more general to show the setting that gives the idea significance.

3. For shorter essays, a separate conclusion is not always needed. It is possible to include in the last supporting paragraph an extended clincher sentence in which you reiterate the thesis sentence and/or make some sort of significant final statement.

4. Since concluding paragraphs often sound "tacked on," make special attempts to link the conclusion to the paragraph that precedes it by repeating an appropriate key word or idea and by utilizing the other connecting devices discussed previously.

Sample Conclusions

1. When the evidence is all in, the arguments against hitchhiking are overpowering. People who do not heed them take a grave risk. Indeed, Thelma Gray and Lucy Taylor might be alive today if they had realized that the stranger's invitation to ride was in reality an invitation to tragedy.

2. So much, then, for humankind's superiority! It looks as if the animals have us beat on every aspect of health. When it comes to sleeping, eating, drinking, exercising, and maintaining activity throughout life, we might as well be mindless. Certainly we act as if we are.

3. Young people who develop these qualities and who learn to be truly loyal to friends will never find themselves friendless. They will have learned the skill most important to the art of friendship.

4. Now the family is ready to start looking for that perfect puppy, the one who will bring pleasure to the entire household for many years. Good luck!

5. Many of the fears of childhood are, perhaps, unavoidable. The world, after all, is a big and fearful place, and there is much the child can learn only from experiencing it. However, the destructive fear that sometimes accompanies the early experience of death can be avoided or, at least, minimized if parents are sufficiently alert to their child's emotional needs. If the child is properly prepared by loving and sensitive parents, there is no reason why his or her first knowledge of death cannot be a constructive, psychologically maturing experience.

Copyright © 1982 by Allyn and Bacon, Inc. Reproduction of this material is restricted to use with *A Guidebook for Teaching Composition*, 2nd Edition, by Gene Stanford and Marie Smith.

DIABETIC ATHLETES: MEETING A SPECIAL CHALLENGE

Diabetes is a serious medical condition that affects one out of every fifty persons. Although medical experts are not completely certain about the exact causes, they know diabetes results from the pancreas' not producing enough insulin to help the body digest and utilize sugar. In spite of their diabetes, dozens, if not hundreds, of American athletes manage to perform as well as athletes without this condition. To do so, they must meet and overcome special challenges.

First of all, in order to keep the condition under control, most diabetics must receive an injection of insulin each day, and most of them give themselves the shots. To prepare for the shot, first they must test the level of sugar in their bodies with a blood or urine test and then calculate the amount of insulin they need and put it into a syringe. The worst part of the process is the shot itself. Shots are never any fun, even for an all-American halfback. Diabetic athletes also have the added burden of making sure they take the equipment for testing and injecting with them whenever they travel to a game or meet.

Another challenge to the diabetic athlete concerns eating. All athletes, of course, must give special attention to their diets when they are in training. For the diabetic athlete, however, diet is especially important. Diabetics must be careful not to eat too many carbohydrates (sugars and starches) and should have a well-balanced diet. This means keeping up with what and how much they eat. If they eat too much food containing sugar, they can go into a coma. On the other hand, if they do not eat enough to balance the insulin they have had, insulin shock can result. Thus, diabetics must plan their meals very carefully, and this makes post-game snacking on pizza and milkshakes almost out of the question.

Because the amount of exercise one gets can affect the rate at which the injected insulin is absorbed, diabetic athletes must carefully balance their food intake and insulin with the amount of exercise they expect to get. A certain amount of regular exercise helps to keep the blood sugar level under control and reduces the need for insulin somewhat. However, too much unanticipated exercise can upset the balance between food and insulin. Thus, diabetic athletes must make adjustments on those days when practice or competition increases their amount of exertion. Should they accidentally miscalculate and eat too little or inject too much insulin, the diabetic athlete risks an insulin reaction, which can lead to coma. For this reason, diabetic athletes must carry with them some source of quickly digested sugar, such as hard candy or sugar cubes, to eat if they get symptoms of a reaction.

Despite these added obstacles that diabetes puts in their paths, diabetic Americans of all ages have distinguished themselves in sports of all kinds.

Copyright © 1982 by Allyn and Bacon, Inc. Reproduction of this material is restricted to use with *A Guidebook for Teaching Composition*, 2nd Edition, by Gene Stanford and Marie Smith.

REPRODUCTION PAGE 75

ESSAY CHECKLIST

INSTRUCTIONS: The following are the logical steps that a writer should take in writing an essay. As you complete each step, check it off and proceed to the next.

_____ 1. Choose a topic you know well.

_____ 2. Narrow the topic to a subject limited enough to be developed in detail in an essay of the length you plan to write.

_____ 3. Write a thesis sentence that indicates your point of view in relation to the restricted subject.

_____ 4. Make sure your thesis sentence contains only one idea.

_____ 5. Make sure your thesis sentence contains no words that may be interpreted in more than one way.

_____ 6. Analyze the thesis to determine what are the parts that must be developed in order to cover the thesis entirely. List the parts.

_____ 7. Decide on the best order for the parts of the thesis.

_____ 8. Begin to write the essay, one paragraph at a time, starting with the introduction.

_____ 9. For each *developed* paragraph, construct a topic sentence and make an outline of the specific details before starting to write it.

_____ 10. Write a conclusion.

_____ 11. Make sure you have provided transitions as needed to guide the reader through the paper.

_____ 12. Proofread the rough draft to make sure it contains no errors in usage or spelling.

_____ 13. Copy the essay over and submit it to the teacher or distribute it to other students to read.

Copyright © 1982 by Allyn and Bacon, Inc. Reproduction of this material is restricted to use with *A Guidebook for Teaching Composition*, 2nd Edition, by Gene Stanford and Marie Smith.

REPRODUCTION PAGE 76

CHART OF DEWEY DECIMAL SYSTEM

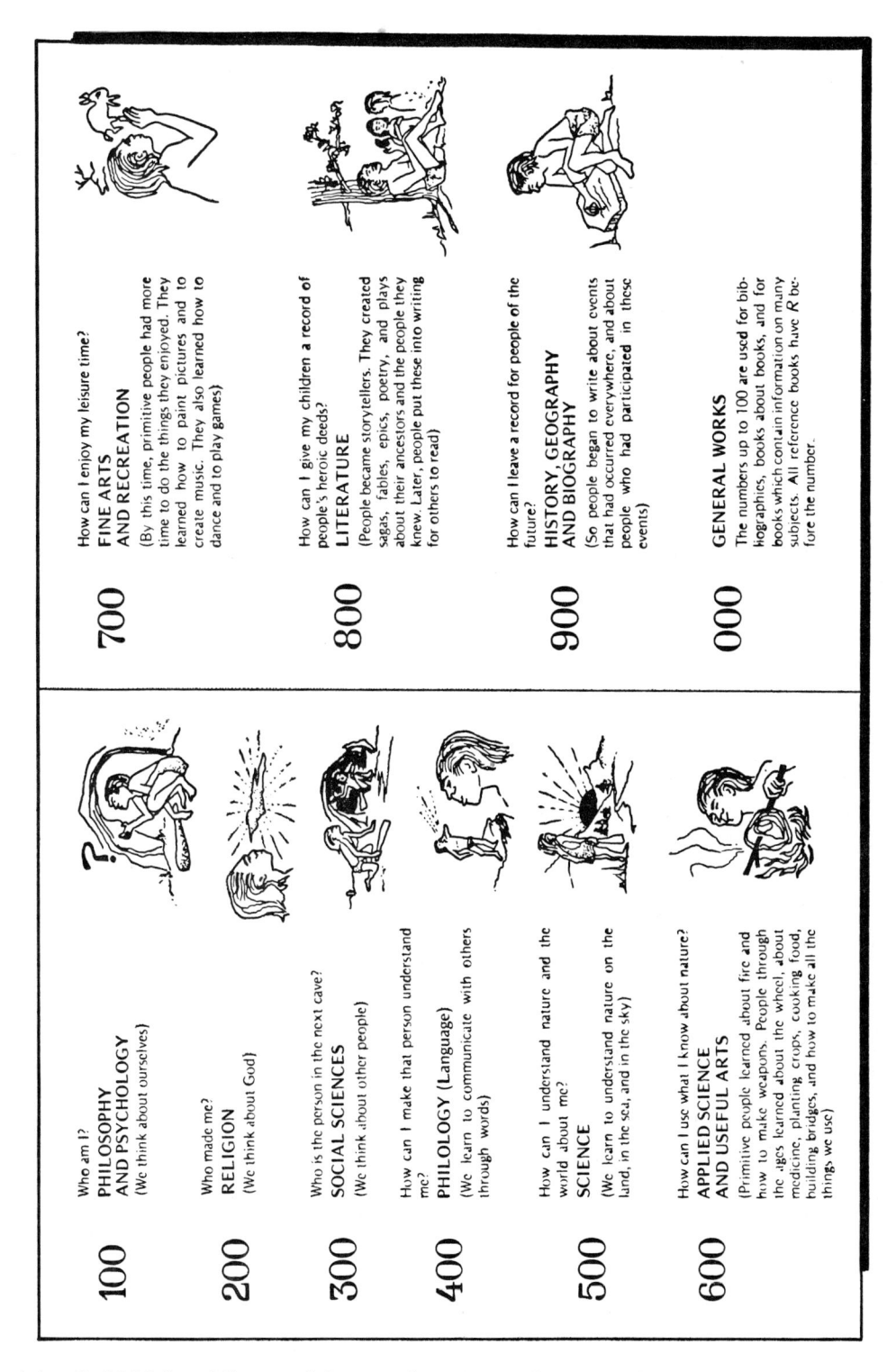

100 **PHILOSOPHY AND PSYCHOLOGY**
Who am I?
(We think about ourselves)

200 **RELIGION**
Who made me?
(We think about God)

300 **SOCIAL SCIENCES**
Who is the person in the next cave?
(We think about other people)

400 **PHILOLOGY (Language)**
How can I make that person understand me?
(We learn to communicate with others through words)

500 **SCIENCE**
How can I understand nature and the world about me?
(We learn to understand nature on the land, in the sea, and in the sky)

600 **APPLIED SCIENCE AND USEFUL ARTS**
How can I use what I know about nature?
(Primitive people learned about fire and how to make weapons. People through the ages learned about the wheel, about medicine, planting crops, cooking food, building bridges, and how to make all the things we use)

700 **FINE ARTS AND RECREATION**
How can I enjoy my leisure time?
(By this time, primitive people had more time to do the things they enjoyed. They learned how to paint pictures and to create music. They also learned how to dance and to play games)

800 **LITERATURE**
How can I give my children a record of people's heroic deeds?
(People became storytellers. They created sagas, fables, epics, poetry, and plays about their ancestors and the people they knew. Later, people put these into writing for others to read)

900 **HISTORY, GEOGRAPHY AND BIOGRAPHY**
How can I leave a record for people of the future?
(So people began to write about events that had occurred everywhere, and about people who had participated in these events)

000 **GENERAL WORKS**
The numbers up to 100 are used for bibliographies, books about books, and for books which contain information on many subjects. All reference books have *R* before the number.

Copyright © 1982 by Allyn and Bacon, Inc. Reproduction of this material is restricted to use with *A Guidebook for Teaching Composition*, 2nd Edition, by Gene Stanford and Marie Smith.

REPRODUCTION PAGE 77

EXERCISE ON THE DEWEY DECIMAL SYSTEM

INSTRUCTIONS: Answer the following questions.

1. List the Dewey Decimal classifications and their numbers.

2. See Activity 18 for suggestions for preparing map of your school library. From the accompanying map of the school library, put the location number of each category of the Dewey Decimal System after its heading in question 1 above.

3. Indicate the Dewey Decimal System category in which each of the following would most likely be found:

    A. Book on Roman Catholicism _____
    B. Book on water skiing _____
    C. Book on astronomy _____
    D. Book of plays _____
    E. Encyclopedia _____
    F. Book on engineering _____
    G. A bibliography _____
    H. A thesaurus _____
    I. Book on government _____
    J. Book on psychology _____

4. True or false

    A. The Dewey Decimal System classifies all books in the library. _____
    B. Painting, photography and music are all found in the 700's. _____
    C. Some books may be classified into two or more categories of the Dewey Decimal System. _____
    D. Dictionaries are found under General Works (000's). _____
    E. Each Dewey Decimal classification has its own subclassifications. _____

Copyright © 1982 by Allyn and Bacon, Inc. Reproduction of this material is restricted to use with *A Guidebook for Teaching Composition,* 2nd Edition, by Gene Stanford and Marie Smith.

SAMPLE ENTRIES FROM THE READERS' GUIDE

ENVIRONMENTAL health
Effects of pollution on health; proceedings of the sixth Berkeley symposium on mathematical statistics and probability, ed. by L. M. LeCam and others. Review
Environment 14:40-2 O '72. S. Norvick
ENVIRONMENTAL movement
Confrontation; when environmentalism confronts economics. il Forbes 110:32-3+ N 15 '72
Conservation: envirometal action line. M. Frome. Field & S 77:80+ D '72
Doomsday syndrome, by J. Maddox. Review Sci N 102:371 D 9 '72. K. Frazier
Environmental challenge to men and institutions; address, September 1972. M. Strong. Nat Parks & Con Mag 46:22-5 N '72
Tips for reducing pollution in your daily living. F. Graham, jr. il Todays Health 50:42-5 N '72
FICTION
Why they aren't writing the great American novel anymore; comparison of 19th century novels with 20th century journalism; with appendices. T. Wolfe. il Esquire 78:152-+ D '72
See also
French fiction
Jews in literature
   Authorship
Elusive plot. D. Eden. Writer 85:9-10+ D '72
   Bibliography
Fiction (cont) W. B. Hill. America 126:549-50; 127:420+ My 20, N 18 '72
   Technique
Your secret writing weapons. P. Gunn. Writer 85:26-7 D '72
GAGE, Joan
(ed) See Graham, R. Mrs Billy Graham: teaching children to believe in God
(ed) See Hope, B. Bob Hope answers his Vietnam critics and tells how he tried to free our prisoners of war
GOODMAN, Paul
Paul Goodman; address, October 22, 1972. G. Dennison. Nation 215:504-6+ N 20 '72 *
GOODMAN, Walter, ca 1873
Courting Cachita; story; excerpt from The pearl of the Antilles, ed. by K. C. Tessendorf. il Américas 24:32-6 O '72
GORDON, Barbara (Wickelgren)
Superior colliculus of the brain; with biographical sketch. il Sci Am 227:10, 72-82 bibliog (p 128) D '72
HACKETT, Walter
Christmas carol; dramatization of story by C. Dickens; reprint from December 1967 issue. Plays 32:81-90 D '72
HECHT, Ben, and MacArthur, Charles
Front page. Criticism
America 127:470-1 D 2 '72 *
HIGHWAY 1, U.S.A.; opera. See Still, W. G.
HIJACKING. See Robberies and assaults
HOPE, Bob
Bob Hope answers his Vietnam critics and tells how he tried to free our prisoners of war; interview, ed. by J. Gage. por Ladies Home J 89:68+ D '72
IRVIN, Robert W.
Exciting options for your '73 car. il Mech Illus 68:82-4 S '72
What's really new in the 1973 cars. il Mech Illus 68:79-85+ O '72
IRVING, Clifford, family
Clifford Irving's children: innocent victims of the hoax that failed. C. Breslin. por Redbook 140:89+ N '72
IRVING, Jules
Curtain at Lincoln Center. J. Kroll. il Newsweek 80:89 N 20 '72 *
JOHNSON, James P. and Churchill, F. O.
Black and bibliographical. Wilson Lib Bull 47:248-50, 374-7 N-D '72
JOHNSON, Lady Bird. See Johnson, C. A. T.

JOHNSON, Mendal
Everything you always wanted to know about sailplans. il Motor B & S 130:48-9+ N '72
JOHNSON, Ted. See Johnson, G. T.
JOHNSON, William
Striking it rich at Snowbird. il Sports Illus 37:65-6+ N 20 '72
KISSINGER, Henry Alfred
Dr Kissinger discusses status of negotiations toward Viet-Nam peace; transcript of news conference, October 30, 1972. Dept State Bull 67:549-58 N 13 '72
Kissinger; interview, ed. by O. Fallaci. New Repub 167:17-22 D 16 '72
Vietnam maxims; excerpt from January 1969 issue of Foreign affairs, ed. by W. F. Buckley, jr. Nat R 24-1318 N 24 '72
   about
Clouds over Paris; with report by H. Hubbard. il pors Newsweek 80:26-7 D 4 '72 *
Facts hard and soft. S. Alsop. Newsweek 80:112 D 18 '72 *
Henry Kissinger: the go between. il por Sr Schol 101:20 N 27 '72 *
Kicking sand. J. Osborne. New Repub 167:9-10 D 16 '72 *
Kissinger: the uses of power, by D. Landau. Review
America 127:499 D 9 '72. B. H. Smith *
Mastermind as mouthpiece. B. Collier. Sat R 55:8-9 N 18 '72 *
Peace by inauguration day? il por Newsweek 80:23-4 N 27 '72 *
Peace talks: putting the heat on Thieu. il por Newsweek 80:41 D 11 '72 *
Peace talks: the last word? il por Newsweek 80:20-1 D 18 '72 *.
This is my battle station. il pors Life 73:36-42 D 1 '72 *
LABOR grievances. See Grievance procedures
LANIER, Doris, and Lightsey, Ralph
Verbal SAT scores and high school averages as predictors. bibliog Intellect 101:127-8 N '72
LEESON, Jeanne Tellier
Third graders in stitches. il Sch Arts 72:8 D '72
LESSER, Murray L.
Sail area for cruising boats. Motor B & S 130:49+ N '72
MACARTHUR, Charles. See Hecht, B jt. auth.
MAGIC flute; opera. See Mozart, J. C. W. A.
MAGIC mountain (amusement park) See Amusement parks
MICE
Chromosome mapping in the mouse. D. A. Miller and O. J. Miller. bibliog il Science 178:949-55 D 1 '72
Genetic mapping of a murine leukemia virus-inducing locus of AKR mice. W. P. Rowe and others. bibliog il Science 178:860-2 N 24 '72
Hemoglobin beta chain structural variation in mice: evolutionary and functional implications. J. G. Gilman. bibliog il Science 178:873-4 N 24 '72
Mice for research; Jackson laboratory. il Chemistry 45:20-1 D '72
MOON
Origin and evolution of the earth-moon system. Sky & Tel 44:368 D '72
   Exploration
   Equipment
Apollo ending as science hits its stride. il Aviation W 97:53-4+ D 4 '72
   Surface
Landing site could add to data on forces that shaped lunar terrain. W. H. Gregory. il Aviation W 97:42-6 D 4 '72

Copyright © 1982 by Allyn and Bacon, Inc. Reproduction of this material is restricted to use with *A Guidebook for Teaching Composition*, 2nd Edition, by Gene Stanford and Marie Smith.

REPRODUCTION PAGE 79

WORKSHEET ON THE *READERS' GUIDE*

1. On the back of this sheet make a list of the magazines subscribed to by your library.

2. Find the meanings for the following abbreviations:

abr	D	m	sup
Ag	ed	Mr	v
Ap	F	My	w
bibliog	il	N	+
bi-m	Ja	no	Sr Schol
bi-w	Je	O	Pop Sci
cond	Jl	S	Good H

3. Explain what is meant by a "See also" reference.

4. Explain each of the items in the following subject entry:

   Automobiles
      Automobile in American life, J. R. Bond. il.
      Read Digest 87:201-2+ S '65

   Automobiles
   Automobile in American Life
   J. R. Bond
   il.
   Read Digest
   87
   201-2+
   S
   '65

5. Using the *Readers' Guide*, find and list the entry for one article on each of the following subjects:

   Eclipses

   College students

   White House

6. For each of the above articles, write down the information needed to find the magazine.

Copyright © 1982 by Allyn and Bacon, Inc. Reproduction of this material is restricted to use with *A Guidebook for Teaching Composition*, 2nd Edition, by Gene Stanford and Marie Smith.

REPRODUCTION PAGE 80

QUIZ ON THE *READERS' GUIDE*

INSTRUCTIONS: Study the Readers' Guide *entries on Reproduction Page 78 and answer the following questions.*

1. Define an author entry. _____

2. Give the example from the list. _____

3. If you were to change it to a subject entry, what would the subject be? _____

4. Define a subject entry. _____

5. Give an example from the list. _____

6. If you were to change it to an author entry, what would the heading be? _____

7. Name an entry that has several magazines. _____

8. Define a cross reference. _____

9. Give an example from the list. _____

10. Name one article that is continued on other pages in the magazine. _____

11. Name one magazine article that has pictures in it. _____

12. List magazines that are published more than once a month. _____

13. Give the author of an article on the Dead Sea Scrolls. _____

Copyright © 1982 by Allyn and Bacon, Inc. Reproduction of this material is restricted to use with *A Guidebook for Teaching Composition*, 2nd Edition, by Gene Stanford and Marie Smith.

REPRODUCTION PAGE 81

THE CARD CATALOG

The card catalog contains cards listing information about every book in the library, fiction and nonfiction alike.

The basic information includes the following: (See card below.)

A. call number—921, First letter of author's name under call number.
B. subject—football
C. author's name—Lou Greenwood
D. author's birthday—1923, and date of death if deceased—(1923-1974)
E. title of the book—*Fourth and Goal*
F. publisher—Prentice Books
G. copyright date—1960
H. number of pages—224
I. illustrations (if any)—illus.
J. other information which may include maps, annotation, tracing line, Library of Congress number, Dewey Decimal classification, and others.

For each book included, there are three types of cards in the card catalog. They are the subject card, author card, and title card. All contain the same information but are listed and placed according to one of the three headings: subject, author or title.

The card catalog is set up alphabetically with drawer labels such as CEL-CRO, RYT-SAM, and VAL-YOU.

Call numbers of books of fiction consist of the letter "F" and the first letter of the author's last name. Story collections may be found with the letters SC in place of the author's initial.

```
921
 G  FOOTBALL
    Greenwood, Lou 1923-
    Fourth and Goal.
    Prentice Books 1960
    244p. illus
```

```
921
 G  FOOTBALL
    Greenwood, Lou 1923-
```

```
921
 G  Greenwood, Lou 1923-
    Fourth and Goal
```

```
921
 G  Fourth and Goal
    Greenwood, Lou 1923-
```

Copyright © 1982 by Allyn and Bacon, Inc. Reproduction of this material is restricted to use with *A Guidebook for Teaching Composition*, 2nd Edition, by Gene Stanford and Marie Smith.

REPRODUCTION PAGE 82

WORKSHEET ON THE CARD CATALOG

1. Name the three types of listings found for each book in the card catalog.

2. List at least eight types of information found on a card in the card catalog.

3. Using whatever information you need from the following list, make a card catalog entry on the line below.

    A book explains the workings of an automobile exhaust system. The author, Ronald Lewis, calls his book *By-products of Combustion*. In it he has diagrams and charts to explain his main points. Pictures of different types of systems help the eader to understand the principles of exhaust systems. Holt and Company were glad to publish his book, which costs $5.95. This cost is not expensive for a modern (1976) 375-page book. Mr. Lewis said that he was glad he waited until he was fifty before he had the book published, since he learned a lot of things while he worked on his son's cars.

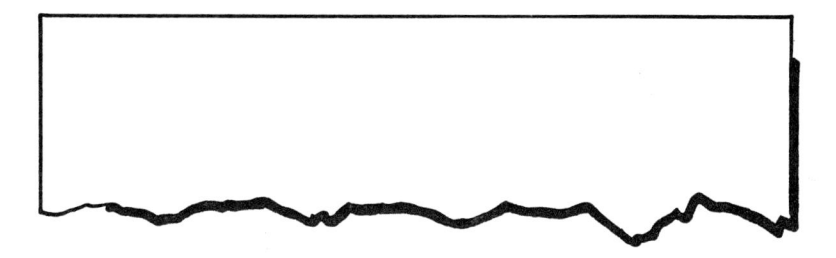

4. Identify the area of the library you would visit to find the following books. If the book is fiction, explain the letters given. If the book is nonfiction, give the Dewey Decimal classification where it is found.

    (a) F.   (b) 944   (c) F.   (d) 095   (e) 655.36
        SC   C   L   W   L

    (a)
    (b)
    (c)
    (d)
    (e)

Copyright © 1982 by Allyn and Bacon, Inc. Reproduction of this material is restricted to use with *A Guidebook for Teaching Composition*, 2nd Edition, by Gene Stanford and Marie Smith.

REPRODUCTION PAGE 83

SCAVENGER HUNT

INSTRUCTIONS: Give the exact place where the following information can be found.

1. What does "vacada" mean in Spanish?
2. What is an "amphilinidea" in science?
3. Give three synonyms for the noun "jinx."
4. What college did Dick Gregory attend?
5. What is the population of Deer Park, Ohio, as of 1980?
6. Who said, "A jest breaks no bones?"
7. What is the title of a 1980 magazine article on air traffic control?
8. How many railroads have served Utica, New York?
9. Name two baseball novels by John Tunis.
10. Give the address and birthdate of Barbra Streisand.
11. Give the date and the cause of the sinking of the *Maine.*
12. Name the play presently on Broadway in the Schubert Theater.
13. What is the tuition for Drew University?
14. What are the dates of the 1970 magazine articles on Oral Roberts University?
15. Identify the world's longest railway tunnel (name or length).
16. Name the first word on page 233 of the book *Moon of Three Rings.*
17. Who won the Academy Award for best actress in 1935?
18. Name the author of "Crystal Moment," a poem.
19. Give the title of an illustrated book on China.
20. Who was on the cover of the October 24, 1979, issue of the *New York Times Magazine?*
21. Give the 1980 population of Syracuse, New York.
22. Give the author and call numbers of a boy scout book on automobiles.
23. Identify the author of a magazine article on pork.
24. Who wrote the opera *Carmen?*
25. What is the first word on page 303 of *Little Women?*

Copyright © 1982 by Allyn and Bacon, Inc. Reproduction of this material is restricted to use with *A Guidebook for Teaching Composition,* 2nd Edition, by Gene Stanford and Marie Smith.

REPRODUCTION PAGE 84

QUIZ ON FINDING INFORMATION IN THE LIBRARY

1. List the categories of the DDS and assign them their correct numbers.

2. Place each of the following books in its most likely DDS category:

    A. *Catholicism, Then and Now* _____
    B. *Japan, A Nation on the Rise* _____
    C. *Fruitbearing Trees of North America* _____
    D. *Waterskiing for Beginners* _____
    E. *Poems of Rod McKuen* _____

3. Match the following:

    A. Glossary   _____ 1. Includes name of book, author and publisher
    B. Index   _____ 2. List of terms (vocabulary) found in text
    C. Title Page   _____ 3. Alphabetical list of sources used in writing the book
    D. Bibliography   _____ 4. Introduction to book
    E. Preface   _____ 5. Alphabetical list of subjects and their pages

4. List a reference book where one would most likely find the following:

    A. Synonym for "illegal" _____
    B. Author of a poem _____
    C. Rivers in Ohio _____
    D. Birthdate of Groucho Marx _____
    E. Population of Chicago _____

5. Identify each part of the following *Readers' Guide* entry:

    The Ranger's Lone Ranger, Paul Eisner, il Sp. Illus., 44:86-8 Je, 7, 1975

6. Answer the following questions about the catalog card on the right.

    A. What is its DDS classification? _____
    B. What does 1923 represent? _____
    C. What kind of card is this: author, title, or subject?
    _____
    D. What is "Doubleday?" _____
    E. Are there pictures in the book? _____

    ```
    876.7
    S  Scott, Walter 1832-1923
       Lady of the Lake
       Doubleday 1965
       313p illus
    ```

Copyright © 1982 by Allyn and Bacon, Inc. Reproduction of this material is restricted to use with *A Guidebook for Teaching Composition*, 2nd Edition, by Gene Stanford and Marie Smith.

REPRODUCTION PAGE 85

QUIZ ON FINDING INFORMATION IN THE LIBRARY

PUT (T) OR (F) IN THE BLANK AT THE RIGHT OF EACH STATEMENT.

1. The index to the *World Almanac* is in the front of the library. _____
2. A book about automobiles would be found in the 600's ("Applied Science"). _____
3. If a book is reprinted using the same material as before, it is called a revised edition. _____
4. The table of contents is arranged in alphabetical order. _____
5. The *Readers' Guide* is an index to magazines. _____
6. The colonial period in United States history is listed in the "g" drawer of the card catalog. _____
7. A bibliography is a list of books. _____
8. *Collier's* is a junior encyclopedia. _____
9. Webster's secondary school dictionary will give all possible meanings of a word. _____
10. *Current Biography* is a logical place to look for a picture of Bing Crosby. _____
11. It is not necessary to know the title of a magazine article to look up the article in the *Readers' Guide*. _____
12. The title card for the book *Dr. Tom Dooley* would be found after the subject DOGS in the card catalog. _____
13. A biography of Abraham Lincoln is in *Who's Who in America*. _____
14. The library receives only two copies of the *Readers' Guide* each year. _____
15. Supplementary material in a book is called the appendix. _____
16. Richard's *Atlas of New York State* is a logical place to look for material about New York State Indians. _____
17. Factual books about sports are in the 700's, a range where books on music and art are also found. _____
18. Biographies of individuals are arranged according to the initial of the author's last name. _____
19. The story collection is marked SC and is found after the 800's on the shelves. _____
20. The Dewey Decimal System divides books into ten classes. _____
21. Cross references are used in the *Readers' Guide,* the card catalog, and encyclopedias. _____
22. *A Night to Remember* is listed in the "A" drawer of the card catalog. _____
23. Nonfiction books are arranged according to their subject matter. _____
24. A class number is the same as the Dewey Decimal number. _____
25. The copyright date is usually found on the back of the title page of a book. _____
26. In the card catalog a subject heading is written either in capitals or in red. _____
27. All reference books in the library may be borrowed overnight. _____
28. Books on folklore are numbered 398. _____
29. When I request back copies of magazines, each magazine should be listed separately on a 3x5 card. _____

Copyright © 1982 by Allyn and Bacon, Inc. Reproduction of this material is restricted to use with *A Guidebook for Teaching Composition,* 2nd Edition, by Gene Stanford and Marie Smith.

QUIZ ON FINDING INFORMATION IN THE LIBRARY

REPRODUCTION PAGE 85

30. Two cents a day is charged for overdue books and $.25 a day for overdue reference books. _____
31. A biography of Christopher Columbus is found in *Webster's Biographical Dictionary*. _____
32. Acknowledgments in a book tell where you may look for more information. _____
33. If I lose my library pass card, I may borrow a card from someone else. _____
34. I can look up a magazine article in the *Readers' Guide* under its title. _____
35. If I do not know the meaning of the abbreviations in the *Readers' Guide*, I should ask the librarian. _____
36. Books written to help you learn French are in the 400's. _____
37. All books in circulation may be renewed indefinitely. _____
38. Statistics on many different subjects will be found in the *World Almanac*. _____
39. A copyright protects authors' rights to have income from their books. _____
40. The logical place to look for pamphlets is the vertical file. _____

II. BELOW ARE SIX DRAWERS OF THE CARD CATALOG. GIVE THE NUMBER OF THE DRAWER IN WHICH YOU WOULD FIND THE FOLLOWING ITEMS.

A	Ba-Bi	Bj-By	C	L-M	T-Z
1	2	3	4	5	6

no. of drawer

10,000 Jokes, Toasts, and Stories _____

The Witch of Blackbird Pond _____

BASKETBALL - FICTION _____

After the Civil War _____

BOATS AND BOATING _____

CARTOONS AND CARICATURES _____

Those 163 Days _____

Mays, Willie _____

MYSTERY AND DETECTIVE STORIES _____

A Time to Stand _____

Copyright © 1982 by Allyn and Bacon, Inc. Reproduction of this material is restricted to use with *A Guidebook for Teaching Composition*, 2nd Edition, by Gene Stanford and Marie Smith.

REPRODUCTION PAGE 85 **QUIZ ON FINDING INFORMATION IN THE LIBRARY**

III. BELOW ARE FOUR CARDS FROM THE CATALOG. USING THESE, ANSWER EACH OF THE QUESTIONS THAT FOLLOW.

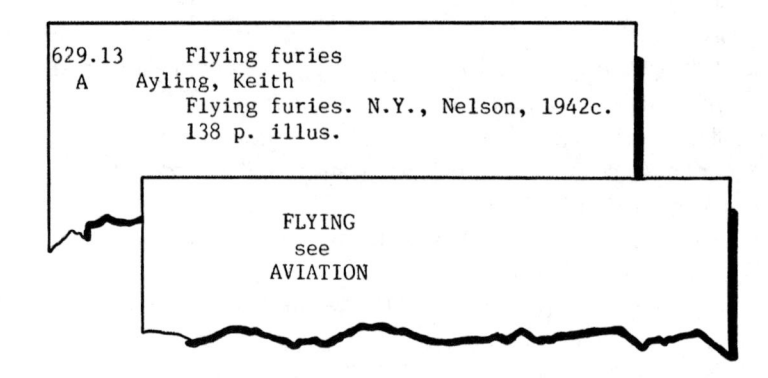

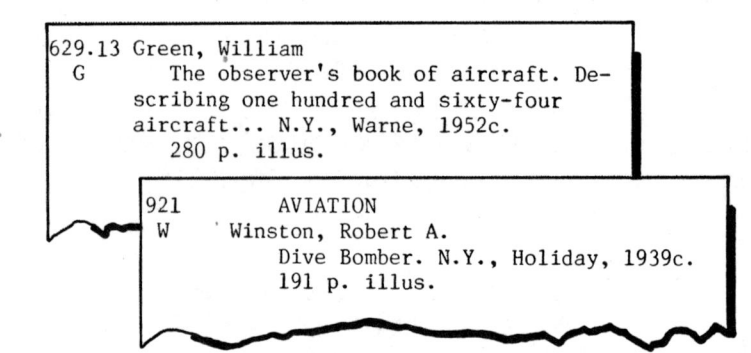

A.
```
629.13      Flying furies
   A     Ayling, Keith
              Flying furies. N.Y., Nelson, 1942c.
              138 p. illus.
```

B.
```
           FLYING
             see
           AVIATION
```

C.
```
629.13 Green, William
   G       The observer's book of aircraft. De-
          scribing one hundred and sixty-four
          aircraft... N.Y., Warne, 1952c.
              280 p. illus.
```

D.
```
921         AVIATION
  W       Winston, Robert A.
              Dive Bomber. N.Y., Holiday, 1939c.
              191 p. illus.
```

1. Which is an author card? _____

2. Which is a title card? _____

3. Which is a subject card? _____

4. Which is a cross-referenced card? _____

5. Which card represents the oldest book? _____

6. Which card represents the longest book? _____

7. What is the title of the book about aviation? _____

8. What is the call number of the book *Flying Furies?* _____

9. Under what letter of the alphabet would you look to find books about flying? _____

Copyright © 1982 by Allyn and Bacon, Inc. Reproduction of this material is restricted to use with *A Guidebook for Teaching Composition,* 2nd Edition, by Gene Stanford and Marie Smith.

QUIZ ON FINDING INFORMATION IN THE LIBRARY   REPRODUCTION PAGE 85

10. What is the title of the book by Keith Ayling? _____

_____

11. Who wrote the book titled *The Observer's Book of Aircraft?* _____

_____

IV. ARRANGE THE FOLLOWING CALL NUMBERS OF BOOKS IN CORRECT ORDER BY NUMBERING THEM FROM 1 TO 8.

359	070.4	822	359	822.08	921	822.3	500
L	F	I	S	C	A	B	C

V. BEFORE THE ITEMS IN THE RIGHT-HAND COLUMN, PUT THE NUMBER OF THE REFERENCE TOOL AT THE LEFT WHICH YOU WOULD USE TO FIND THE ANSWER. (SOME NUMBERS WILL BE USED MORE THAN ONCE.)

1. *Richard's Atlas of New York State*
2. *Current Biography*
3. *World Almanac*
4. *Card Catalog*
5. *Readers' Guide*
6. *Encyclopaedia Britannica*
7. *Who's Who in America*
8. *Goode's World Atlas*
9. *Webster's Biographical Dictionary*

_____ A magazine article about U.S. space efforts.
_____ Biographical information about John F. Kennedy
_____ A description of the life of the Iroquois Indians
_____ Name of a book about skin diving
_____ Names of the members of the President's cabinet
_____ All possible meanings of the word "induction"
_____ Biography of Charles A. Lindbergh
_____ Map of the U.S.S.R.
_____ The author of the book *Day of Infamy*
_____ Biography of John Glenn (with a picture)

VI. SHOW HOW THE FOLLOWING BIOGRAPHIES WOULD BE ARRANGED ON THE SHELVES BY NUMBERING THEM FROM 1-5.

Sir Walter Raleigh by Nina Baker Brown   _____
The Wright Brothers by Quentin Reynolds   _____
Ethan Allen and the Green Mountain Boys by Slater Brown   _____
Lou Gehrig by Frank Graham   _____
Bing Crosby's Own Story: Call Me Lucky   _____

Copyright © 1982 by Allyn and Bacon, Inc. Reproduction of this material is restricted to use with *A Guidebook for Teaching Composition,* 2nd Edition, by Gene Stanford and Marie Smith.

REPRODUCTION PAGE 85   QUIZ ON FINDING INFORMATION IN THE LIBRARY

VII. ARRANGE THE FOLLOWING FICTION BOOKS IN THE ORDER IN WHICH THEY WOULD BE PLACED ON THE SHELVES BY NUMBERING THEM FROM 1-10.

Captain Blood by Rafael Sabatini   _____
The Swiss Family Robinson by Johann Wyss   _____
Twenty Thousand Leagues under the Sea by Jules Verne   _____
Jane Eyre by Charlotte Bronte   _____
We Were There at the Battle of the Bulge by David Sheperd   _____
The Scarlet Pimpernel by Baroness Orczy   _____
Adventures of Sherlock Holmes by A. Conan Doyle   _____
Drums along the Mohawk by Walter Edmonds   _____
Masked Prowler by John George   _____
The Old Man and the Sea by Ernest Hemingway   _____

VIII. TELL WHAT INFORMATION IS FOUND IN ANY SEVEN OF THE FOLLOWING PARTS OF A BOOK.

Copyright date _____

Preface _____

Title Page _____

Index _____

Table of Contents _____

Introduction _____

Appendix _____

Bibliography _____

IX. IN THE ANSWERS TO THE QUESTIONS BELOW, NO BOOK MAY BE USED TWICE.

A. Name three places in our library where you would look for information on the man who is now President of the United States.

1. _____ 2. _____

3. _____

B. Name two places where you would look for material on atomic energy.

1. _____ 2. _____

Copyright © 1982 by Allyn and Bacon, Inc. Reproduction of this material is restricted to use with *A Guidebook for Teaching Composition*, 2nd Edition, by Gene Stanford and Marie Smith.

REPRODUCTION PAGE 86

TEN STEPS FOR WRITING A RESEARCH REPORT

1. *Select a topic.* Choose something you care about. Spending time and effort on a topic of no interest to you leads to poor results.

2. *Narrow the topic.* Find smaller subjects within the major topic, making certain that the subtopics can be handled well in a relatively small paper.

3. *Formulate a thesis statement.* Reduce the narrowed topic area to a statement that can be proven or that can be argued with pros and cons. Identify the various aspects of your thesis that you will want to research. These tentative categories will help you formulate your outline (#6 below) in a logical fashion.

4. *Gather information.* Use the card catalog, *Readers' Guide*, encyclopedias, and any other available source. As each source is used, record it in a working bibliography (a numbered list of sources which includes the bibliographical information of each source).

5. *Take notes:* Use an orderly process to record information pertinent to proving the thesis sentence. This is most effectively done on note cards, with each one numbered to show its place in the sequence and lettered to show the source used, as recorded in the working bibliography. Note cards should include quotes, paraphrases, and summations in addition to general knowledge the student may find.

6. *Outline.* Arrange the notes into the best order for proving the thesis sentence. If little work is done on the outline, then more work will be required in writing the paper. Conversely, a thorough outline will make writing the paper a relatively simple task.

7. *Write the first draft.* Following the outline and using the note cards, write the first draft of your paper.

8. *Proofread.* Go over the first draft to find errors and be certain thoughts are presented in the best possible way. This is also the time to make sure that quotes, paraphrases, and footnotes are in order.

9. *Write the final paper.* Using the corrected first draft, consider the revisions, changes, and arrangement of the footnotes and write the final paper.

10. *Proofread the final draft.* Read the final copy carefully to make absolutely certain there are no errors in mechanics, form, or expression. The final copy includes a title page, the paper itself, and a bibliography.

Copyright © 1982 by Allyn and Bacon, Inc. Reproduction of this material is restricted to use with *A Guidebook for Teaching Composition*, 2nd Edition, by Gene Stanford and Marie Smith.

REPRODUCTION PAGE 87

IDEAS FOR RESEARCH PAPERS

a musician	water pollution	China
a poet	insecticides	Japan
an inventor	pioneers	competition
a sports hero	assassinations	miracles
an author	antiques	crime
a movie star	women's rights	origins of English
a political leader	electronics	UFO's
water skiing	guns	comic books
snow skiing	hunting	American Indians
hobbies	major weapons	the Amish
travels	working women	helicopters
movies	women's liberation	unions
marriage	men's liberation	the police
family life	inflation	patriotism
boating safety	coin collecting	national defense
flying	art	self-defense
archery	music	Socialism
lacrosse	cooking	Communism
horse racing	insects	teenage drivers
witches	farming	the United Nations
superstitions	photography	masonry
hypnotism	human-made satellites	bicycles
ESP	propaganda techniques	democracy
violence	capitalism	hockey
dreams	busing	education
the White House	suicide	Watergate
architecture	juvenile delinquency	forest preservation
ceramics	alcohol	dinosaurs
wild animals	tobacco	the Middle East
blindness	marijuana	Russia
space travel	hard drugs	wars
trees	population explosion	roller derby
oceans	food shortages	ice skating
snakes	dancing	recycling
spiders	heart transplants	human rights
student rights	ghettos	stamp collecting
giving blood	religions: Jewish	the stock market

Copyright © 1982 by Allyn and Bacon, Inc. Reproduction of this material is restricted to use with *A Guidebook for Teaching Composition*, 2nd Edition, by Gene Stanford and Marie Smith.

IDEAS FOR RESEARCH PAPERS   REPRODUCTION PAGE 87

18-year-old vote	religions: Roman Catholic	scouting
ants	religions: Protestant	dogs
whales	religions: eastern	horses
rare animals	forts	poetry
logic	storms	fairy tales
plants	weather problems	energy shortage
clothing styles	canals	cars
national parks	Greek philosophy	shoes
air pollution	mail carriers	frogs
coins and money	circus	holidays
newspapers	Eskimos	etiquette
motorcycles	TV shows	pets
blood pressure	lumber business	realism
occupations	dating	epilepsy
retardation	exercise	part-time jobs
coaches		

Copyright © 1982 by Allyn and Bacon, Inc. Reproduction of this material is restricted to use with *A Guidebook for Teaching Composition,* 2nd Edition, by Gene Stanford and Marie Smith.

REPRODUCTION PAGE 88

SAMPLE NOTE CARDS

INSTRUCTIONS: Your teacher will discuss with you the techniques demonstrated below for making sure your note cards are of maximum use to you in preparing your paper.

Passage from Article

    The government is doing several things to help control automobile pollution. Laws requiring the installation of pollution control equipment on all models have done much to decrease emission pollution. These standards are to be even more stringent in the years ahead.

Note Cards Recording These Ideas

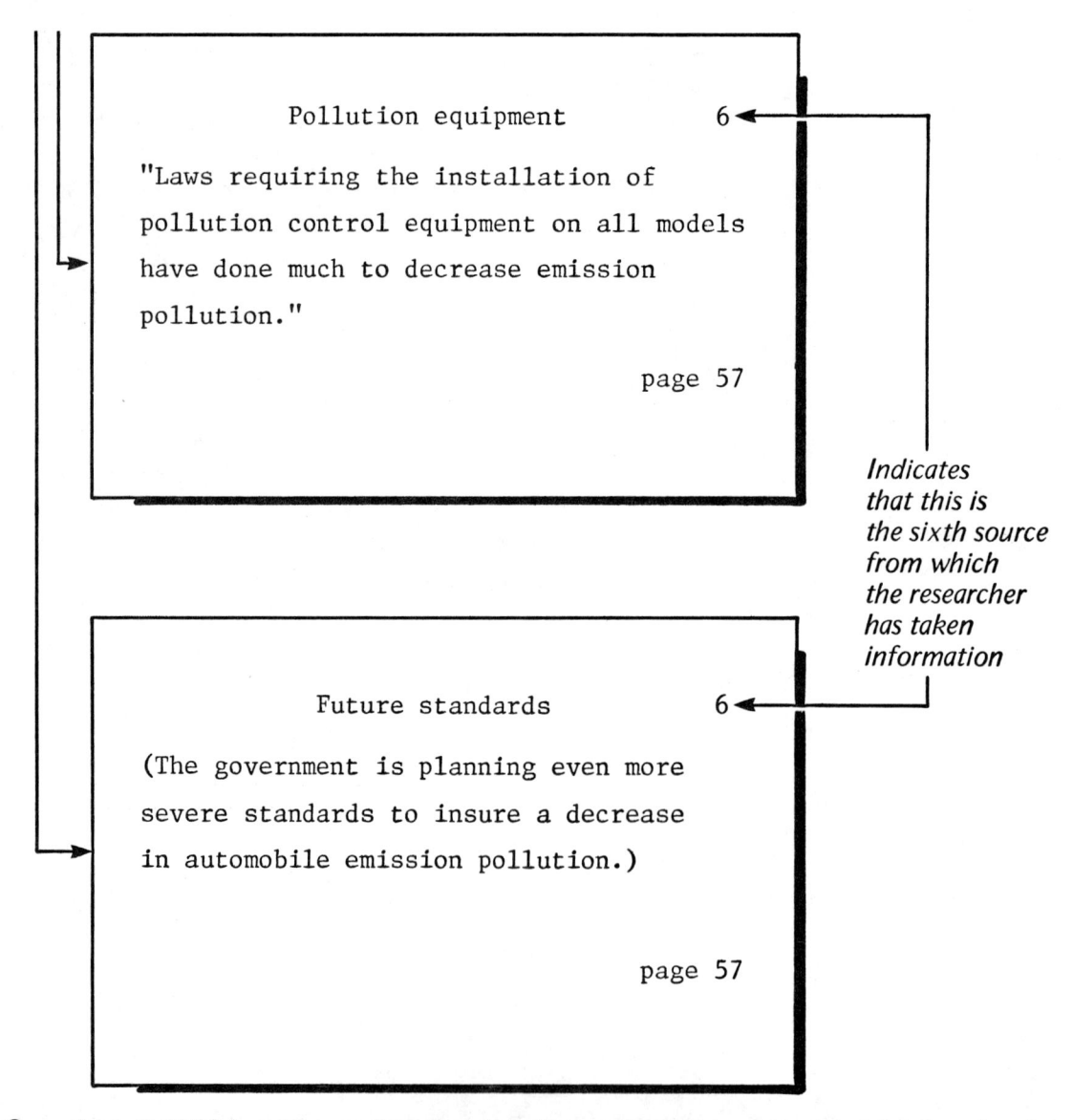

```
              Pollution equipment          6

   "Laws requiring the installation of
   pollution control equipment on all models
   have done much to decrease emission
   pollution."

                                    page 57
```

Indicates that this is the sixth source from which the researcher has taken information

```
              Future standards             6

   (The government is planning even more
   severe standards to insure a decrease
   in automobile emission pollution.)


                                    page 57
```

Copyright © 1982 by Allyn and Bacon, Inc. Reproduction of this material is restricted to use with *A Guidebook for Teaching Composition*, 2nd Edition, by Gene Stanford and Marie Smith.

REPRODUCTION PAGE 89

WORKSHEET ON NOTE TAKING

INSTRUCTIONS: Assume that you are writing a paper on automobile pollution with the thesis statement, "Unless drastic measures are taken, automobile pollution will become an extremely serious problem." Imagine that the passages below are taken from page 57 of a magazine article you found in the library. It is the third source of information you have used. Fill in the note cards, as your teacher has instructed, with either quotations or paraphrases.

Less direct but still effective control came about when gas was in small supply and the number of miles driven was greatly reduced.

Mileage standards are being emphasized through publicizing EPA highway standards. Also the nation's car manufacturers are being encouraged to design and build cars which can deliver 40 mpg or better.

Ray Simon has said, "All Americans must make a strong effort to change their driving habits." With this kind of support from Washington, it seems reasonable to believe that automobile pollution will become less and less a factor in America's fight to clean up its air.

Copyright © 1982 by Allyn and Bacon, Inc. Reproduction of this material is restricted to use with *A Guidebook for Teaching Composition*, 2nd Edition, by Gene Stanford and Marie Smith.

REPRODUCTION PAGE 90

THE BIBLIOGRAPHY

INSTRUCTIONS: You will considerably simplify your task of gathering and recording information from various sources if you will learn the following techniques for preparing bibliography cards.

A bibliography is an alphabetized list of all information sources (books, magazines, encyclopedias, pamphlets, and interviews, for example) used by an individual in writing an article, book, or paper.

The information that will ultimately go into the bibliography is obtained from each source as it is used. This information is usually written on 3 x 5 index cards. A separate card is kept for each source of information and is numbered to correspond to the number on the note cards from that source. Thus, each card represents one source, even though many pieces of information were obtained from that single source.

The following is a sample bibliography card for a book, the sixth source consulted by this researcher:

Type of source:	book 6	←—Number of
Author's name:	Curtiss, John L.	source
Title:	After the Fact	
Place of publication:	New York, New York	
Publisher's name:	Randolph Williams Co.	
Copyright date:	1963	

Once the researcher has recorded this information on the bibliography card, he or she can return the book to the library, can prepare the bibliography using only the bibliography cards, and can write the paper using only the notes on the note cards. Hence, the researcher does not have to keep all the works consulted until the paper is finished.

FORMS FOR OTHER TYPES OF SOURCES:

Magazine: Type (magazine)
              Author's name
              Article title (in quotation marks)
              Magazine title (underlined)
              Volume number and page
              (separated by colon)
              Date

Newspaper: Type (newspaper)
              Author (if given)
              Title of article (in quotation marks)
              Name of newspaper
              Date
              Page number

Encyclopedia: Type (encyclopedia)
              Author's name (if article is signed)
              Topic (in quotation marks)
              Title of encyclopedia (underlined)
              Year of edition
              Copyright date
              Volume and number
              Page

Interview: Type (interview)
              Name of person interviewed
              Date of interview
              Place of interview

Copyright © 1982 by Allyn and Bacon, Inc. Reproduction of this material is restricted to use with *A Guidebook for Teaching Composition,* 2nd Edition, by Gene Stanford and Marie Smith.

REPRODUCTION PAGE 91

WORKSHEET ON BIBLIOGRAPHY CARDS

INSTRUCTIONS: Fill out seven bibliography cards using the information below.

1. Book: *The Outsiders*   publisher — Bantam
   author — S.E. Hinton   place — Boston
   page — 47   date — 1962

2. Book: *Sister Carrie*   publisher — Charles E. Merrill
   author: Theodore Dreiser   place — Columbus, Ohio
   page — 132   date — 1969

3. Book: *The Word*   publisher — Simon and Schuster
   author — Irving Wallace   place — New York
   page — 308   date — 1972

4. Magazine: *Newsweek*   date — May 14, 1968
   article — "The Space Probe"   volume — 178
   pages — 47-49   author — Ralph Neely

5. Magazine: *Time*   date — November 20, 1972
   article — "A Future That Is Up for Grabs"   volume — 100
   pages — 27-31   author — none

6. Magazine: *Today's Education*   date — November 1972
   article — "The Picture of America"   volume — 61
   pages — 28-30   author — Charles B. Johnson, Jr.

7. Encyclopedia: *Colliers*   publisher — Crowell Co. of Boston
   author — Winston Bragg   volume — 22
   subject — whales   printed — 1954
   page — 476

Copyright © 1982 by Allyn and Bacon, Inc. Reproduction of this material is restricted to use with *A Guidebook for Teaching Composition*, 2nd Edition, by Gene Stanford and Marie Smith.

REPRODUCTION PAGE 92

OUTLINING WORKSHEET

1. Sort out the following items and fit them into the form listed below:

    Title — What I like about my hometown
    Main headings — location, school, facilities, people
    Unsorted list — friendly, near a large city, superior library, on a river, well-trained teachers, parks, charitable, balanced curriculum, in the mountains, modern classrooms, recreation center, theaters

    Title —

    I.
       A.
       B.
       C.
    II.
       A.
       B.
       C.
       D.
    III.
       A.
       B.
       C.
    IV.
       A.
       B.

2. Now, without any heading outline for a guide, sort out the following and put them in a reasonable outline form.

Bull dog	As Seeing Eye dog
Irish setter	English setter
Golden retriever	Sheep dog
Kinds of dogs	German shepherd
Poodles	Sport dogs
Working dogs	House dogs
Labrador retriever	Cocker spaniel
As police dog	As guard dogs
Retrievers	Setters

Copyright © 1982 by Allyn and Bacon, Inc. Reproduction of this material is restricted to use with *A Guidebook for Teaching Composition*, 2nd Edition, by Gene Stanford and Marie Smith.

NOTE CARD WORKSHEET

INSTRUCTIONS: Following your teacher's directions, number the cards shown below in the order you believe would be most effective in a research paper.

Cars Manufactured — 3

"Each day in Detroit, more than 18,000 cars come off the assembly line." pg. 84

Equipment cuts 30% — 3

(If every car made was equipped with the devices already invented and tested, pollution from the automobile could be cut by at least 30%.) pg. 16

Future standards — 1

(The government is planning even more severe standards to insure a decrease in automobile emission pollution.) pg. 57

Conclusion — 4

"If these measures are taken, if this advice is followed, America will begin to rid itself of air pollution from the automobile." pg. 114

Copyright © 1982 by Allyn and Bacon, Inc. Reproduction of this material is restricted to use with *A Guidebook for Teaching Composition*, 2nd Edition, by Gene Stanford and Marie Smith.

REPRODUCTION PAGE 93   NOTE CARD WORKSHEET

New equipment   4

(Invention of new equipment like pcv and catalytic converter is a large step forward.)   pg. 111

Tires, gas, etc.   2

(Radial tires, nonleaded gas and smaller cars all aid in the drive to decrease the problem of automobile pollution.) pg. 117

Simon quote   1

" 'All Americans must make a strong effort to change their driving habits.' " pg. 57

Auto pollution #1   4

"Of all the threats to clean air that our country faces, automobile pollution has earned the right to be our number one priority." pg. 12

Copyright © 1982 by Allyn and Bacon, Inc. Reproduction of this material is restricted to use with *A Guidebook for Teaching Composition*, 2nd Edition, by Gene Stanford and Marie Smith.

CARS I WOULD NOT WANT TO OWN

There are over a quarter of a million automobiles sold in the United States each year. Many types are available; foreign cars and American cars, convertables and sedans, big cars and little cars. This variety is the result of the wide range of tastes of the driving population. There is three kinds of cars which doesn't suit my taste at all, and which I would never own. One type is impractical, another is little and ugly, and a third is poorly made.

An example of an impractical car is the Excalibur SS, perhaps you have never seen one of these cars. It bears a strong resemblance to the Dusenberg of years ago or to an old MG, early 1951 or 1952. One of the things I don't like about it are that it only comes in a convertable model. That's fine in the summer or on a sunny day, but when it rains or when winter comes, its rather impractical. Winter is perhaps the roughest though. Mainly because the car is not equipped with a heater. And the softtop has plastic side windows and a plastic rear window that leaks and yellows in the sun and becomes briddle with age. This car is fitted with a 327 cubic inch engine from the Corvette Stingray. The car does not weigh more than 200 pounds, compared to the Corvette, which weighs approximately 3200 pounds this year. With over 350 horsepower and so little weight, the Excalibur is very dangerous, you can't come near controlling shortcommings with a $10,000 price tag, you have a very impractical car.

A car that I wouldn't want is one of those ugly little foreign "bugs" you see everywhere. The Volkswagen is a good example, this simply isn't my idea of a car with good looks. In addition, its to small for safety. If you were hit in the side by a large car or by a truck, you'd be finished. You also can't ride for great distances in comfort, because the engine is to noisy and the interior is cramped. Another shortcomming is that Volkswagen's are to common. I don't want a car that every mothers son has, and if you look around any large parking lot in this city, you are bound to see at least ten Volkswagen's. Besides being so common, this car is to underpowered for freeway driving. Its almost impossible to pass a car on the expressway at sixty miles per hour, if there is a stiff crosswind blowing, you would think you were on a roller coaster. This is both unpleasant and unsafe.

The third type of car that I wouldn't like to own is one that is cheaply made. Ford Mustangs fall into this class—my family owned one once, and before we got rid of it the muffler fell off at least five times. By the time we sold it six months later, there was rattles in every corner. Meanwhile, the paint had started peeling off, to say nothing of the first layer of chrome on the bumpers. To top it off, whenever the driver made a hard left turn, the door on the passenger's side would fly open. My uncle own a Cougar, and it doesn't have these problems.

John Richardson
(10th grade student)

Copyright © 1982 by Allyn and Bacon, Inc Reproduction of this material is restricted to use with *A Guidebook for Teaching Composition,* 2nd Edition, by Gene Stanford and Marie Smith.

LOOK-ALIKES/SOUND-ALIKES

1. accent — ascent — assent
2. accept — except
3. access — excess
4. adapt — adept — adopt
5. advice — advise
6. affect — effect
7. allay — alley — alleys — allies — ally
8. already — all ready
9. altogether — all together
10. allude — elude
11. altar — alter
12. always — all ways
13. an — and
14. angel — angle
15. ante — auntie — anti-
16. appraise — apprise
17. are — or — our — ore
18. assure — insure
19. attendance — attendants
20. bail — bale
21. ball — bole — boll — bowl
22. baring — barring — bearing
23. bear — bare
24. beat — beet
25. berry — bury
26. berth — birth
27. biding — bidding
28. blew — blue
29. boar — bore
30. board — bored
31. boarder — border
32. born — borne
33. brake — break
34. bread — bred
35. breadth — breath — breathe
36. brewed — brood
37. bridal — bridle
38. build — billed
39. Calvary — cavalry
40. capital — capitol
41. carat — caret — carrot
42. casual — causal
43. ceiling — sealing
44. cent — scent — sent
45. choose — chose
46. chord — cord
47. cite — sight — site
48. clothes — cloths
49. coarse — course
50. coma — comma
51. complement — compliment
52. confidant — confident
53. conscience — conscious
54. conscientiousness — consciousness
55. consul — council — counsel
56. coral — corral
57. core — corps — corpse
58. costume — custom
59. creak — creek
60. crews — cruise
61. dairy — diary
62. days — daze
63. dear — deer
64. decease — disease
65. decent — descent — dissent
66. dependence — dependents
67. desert — desert — dessert
68. detract — distract
69. device — devise
70. die — dye
71. dining — dinning
72. dual — duel
73. due — do
74. emigrate — immigrate
75. envelop — envelope
76. ever — every

Copyright © 1982 by Allyn and Bacon, Inc. Reproduction of this material is restricted to use with *A Guidebook for Teaching Composition*, 2nd Edition, by Gene Stanford and Marie Smith.

LOOK-ALIKES/SOUND-ALIKES REPRODUCTION PAGE 95

77. exalt – exult
78. extant – extent – extinct
79. faint – feint
80. fair – fare
81. fir – fur
82. flair – flare
83. flea – flee
84. flour – flower
85. forbear – forebear
86. foreword – forward
87. formally – formerly
88. forth – fourth
89. gilt – guilt
90. grip – gripe
91. hail – hale
92. hair – hare
93. hart – heart
94. heal – heel
95. hear – here
96. hoard – horde
97. hole – whole
98. holy – wholly
99. hoping – hopping
100. human – humane
101. idle – idol
102. its – it's
103. knew – new
104. later – latter
105. lead – lead – led
106. least – lest – leased
107. lessen – lesson
108. lie – lye
109. lightening – lightning
110. loan – lone
111. loose – lose – loss
112. mail – male
113. main – mane
114. manner – manor
115. maybe – may be
116. meat – meet

117. medal – meddle – metal – mettle
118. minor – miner
119. moral – morale
120. morning – mourning
121. of – off
122. on – one – won
123. pail – pale
124. pain – pane
125. pair – pare – pear
126. passed – past
127. peace – piece
128. pedal – peddle – petal
129. personal – personnel
130. pray – prey
131. precede – proceed
132. principal – principle
133. quiet – quite
134. right – rite – write
135. sail – sale
136. shear – sheer
137. shone – shown
138. sole – soul
139. stair – stare
140. stationary – stationery
141. steal – steel
142. tail – tale
143. then – than
144. their – there – they're
145. therefor – therefore
146. though – through – threw – thorough
147. to – too – two
148. tolled – told
149. vain – vane – vein
150. vice – vise
151. waist – waste
152. weather – whether
153. were – we're – where
154. whose – who's
155. yolk – yoke
156. your – you're – yore

Copyright © 1982 by Allyn and Bacon, Inc. Reproduction of this material is restricted to use with *A Guidebook for Teaching Composition,* 2nd Edition, by Gene Stanford and Marie Smith.

SPELLING DEMONS

there — their — they're
its — it's
to — too — two
forty
definite — definitely
occurred — occurrence
loneliness — lonely
receive, conceive, etc.
thorough
friend
psychology
cite — site — sight
height — weight — freight
congratulations
flow — flowed
fly — flew
tie — tied
fry — fried — try — tried
occasion
incidentally — accidentally
professor — profession
principle — principal
immediately
accept — except
led — lead
effect — affect
similar
truly — duly
whole — wholly
fire — fiery
maintenance
cemetery

athlete
confidence
relevant
privilege
grammar
background
college
supposedly
undoubtedly
sense — since — scents
consider
overcoming — coming
recognize
passed — past
recommend
piece — peace
always
pastime
lose — loose
chose — choose
temperature
miniature
whether — weather
tragedy
than — then
separate
cloths — clothes
conscious
conscience
boundary
a lot

Copyright © 1982 by Allyn and Bacon, Inc. Reproduction of this material is restricted to use with *A Guidebook for Teaching Composition*, 2nd Edition, by Gene Stanford and Marie Smith.

SENTENCE CARDS FOR SPELLING GAME

1. I really like them; their my friends.
2. She excepted our invitation to go to the game.
3. Don't ask me; its they're decision.
4. I was relieved to find that I past my math test.
5. We had very bad whether last week.
6. Don't worry; everything will be all right.
7. I walked right in to the wall.
8. She was very impolite; she didn't have any manors.
9. It was a beautiful site to see.
10. Sam forgot about his piano lessen.
11. In England we saw many beautiful feudal manners.
12. It's a locale store.
13. She threw the fruit away; it was a real waist.
14. I really liked the play, irregardless of what the critics said.
15. This rule is generally true; however, their are a few acceptions.
16. I all ready paid that bill.
17. May I sit down?
18. Whose their?
19. I don't no witch book you want.
20. Who do you wish to sea?
21. I received too lovly Christmas cards.
22. Your the best friend I've ever had.
23. Linda wrote the letter, stamped the envelope, ceiled, and maled it.
24. Were very disappointed with Sue's performance.
25. Liberty is a basic human rite.
26. Hours past while we weighted.
27. I gave her good advise.
28. I think that Bobby is taller then she.
29. She looked beautiful in her wedding gown as she walked down the isle.
30. He was a fine person; I believe his sole will go to heaven.
31. I studied the principals of geometry for more than three ours.
32. Their was no apparent effect.
33. The door handle was very lose; it must of fallen off.
34. The road was a dead end; it lead too a grassy field.
35. Its to hard to understand; let's forget it.
36. They were making to much noise; I tolled them to be quite.
37. The highway was long, narrow and strait.
38. Eugene O'Neill was a great playwrite.
39. Jennifer all ways ware tie-died jeans.
40. She had two go a way on vacation.
41. This year they're were fewer at the party then last.
42. We studied the ancient rights and rituals.
43. The principle suspended five students.
44. Everyone attended accept Jill.
45. Mr. Young was the soul survivor of the crash.
46. That's you're coat.
47. The coral straights are about a mile from the Canary Aisles.
48. Who's dog is that?
49. Forget it; its all in the passed.
50. Our house is being built on a new cite.
51. Since Carried died her hair black, she looks like a which.
52. She tried too advice me.

Copyright © 1982 by Allyn and Bacon, Inc. Reproduction of this material is restricted to use with *A Guidebook for Teaching Composition*, 2nd Edition, by Gene Stanford and Marie Smith.

REPRODUCTION PAGE 97 **SENTENCE CARDS FOR SPELLING GAME**

53. I am sole air to the company fortune.
54. I don't care weather you bring the pizza or the drinks.
55. She eats to much candy; she's gaining alot of wait.
56. I agree; your one-hundred percent rite.
57. It was a vary boaring experience.
58. She fell down the stares and broke her leg.
59. Lisa was speeding when the light changed; she slammed on the breaks.
60. He burned the rug with the acid and lie.
61. The plain sored threw the sky as it made its assent.
62. The police told us too excess the damage.
63. The Carters adapted a three-month old baby.
64. He was robbed in a narrow, dark allay.
65. What you are doing is all together wrong.
66. She eluded to the classics on several occasions.
67. Don't altar your plans on are account.
68. You an Margaret look a like.
69. Little Elizabeth has a face like an angle.
70. Don't be sew ante-social.
71. The insurance agent apprised our house.
72. The diamonds are assured for one thousand dollars.
73. The family was not in attendence.
74. I baled you out of jail the last time.
75. Diane ate the hole bole of fruit.
76. The hunter shot but mist the bare.
77. Alice dyed Friday; they berried her too days latter.
78. We all celebrated her berthday.
79. The wind was fierce; it blue all night.
80. I served on the Bored of Education.
81. The dress had a pretty, embroidered border.
82. I was bourne in February.
83. The entire bridle party was dressed in blew.
84. We didn't have any cash, so the car sailsman build us a month latter.
85. The capitol of New York State is Albany.
86. There weren't any carats in the salad.
87. It was a vary fragrant cent.
88. I choose this option.
89. The chord snapped and the plant feel.
90. Leigh brought all knew cloths.
91. She confused the coma and the semicolon.
92. I complemented her on her great ideas.
93. She was very confidant.
94. She wasn't conscience of the problem.
95. The book was designed to expand the readers' conscientiousness.
96. I was late for the student counsel meeting.
97. John joined the Piace Core.
98. Every culture has its own set of traditions and customs.
99. The water emptied into a little creek.
100. Her parents went on a luxury crews.
101. The hunter shoot three dear.
102. Cancer is a serious decease.
103. Her helplessness and dependents are irritating.
104. We had ice cream for desert.
105. Their was so much noise, that I was detracted.
106. The experts devised a good plan.
107. We had diner at five-thirty.
108. It was a two-fold situation; it had a duel purpose.

Copyright © 1982 by Allyn and Bacon, Inc. Reproduction of this material is restricted to use with *A Guidebook for Teaching Composition*, 2nd Edition, by Gene Stanford and Marie Smith.

SENTENCE CARDS FOR SPELLING GAME

REPRODUCTION PAGE 97

109. They decided to make Eddie due the work.
110. They emigrated to this country fifty years ago.
111. I don't no to what extant she agreed.
112. David was dizzy, pail, and feint.
113. The bus fair was increased alot.
114. Our Christmas tree was a northern fur.
115. You have a flare with words.
116. Max, our dog, has flees.
117. The receipt required eggs, flower, and milk.
118. The lunch line was to long, so we pushed foreword.
119. The meeting was conducted very formerly.
120. Darlene ranked forth in the beauty contest.
121. The police new that she was gilty by the sick look on her face.
122. The karate expert had a tight gripe on his opponent.
123. Snow, sleet, and hail feel for hours.
124. The small hair dodged off into the woods.
125. Dr. Barnard performed the first hart transplant.
126. The heal came off my knew shoes.
127. The music was so loud that I couldn't here the speaker.
128. Tomorrow is a wholly day.
129. The answer alludes me at the present.
130. The statue represented an old Egyptian idel.
131. Our city boasts the leased number of accidents.
132. The thunder and lightening scarred Missy.
133. Michael implied for a lone.
134. Go threw the mane entrance.
135. Stake is my favorite meet.
136. The brave soldier received a special honorary metal.
137. The accident occured at midnight.
138. The tempature rose thirty degrees.
139. The old lady looked vary lonly.
140. After I gradate from high school I am hopping to go too collage.
141. Meeting the king was a great honer and privledge.
142. I hate spelling, puntuation, and grammar.
143. We made gravestone rubbings at the cemetary.
144. She had changed so much that I didn't reconize her.
145. *Othello* is one of Shakespeare's tradgedies.
146. Joan ownes fourty albums.
147. I'm definitly in favor of your suggestion.
148. I mean this vary sincerly.
149. Use your common scents.
150. She did a comprehensive, through job.
151. You are my friend; I beleive everything you say.
152. Allow me to congradulate you on your new appointment.
153. I tryed my best to be a good athelete.
154. Psychology and phylosophy are two entirely seperate feilds.
155. I didn't do it on purpose; it was an incident.
156. What's your favorite pasttime?
157. The minature is very simular to the original.
158. What do you consider relevent?
159. I don't like fir coats; I perfer lether.
160. The cut looked soar; it didn't heel vary well.

Copyright © 1982 by Allyn and Bacon, Inc. Reproduction of this material is restricted to use with *A Guidebook for Teaching Composition*, 2nd Edition, by Gene Stanford and Marie Smith.

REPRODUCTION PAGE 97 **SENTENCE CARDS FOR SPELLING GAME**

161. He though the ball threw the window.
162. The captain saluted and boughed.
163. The sky was a pail blew.
164. Cite all references
165. There were fewer car accidents this year than last.
166. The principal gave all the students a two-week vacation.
167. Of the two, you're the better dancer.
168. It's your party; do as you please.
169. Who's at the door?
170. Everything is all right.
171. May I give my opinion?
172. Everyone must listen; there are no exceptions.
173. I am very confident that everything will be fine.
174. The old man was losing his sight.
175. The cow escaped from the corral.
176. I can't draw a straight line.
177. There is less water in this container than in the other.
178. We were never formally introduced.

Copyright © 1982 by Allyn and Bacon, Inc. Reproduction of this material is restricted to use with *A Guidebook for Teaching Composition*, 2nd Edition, by Gene Stanford and Marie Smith.

REPRODUCTION PAGE 98

GAME BOARD

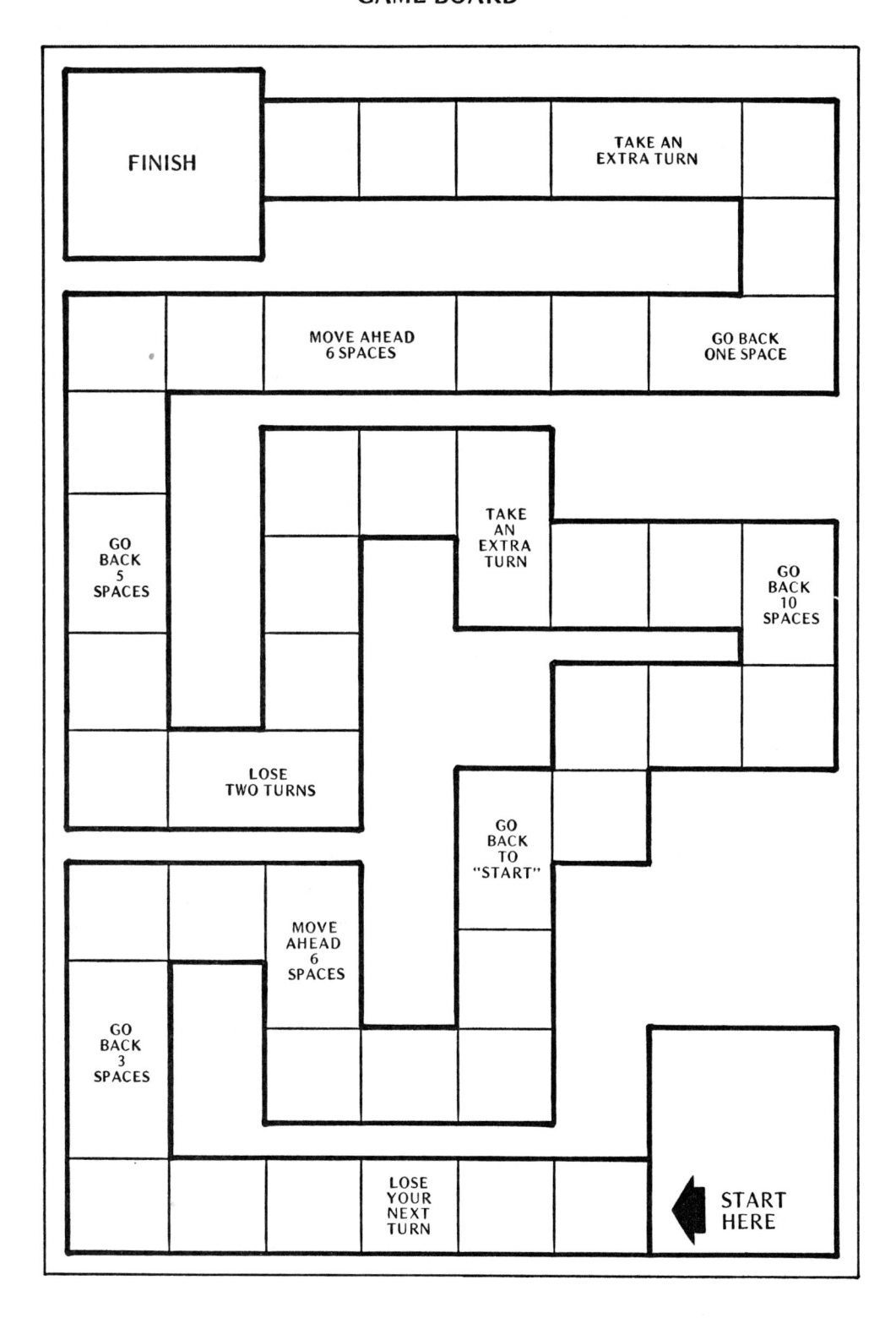

FINISH	TAKE AN EXTRA TURN
	MOVE AHEAD 6 SPACES / GO BACK ONE SPACE
GO BACK 5 SPACES	TAKE AN EXTRA TURN / GO BACK 10 SPACES
	LOSE TWO TURNS / GO BACK TO "START"
GO BACK 3 SPACES	MOVE AHEAD 6 SPACES
	LOSE YOUR NEXT TURN / START HERE

Copyright © 1982 by Allyn and Bacon, Inc. Reproduction of this material is restricted to use with *A Guidebook for Teaching Composition*, 2nd Edition, by Gene Stanford and Marie Smith.

REPRODUCTION PAGE 99

INSTRUCTIONS FOR SPELLING GAME

1. Approximately four persons can play this game.

2. Lay the game board on the floor or other flat surface such as a table or desk.

3. Give the answer key to one person (either a player or someone who wants to watch but not play). This person will consult the answer key when necessary to check an answer and hence will be referred to as "the Judge." Warn the Judge not to let anyone see the answers.

4. Shuffle and stack all the sentence cards. Place them face down near the game board.

5. Roll dice or draw lots or guess a number to determine who goes first.

6. Place your markers in the space labeled "Start" on the game board.

7. The first player draws a sentence card from the top of the stack. The player reads it and determines whether or not all of the words are spelled according to acceptable standard English. Sentences may contain one or more errors.

8. If the player decides that there are no spelling errors in the sentence, he or she must show it to the other players to see whether they agree. If they don't agree, the Judge checks the answer key. If the Judge upholds the player's opinion, then the player may move ahead two spaces. If the player is wrong (that is, if the sentence does contain misspelled words), then he or she loses the next turn.

9. If the player decides that a word or words in the sentence are misspelled, he or she must identify each, correctly spell each, and explain the correction. If the Judge and other players agree with the player's correction(s), the player may move ahead the number of spaces equal to the number of misspelled words in the sentence. If the other players do not agree, then the group must discuss the question until they reach agreement. If they cannot agree, they must consult the Judge, whose answer, based on the key, overrules all other players. The Judge must explain the answer to the other players. If the player's answer is upheld by the Judge, then the player may move ahead as many spaces as there are misspelled words in the sentence; otherwise, the player may not move ahead or take his or her next turn.

10. The player whose marker reaches the "Finish" space first is the winner.

Copyright © 1982 by Allyn and Bacon, Inc. Reproduction of this material is restricted to use with *A Guidebook for Teaching Composition*, 2nd Edition, by Gene Stanford and Marie Smith.

REPRODUCTION PAGE 100

ANSWER KEY FOR SPELLING GAME

1. they're	(1)
2. accepted	(1)
3. it's, their	(2)
4. passed	(1)
5. weather	(1)
6. no error	(1)
7. into	(1)
8. manners	(1)
9. sight	(1)
10. lesson	(1)
11. manors	(1)
12. local	(1)
13. waste	(1)
14. regardless	(1)
15. there, exceptions	(2)
16. already	(1)
17. no errors	(2)
18. who's there	(2)
19. know, which	(2)
20. whom, see	(2)
21. received, two, lovely	(3)
22. you're	(1)
23. sealed, mailed	(2)
24. we're	(1)
25. right	(1)
26. passed, waited	(2)
27. advice	(1)
28. than	(1)
29. aisle	(1)
30. soul	(1)
31. principles, hours	(2)
32. there	(1)
33. loose, have (not of)	(2)
34. led, to	(2)
35. it's, too	(2)
36. too, told, quiet	(3)
37. straight	(1)
38. playwright	(1)
39. always, wears, tie-dyed	(3)
40. to, away	(2)
41. there, than	(2)
42. rites	(1)
43. principal	(1)
44. except	(1)
45. sole	(1)
46. your	(1)
47. straits, isles	(2)
48. whose	(1)
49. it's, past	(2)
50. site	(1)
51. dyed, witch	(2)
52. to, advise	(2)
53. heir	(1)
54. whether	(1)
55. too, a lot, weight	(3)
56. you're, right	(2)
57. very, boring	(2)
58. stairs	(1)
59. brakes	(1)
60. lye	(1)
61. plane, soared, through, ascent	(4)
62. to, access	(2)
63. adopted	(1)
64. alley	(1)
65. altogether	(1)
66. alluded	(1)
67. alter, our	(2)
68. and, alike	(2)
69. angel	(1)
70. so, antisocial	(2)
71. appraised	(1)
72. insured	(1)
73. attendance	(1)
74. bailed	(1)
75. whole, bowl	(2)
76. missed, bear	(2)
77. died, buried, two, later	(4)

Copyright © 1982 by Allyn and Bacon, Inc. Reproduction of this material is restricted to use with *A Guidebook for Teaching Composition*, 2nd Edition, by Gene Stanford and Marie Smith.

REPRODUCTION PAGE 100   ANSWER KEY FOR SPELLING GAME

78.	birthday	(1)		118.	too, forward	(2)
79.	blew	(1)		119.	formally	(1)
80.	Board	(1)		120.	fourth	(1)
81.	border	(1)		121.	knew, guilty	(2)
82.	born	(1)		122.	grip	(1)
83.	bridal, blue	(2)		123.	hale, fell	(2)
84.	car salesman, billed, later	(3)		124.	hare	(1)
				125.	heart	(1)
85.	capital	(1)		126.	heel, new	(2)
86.	carrots	(1)		127.	hear	(1)
87.	very, scent	(2)		128.	holy	(1)
88.	no error	(2)		129.	eludes	(1)
89.	cord, fell	(2)		130.	idol	(1)
90.	new, clothes	(2)		131.	least	(1)
91.	comma	(1)		132.	lightning, scared	(2)
92.	complimented	(1)		133.	applied, loan	(2)
93.	confident	(1)		134.	through, main	(2)
94.	conscious	(1)		135.	steak, meat	(2)
95.	consciousness	(1)		136.	medal	(1)
96.	council	(1)		137.	occurred	(1)
97.	Peace Corps	(2)		138.	temperature	(1)
98.	customs	(1)		139.	very, lonely	(2)
99.	creek	(1)		140.	graduate, hoping, to, college	(4)
100.	cruise	(1)				
101.	shot, deer	(2)		141.	honor, privilege	(2)
102.	disease	(1)		142.	punctuation, grammar	(2)
103.	dependence	(1)		143.	cemetery	(1)
104.	dessert	(1)		144.	recognize	(1)
105.	distracted	(1)		145.	tragedies	(1)
106.	no error	(2)		146.	owns, forty	(2)
107.	dinner	(1)		147.	definitely, favor	(2)
108.	dual	(1)		148.	very, sincerely	(2)
109.	do	(1)		149.	sense	(1)
110.	immigrated	(1)		150.	thorough	(1)
111.	know, extent	(2)		151.	friend, believe	(2)
112.	pale, faint	(2)		152.	congratulate	(1)
113.	fare, a lot	(2)		153.	tried, athlete	(2)
114.	fir	(1)		154.	psychology, philosophy, separate, fields	(4)
115.	flair	(1)				
116.	fleas	(1)		155.	accident	(1)
117.	recipe, flour	(2)		156.	pastime	(1)

Copyright © 1982 by Allyn and Bacon, Inc. Reproduction of this material is restricted to use with *A Guidebook for Teaching Composition*, 2nd Edition, by Gene Stanford and Marie Smith.

ANSWER KEY FOR SPELLING GAME   REPRODUCTION PAGE 100

157. miniature, similar, original	(3)	
158. relevant	(1)	
159. fur, prefer, leather	(3)	
160. sore, heal, very	(3)	
161. threw, through	(2)	
162. bowed	(1)	
163. pale, blue	(2)	
164. no error	(2)	
165. no error	(2)	
166. no error	(2)	
167. no error	(2)	
168. no error	(2)	
169. no error	(2)	
170. no error	(2)	
171. no error	(2)	
172. no error	(2)	
173. no error	(2)	
174. no error	(2)	
175. no error	(2)	
176. no error	(2)	
177. no error	(2)	
178. no error	(2)	

Copyright © 1982 by Allyn and Bacon, Inc. Reproduction of this material is restricted to use with *A Guidebook for Teaching Composition,* 2nd Edition, by Gene Stanford and Marie Smith.

REPRODUCTION PAGE 101

SPELLING PROOFREADING EXERCISE

INSTRUCTIONS: Underline each word misspelled and write it correctly and legibly above the line.

Recently I learned a very important lesson about releiving my own problems rather than expecting others to help me bare my troubles. I had been feeling pretty blue for some time. My dog, who had been with me sinse I was a little more then a baby, just layed down one evening, on the bear basement floor, and dyed. Of coarse, I new he had lead a good life, and he was definately not young, having lived six years, or about the same as fourty-two years in the life of a humane being. Therefore, his death shouldn't have been considered a tradgedy. But it was, nonetheless, a truely sad occassion, and I couldn't seem to get over the affect of loosing such a good old faithful friend.

One day it occured to me that I had not really tryed to do anything about overcomming the indefinate sence of loneliness that was making me feel depressed all the time, ever sinse my dog dyed. I hadn't truely tryed to except the fact that the death had occured, weather I choose to reconize it or not; and the time had come, I knew, when I must use good sence and move on into new activitys, seperating myself from the passed.

I decided to follow the principal of replacement in training myself to a new and better attitude. I would replace the fun I use to have with Beau with other pleasures and persuits. (Incidently, this method is good phsychology, and I recommend it to anyone who has alot of problems acheiving piece of mind after loosing a pet.)

The first thing I did on the evening this idea finally occured to me was to check the temparture on the thermometer outside my window. Sure enough, it was a lovely warm 70 degrees, perfect gardening whether, and I knew I'd be alright planting flower seeds. I quickly through on my gardening cloths and went to the garage to get the tools I had recieved as a birthday gift. I also took alot of seeds I had layed away for the spring day when the temperature would be alright for planting.

Bearing these things with me to the back yard, I began to plant seeds along the boundry of our yard. I choose a place where the sun almost allways shone. I felt better at once, as soon as I began digging in the warm soil. Gardening has allways been a soothing passtime for me, and immediatly it began to divert my mind from poor Beau's death.

I did feel a little guilty about going ahead with the flower garden without waiting for my little brother, but I beleive the older child should have some priveleges that definately belong to him, so my conscious didn't hurt me to badly. My gardening soothed my spirit, and the whole experience lead me to a realization that life goes on, and one must move with it and not let any tradegy, wether major or miner, effect him to much.

Copyright © 1982 by Allyn and Bacon, Inc. Reproduction of this material is restricted to use with *A Guidebook for Teaching Composition*, 2nd Edition, by Gene Stanford and Marie Smith.

REPRODUCTION PAGE 102

GUIDE TO PUNCTUATION

The Comma (,)

The comma is used:

1. To set off appositives (words that clarify or identify that which precedes or comes before it):

    Kristin, my younger sister, is going to Washington.

2. To set off a direct address (words that tell to whom a remark is directed):

    Listen, Diane, you'd better not be late again.

3. To set off a quotation:

    "Don't hit the telephone pole," shrieked the driver education teacher, "or you'll go back to study hall forever."

4. After each word in a series:

    The store was all out of peanuts, popcorn, and pretzels.

5. Following an introductory participial phrase:

    Hearing the bell, I ran!

6. Following such words as yes, no, oh, well, incidentally, and so forth:

    Oh, what a beautiful dog.

7. Before the state in an address and after the state if the sentence continues.

    I lived in Albany, New York, for two years.

8. Between the day of the month and the year, and after the year if the sentence continues.

    I remember February 18, 1976, as the happiest day of my life.

9. Before a coordinating conjunction in a compound sentence.

    John came on a motorcycle, and Alan arrived on a horse.

10. To set off a nonrestrictive clause.

    The boys, who drove their own cars, left early.

11. After an introductory subordinant clause:

    When I heard the bell, I ran for class.

Copyright © 1982 by Allyn and Bacon, Inc. Reproduction of this material is restricted to use with *A Guidebook for Teaching Composition,* 2nd Edition, by Gene Stanford and Marie Smith.

REPRODUCTION PAGE 102   GUIDE TO PUNCTUATION

The Colon (:)

The colon is used:

1. To introduce a quotation:

    We can fully understand Cassius's philosophy when he says:
    "The fault, dear Brutus, is not in our stars,
    But in ourselves, that we are underlings."

2. To set up or prepare the reader for a list or a series:

    The reasons for his dismissal include: tardiness, incompetence, dishonesty, and disrespect.
    Will the following people report to the office: Mary, Kevin, Bill, and Jo-Ann.
    The recipe calls for the following: butter, sugar, milk, and salt.

The Semicolon (;)

The semicolon is used:

1. To separate two independent clauses when the conjunction has been omitted:

    It rained all afternoon; we stayed in the house and watched television.

2. To separate items in a series that contain commas:

    The dinner list included: Martin Norton, Ph.D.; Kelly Gaffney, M.D.; and Henry Owens, D.D.S.

Quotation Marks (" ")

Quotation marks are used:

1. To indicate titles of poems, essays, short stories, songs, and articles:

    My favorite poem is "Dover Beach."

    Edgar Allen Poe's short story, "The Masque of the Red Death," is frightening.

    The song title "Somebody Done Somebody Wrong Song" is the longest on the record.

    Do you like the poem "Ode to a Grecian Urn"?

2. To quote a person's direct comments:

    "It's nice to see you," said Mrs. Benson.

    "Where have you been?" asked Mary. "I've been waiting for an hour."

Copyright © 1982 by Allyn and Bacon, Inc. Reproduction of this material is restricted to use with *A Guidebook for Teaching Composition*, 2nd Edition, by Gene Stanford and Marie Smith.

GUIDE TO PUNCTUATION   REPRODUCTION PAGE 102

Underline (_____)

The underline is used where italics are used in print:

1. To indicate the titles of novels, plays, paintings, and magazines:

    Picasso's *Guernica* is a famous painting.

    Daniel Defoe's *Moll Flanders* is one of the first British novels.

    Samuel Beckett's *Waiting for Godot* is one of the best modern plays.

    Do you read *Time* magazine?

The Apostrophe (')

The apostrophe is used:

1. To indicate possession. (Add an apostrophe and an "s" to most words to create the singular possessive form.):

    That is Alice's purse.

    Here is Jan's letter.

    Mrs. Jones's son is a doctor.

2. To indicate possession of a plural word. (Add an apostrophe for most words ending in "s."):

    She is one of hundreds who belong to the Teachers' Association.

    Check *The Readers' Guide to Periodical Literature*.

    The Joneses' house burned down.

    In cases where the plural is not formed by adding an "s," an apostrophe and then an s should be added to form the possessive.

    | child (singular) | children (plural) | children's (plural possessive) |
    | woman (singular) | women (plural) | women's (plural possessive) |

    Don't use apostrophes with possessive pronouns—theirs, ours, yours, mine, hers, his, its.

3. To indicate the omission of a letter in a contraction:

    I didn't go. (didn't—did not; the apostrophe takes the place of the "o" in "not.")

    I wasn't at home. (wasn't—was not; the apostrophe takes the place of the "o" in "not.")

Note: "its" is a possessive pronoun meaning "belonging to it" and does not have an apostrophe. "It's" is a contraction meaning "it is," and the apostrophe substitutes for the "i" in "is."

Copyright © 1982 by Allyn and Bacon, Inc. Reproduction of this material is restricted to use with *A Guidebook for Teaching Composition*, 2nd Edition, by Gene Stanford and Marie Smith.

The Period (.)

The period is used:

1. To end a complete sentence:

    I cannot find my car keys.

    Tomorrow is Saturday.

2. To punctuate abbreviations:

    "Street" is abbreviated "St."

    "Mister" is abbreviated "Mr."

    "Missus" is abbreviated "Mrs."

    "Governor" is abbreviated "Gov."

Note: when an abbreviation comes at the end of a sentence, only one period is used.

The Question Mark (?)

The question mark is used:

1. As the end punctuation of an interrogative sentence (one that asks a question):

    Where is the bank?

    What is your name?

    Who is that man over there?

    When are you leaving?

Copyright © 1982 by Allyn and Bacon, Inc. Reproduction of this material is restricted to use with *A Guidebook for Teaching Composition*, 2nd Edition, by Gene Stanford and Marie Smith.

SENTENCE CARDS FOR PUNCTUATION GAME

1. Mr. Martin who is our principal has been transferred.
2. We left on Sunday and arrived home the next day.
3. I bought records jeans and beads.
4. The test was difficult everyone failed.
5. Who wrote the poem The Road Not Taken.
6. The following people were late Bill Mary Bob Martin and Maureen.
7. Roads were slippery therefore we drove very carefully.
8. Where are you going.
9. The essays were interesting however there were many spelling errors.
10. Yes I agree.
11. The old ski lodge was torn down in August and a new one was built the next year.
12. Anne is a thoughtful friendly girl.
13. Robert Dobbs M.D. is her family doctor.
14. We visited Darwin White and Company Incorporated.
15. Mrs Waters Mr Moore and Ms Woodruff are school board members.
16. When I finally received my driver's license I was very excited.
17. Disturbed by the thunder the dog howled all night.
18. Stop that right now she yelled or I'll spank you.
19. Out out brief candle whispered the young actor.
20. May I quote asked Mrs. Green.
21. Oh you do look tired.
22. On February 23 1976 Sally leaves for Boston.
23. Allison was born in Maple Tree Falls Nebraska on May 9 1956.
24. The Mill on the Floss a sensitive poignant novel by George Eliot is a classic.
25. Seventeen is my favorite magazine my parents read Time.
26. Mrs. Conway said to check *The Readers Guide to Periodical Literature.*
27. He that hath the steerage of my course direct my sails read Larry who plays Hamlet.
28. What's so funny asked Cindy.
29. It's your house not theirs.
30. Go to the ladies department.
31. Carolyns friends are very nice.
32. James books are torn ripped and yellowed with age.
33. That car looks like the Smiths.
34. The students desks are dirty.
35. The childrens toys are broken.
36. The following people were not present: Mary Harvey, C.P.A.; Jason Barnes, M.D.
37. That's fine with me.
38. I bought flowers, candy, and clothes.
39. The book is a bestseller; everyone is reading it.
40. It is your decision, not mine.

Copyright © 1982 by Allyn and Bacon, Inc. Reproduction of this material is restricted to use with *A Guidebook for Teaching Composition,* 2nd Edition, by Gene Stanford and Marie Smith.

REPRODUCTION PAGE 104

INSTRUCTIONS FOR PUNCTUATION GAME

1. The object of the game is to match cards bearing punctuation marks with sentences that require those marks in order to be punctuated correctly. The first player to get rid of all his or her cards by properly matching sentences with punctuation marks is the winner.

2. Three to five persons can play this game.

3. Choose one person to serve as the Judge and hand him or her the answer key. This person will consult the answer key to determine whether a player has made a correct match. If necessary, the Judge can also be a player.

4. Shuffle the sentence cards (large ones) and place them in a stack face down.

5. Shuffle the punctuation mark cards (small ones) and place them in a stack face down.

6. Beside each stack of cards, turn one card face up as the beginning of a discard pile.

7. Have one player serve as dealer and give each player two sentence cards and two punctuation mark cards without looking at them.

8. The player to the right of the dealer goes first. First, the player draws a card from *either* the sentence card stack or the punctuation mark card stack. Or, the player can take either the sentence card or punctuation mark card that has been placed face up on the discard pile. Whichever choice the player takes, he or she draws only one card. Then the player attempts to match sentence cards and punctuation mark cards in order to punctuate the sentences correctly. For example, if the player has a sentence card that needs a semicolon and a comma in order to be correctly punctuated and if there are a semicolon and a comma among his or her punctuation mark cards, the player can put the two punctuation mark cards with the sentence card and have a "match." If a player thinks he or she has a match, the player tells the group of a wish to discard those cards and they check to make sure the player has punctuated the sentence(s) correctly. If they all agree that the punctuation is right (and the Judge concurs after consulting the answer key), the player may discard the cards used for the "match" by placing them face up on the respective piles. If the player has punctuated the sentence incorrectly, according to the other players and/or the Judge, then he or she cannot discard the cards and also loses the next turn.

9. Players can discard "matches" only when it is their turn. The do so *after* drawing one new card from one of the four piles.

10. Play continues until one player has discarded all his or her cards by matching.

11. If players use all the cards in the stacks of sentence cards or punctuation mark cards, they shuffle all but the top card in the discard pile and turn these face down to use as a new stack.

Copyright © 1982 by Allyn and Bacon, Inc. Reproduction of this material is restricted to use with *A Guidebook for Teaching Composition*, 2nd Edition, by Gene Stanford and Marie Smith.

ANSWER KEY FOR PUNCTUATION GAME

1. Martin, principal,
2. no error
3. records, jeans, and beads
4. difficult;
5. "The Road Not Taken"?
6. late: Bill, Mary, Bob, Martin, and Maureen
7. slippery; therefore,
8. going?
9. however,
10. Yes,
11. August,
12. thoughtful,
13. Dobbs, M.D.,
14. Darwin, White, and Company, Incorporated
15. Mrs. Waters, Mr. Moore, and Ms. Woodruff
16. license,
17. thunder,
18. "Stop . . . now," yelled, "or . . . you."
19. "Out, out . . . candle,"
20. "May . . . quote?"
21. Oh,
22. February 23, 1976, Sally
23. Maple Tree Falls, Nebraska, May 9,
24. *The Mill on the Floss*, a sensitive, Eliot,
25. *Seventeen* magazine; *Time*
26. *The Readers' Guide to Periodical Literature*
27. "He . . . sails," Larry, *Hamlet*
28. "What's . . . funny?"
29. house,
30. ladies'
31. Carolyn's
32. James's torn, ripped,
33. Smiths'
34. students'
35. children's
36. no errors
37. no errors
38. no errors
39. no errors
40. no errors

Copyright © 1982 by Allyn and Bacon, Inc. Reproduction of this material is restricted to use with *A Guidebook for Teaching Composition*, 2nd Edition, by Gene Stanford and Marie Smith.

REPRODUCTION PAGE 106

PUNCTUATION PROOFREADING EXERCISE

INSTRUCTIONS: Add all necessary marks of punctuation.

Painting is a multi-faceted versatile and diverse field. There are many different distinctive types of painting such as naturalistic non-representational geometric biomorphic symbolic and literal etc Good artists always consider the possibilities open to them they carefully decide how to communicate their feelings what colors to use what style technique and manner to employ. Competent serious artists use their medium explore its range and scope and attempt to bring both their medium and their message into harmonious lucid focus. Its the artists job according to many experts to convey the message as expressively as possible. Many of the paintings that we laugh off and label simple silly and childish are really the products of enormous effort tenacious unending hard work and limitless creative decision Don't be like one of my neighbors who said that painting is crooked and any two year old could do better Next time you view a painting give it a fair chance consider its message its purpose its expressiveness Dont just decide on face value whether or not its good.

Copyright © 1982 by Allyn and Bacon, Inc. Reproduction of this material is restricted to use with *A Guidebook for Teaching Composition*, 2nd Edition, by Gene Stanford and Marie Smith.

COMMA EXERCISE

INSTRUCTIONS: Commas have been deleted from the following paragraph. Using your Guide to Punctuation on Reproduction Page 102, insert commas where needed and put the number of the rule above the comma.

My summer as a volunteer at Children's Hospital in Buffalo New York was a time when I learned to think about people besides myself developed a sense of responsibility and decided that I wanted a career working with children. Lucy who supervised my work in the playroom explained how important it was for me to come regularly be on time and take care of equipment. Although I tried to be mature I sometimes goofed off but after a little boy almost got hurt because I was careless I became much more careful. I soon forgot about my own interests and concerns and learned to concentrate on the children and what they wanted. I was sad when I had to leave but one little boy made me feel better. He said "You finish school so you can come back and work here all the time." You know I think I will.

Copyright © 1982 by Allyn and Bacon, Inc. Reproduction of this material is restricted to use with *A Guidebook for Teaching Composition,* 2nd Edition, by Gene Stanford and Marie Smith.

REPRODUCTION PAGE 108

SENTENCE CARDS FOR USAGE GAME

1. The road is froze.
2. He don't want to stay any longer.
3. Sarah is the nicest of the two.
4. Each of you are expected to listen.
5. She must of went to the store with her brother.
6. I couldn't care less.
7. I don't remember never having seen that film.
8. He did it all herself.
9. There isn't no candy left.
10. Don't let no one see these exam papers
11. Everyone made their own lunch.
12. Drive very careful.
13. She looked very nicely in her new dress.
14. Us students know a lot about our school.
15. I think that politics are interesting.
16. My scissors is broken.
17. Patience and honesty are fine virtues.
18. Bring them papers over here.
19. Ham and eggs are my favorite meal.
20. Field trips is more better than homework.
21. Mrs. Hayden is more nice than Mr. Gray.
22. The television is broke.
23. There isn't nothing more to say.
24. Them shoes is mine.
25. Buy three dozen of eggs.
26. We has all the time in the world.
27. We had just began when it started to rain.
28. We sung for two hours.
29. Leslie and me washed, dried, and polish the car.
30. Harold is old-fashion and prejudice.
31. When you finish wiped the dishes, you can leave.
32. This is between Mary and I.
33. Her and her brother are my cousins.
34. Alls you got to do is read the directions.
35. She must not of been very happy.
36. You are smarter than her.
37. They has got my folder.
38. She's the beautifullest person I ever meet.
39. I tried to be honest with he.
40. Communications are a new and exciting field.
41. We will run, jump, do some racing, jogging, and exercising.
42. He's more skinnier than me.
43. We swum all afternoon.
44. I was all shoken up by the accident.
45. The child snuck down the stairs quiet.
46. They had a real nice day.
47. We was home by nine o'clock.
48. Yesterday I went ice skating and come home exhausted.
49. The job, although interesting and exciting, weren't exactly what I wanted.
50. To who do you wish to speak?
51. I seen Jill downtown.
52. John one of two hundred boys participating, are winning every event.
53. Mrs. Fine, which is my typing teacher, is retiring.
54. There is two kind of books—dull and interesting.
55. I read where she got sick.
56. Each of the five hundred team members are signed up.

Copyright © 1982 by Allyn and Bacon, Inc. Reproduction of this material is restricted to use with *A Guidebook for Teaching Composition*, 2nd Edition, by Gene Stanford and Marie Smith.

SENTENCE CARDS FOR USAGE GAME

REPRODUCTION PAGE 108

57. Whom may I ask are you?
58. I wish to see Cathy and he.
59. The weatherman forecasted rain for tonight.
60. I was very tired when I finally sit down.
61. This is a occasion to remember.
62. Karen and me is friends.
63. The perfume smelled beautifully.
64. That music sounds well.
65. Ask whoever you wish.
66. That pair of shoes are beautiful.
67. My pants is torn.
68. There is less apples in that bag.
69. You done everything real good.
70. There isn't any more potatoes.
71. Him and me went to the concert.
72. I am older than she.
73. This is between David and me.
74. This problem is among the two school boards.
75. Either Marty or Jeff are going to go to Yale.
76. Stealing these books are prohibited.
77. There isn't any quick answers.
78. The media are always objective.
79. I got into my car, fastened my seatbelt, checked my mirrors, locked the door, turned on the motor, and starting driving away.
80. They got a nice house.
81. Mary has often spoke of you.
82. Following training, the dog reverted back to his old ways.
83. Lisa sprung her ankle.
84. Annie had took all my cigarettes.
85. Lenny loaned he ten dollars.
86. That was the worstest game I ever seen.
87. The both of us went together.
88. My sister she is very irritating.
89. They did that there art work all by theirselves.
90. Joanne's childrens is real fresh.
91. That there girl is Kevin's sister.
92. We will leave the door opened.
93. By this time next week, we will have already went.
94. She must of gave me the keys.
95. She went with they to the movies.
96. One of my friends and I is going to New York.
97. Ceramics are my favorite hobby.
98. Mr. Mitchell and his wife, two of our best customers, is sick.
99. Neither Kristin nor Juanita are old enough to vote.
100. She came in, sat down, and starts talking.
101. I was suppose to write an essay.
102. I sat down and rest.

Copyright © 1982 by Allyn and Bacon, Inc. Reproduction of this material is restricted to use with *A Guidebook for Teaching Composition*, 2nd Edition, by Gene Stanford and Marie Smith.

REPRODUCTION PAGE 109

INSTRUCTIONS FOR USAGE GAME

1. Approximately four persons can play this game.

2. Lay the game board on the floor or other flat surface such as a table or a desk.

3. Give the answer key to one person (either a player or someone who wants to watch but not play). This person will consult the answer key when necessary to check an answer, and hence will be referred to as "the Judge." Warn the Judge not to let anyone see the answers.

4. Shuffle and stack all the sentence cards. Place them face down near the game board.

5. Roll dice or draw lots or guess a number to determine who goes first.

6. Place your markers in the space labeled "Start" on the game board.

7. The first player draws a sentence card from the top of the stack. The player reads it and determines whether or not it contains any error(s) in standard English. Sentences may contain no, one, two, or three errors.

8. If the player decides there are no usage errors in the sentence, he or she must show it to the other players to see whether they agree. If they don't agree, the Judge checks the answer key. If the Judge upholds the player's opinion, then the player may move ahead two spaces. If the player is wrong (that is, if the sentence does contain one or more usage errors), then he or she loses the next turn.

9. A player who decides that the sentence does not contain a usage error must identify each error, correct it, and explain the correction to the other players. If the Judge and other players agree with the correction, the player may move ahead the number of spaces equal to the number of usage errors in the sentence. If the other players do not agree, then the group must discuss the issue until they reach agreement. If they cannot agree, they must consult the Judge. The Judge's answer, based on the key, overrules all other players. The Judge must explain the answer to the other players. If the player's answer is upheld by the Judge, then the player may move ahead as many spaces as there are usage errors in the sentence. If the player is wrong, he or she loses the next turn.

10. The player whose marker reaches the "Finish" space first is the winner.

Copyright © 1982 by Allyn and Bacon, Inc. Reproduction of this material is restricted to use with *A Guidebook for Teaching Composition*, 2nd Edition, by Gene Stanford and Marie Smith.

ANSWER KEY FOR USAGE GAME

1.	frozen	(1)	39.	him	(1)
2.	doesn't	(1)	40.	is (not are)	(1)
3.	nicer	(1)	41.	run, jump, race, jog, and exercise.	(3)
4.	is	(1)	42.	He's skinnier than I	(2)
5.	must have gone	(2)	43.	swam	(1)
6.	no error	(2)	44.	shaken up	(1)
7.	ever	(1)	45.	sneaked quietly	(2)
8.	himself	(1)	46.	really (or very)	(1)
9.	any	(1)	47.	were	(1)
10.	anyone	(1)	48.	came	(1)
11.	his or her (not their)	(1)	49.	The job .... wasn't	(2)
12.	carefully	(1)	50.	whom	(1)
13.	nice	(1)	51.	I saw	(1)
14.	We	(1)	52.	John ... is	(1)
15.	politics is	(1)	53.	who (not which)	(1)
16.	scissors are	(1)	54.	are ... kinds	(2)
17.	no error	(2)	55.	that (not where)	(1)
18.	those	(1)	56.	Each .... is	(1)
19.	is	(1)	57.	Who	(1)
20.	are better	(2)	58.	him	(1)
21.	nicer	(1)	59.	forecast	(1)
22.	broken	(1)	60.	sat	(1)
23.	anything	(1)	61.	an	(1)
24.	Those ... are	(1)	62.	I are	(2)
25.	dozens	(1)	63.	beautiful	(1)
26.	have	(1)	64.	good	(1)
27.	begun	(1)	65.	whomever	(1)
28.	sang	(1)	66.	is	(1)
29.	I, polished	(2)	67.	are	(1)
30.	old-fashioned, prejudiced	(2)	68.	are fewer	(2)
31.	wiping	(1)	69.	did ... really well	(3)
32.	me (not I)	(1)	70.	aren't	(1)
33.	She	(1)	71.	He and I	(2)
34.	All you have	(2)	72.	no error	(2)
35.	have (not of)	(1)	73.	no error	(2)
36.	she	(1)	74.	between	(1)
37.	have	(1)	75.	Either ... is	(1)
38.	most beautiful person I ever met	(2)	76.	Stealing ... is	(1)

Copyright © 1982 by Allyn and Bacon, Inc. Reproduction of this material is restricted to use with *A Guidebook for Teaching Composition*, 2nd Edition, by Gene Stanford and Marie Smith.

REPRODUCTION PAGE 110   ANSWER KEY FOR USAGE GAME

77.	aren't	(1)	90.	children are really	(1)
78.	no error	(2)	91.	That (not that there)	(1)
79.	drove	(1)	92.	open	(1)
80.	have	(1)	93.	gone	(1)
81.	spoken	(1)	94.	must have given	(2)
82.	reverted (not reverted back)	(1)	95.	them	(1)
83.	sprained	(1)	96.	are	(1)
84.	had taken	(1)	97.	Ceramics is	(1)
85.	lent (not loaned) him	(2)	98.	are	(1)
86.	worst . . . saw	(2)	99.	Neither . . . is	(1)
87.	Both (not the both)	(1)	100.	started	(1)
88.	My sister is	(1)	101.	supposed	(1)
89.	did that (not that there), themselves	(2)	102.	rested	(1)

Copyright © 1982 by Allyn and Bacon, Inc. Reproduction of this material is restricted to use with *A Guidebook for Teaching Composition*, 2nd Edition, by Gene Stanford and Marie Smith.

THE GRAMMAR WITCH

Once upon a time a long time ago in a green asbestos-shingled cottage by a deep dark lake with monsters in its depth their was a lady who was known as the grammer witch. The number of people who was lost in her grammer ovens were never known for sure but it must of been high according to the local gossip about who's family had lost it's third member and who's family had lost it's forth fifth sixth ect.

She was also one of those witches who doesn't care about others misusing grammer as long as they try really try as hard as her. Alot of people don't feel that way, they think your a social outcast who's need for grammer and usage lessons outweighs any good points, that you might have. Either they or she are wrong its obvious in there attitude.

Anyhow this witch used to set down by the lake as comfortable as she can be and watch for unwary victims who she could entice into her grammer ovens, their were many a weary traveler she caught on there way past her cottage. Going home from work. She would lay in wait ten hours at a time, thats a long tiring time to set in one place. As a matter of fact ten hours are to long to do any one thing it seems to me. However remember she was a witch and there not like the rest of us

Well she would lay their and wait and turn over in her mind all the grammer lessons she would teach to whoever she caught. No matter whom they were. Agreement of verbs and subjects were her favorite lesson and she would teach them to absolutely anyone, she wasn't particular. A businessman for instance along with alot of employees were her favorite victims. It was them who aroused in her a regular frenzy of teaching and inspired her to pedagogical extreams that were her's alone.

Be that as it may since the victims she lured in and tried to teach, were seldom fascinated by her efforts she usually ended up in a violent towering rage, and popped them screaming writhing and sobbing into her ovens which always had clouds of smoke pouring from their chimneys.

Now that may sound cruel inhuman and atrocious to you but if so your not thinking enough about how hard all this was on the poor frustrated grammer witch. Think how she must of felt when whomever she was trying to teach just ignored her fine lessons, and acted

Copyright © 1982 by Allyn and Bacon, Inc. Reproduction of this material is restricted to use with *A Guidebook for Teaching Composition,* 2nd Edition, by Gene Stanford and Marie Smith.

REPRODUCTION PAGE 111

as if they thought they're lives would be perfectly happy without knowing grammer isn't that disgusting.

One day in her ovens a quite routine day actually their was a businessman who she'd caught on his way home from work a truck driver who's truck had staled near her cottage a high school student who had forgotten to do his homework and three pastry cooks who she felt convinced she could never educate to the joys of grammer. Poor things. There attitude was not good. The others were less willing than the high school student, although they were to tell the truth somewhat smarter than him. I would not like to be him. Would you? Oh well.

Now if your wondering why this short unhappy story of the grammer witch is indeed short which is seldom the case of stories these days let me remind you dear students that on another day at another hour you might well have another story to read carefully trying to catch all errors in grammer and that other story will have spelling problems in it thus this story—or another one like it—cant be to long, isn't that right. Oh well.

Copyright © 1982 by Allyn and Bacon, Inc. Reproduction of this material is restricted to use with *A Guidebook for Teaching Composition*, 2nd Edition, by Gene Stanford and Marie Smith.

REPRODUCTION PAGE 112

AVOIDING PRETENTIOUS LANGUAGE

INSTRUCTIONS: For each of the following words, write a synonym that is more common and less pretentious.

1. desire
2. uttered
3. conveyed
4. edifice
5. heavens
6. pass away
7. veracity
8. poverty stricken
9. loquacious
10. solar body
11. heavenly body
12. gentleman
13. consumed
14. prevaricate
15. inception
16. initiate
17. inebriated
18. astronomical
19. consequently
20. fraught with peril
21. nonmotile
22. illuminate
23. truncated
24. disseminate
25. give pleasure to
26. human frailty
27. hirsute
28. elucidate
29. predicated
30. circumvent
31. unfortunate culmination
32. arrive at a determination
33. to occupy a position of prominence
34. to rectify a misapprehension
35. predilection for laborious effort

Copyright © 1982 by Allyn and Bacon, Inc. Reproduction of this material is restricted to use with *A Guidebook for Teaching Composition*, 2nd Edition, by Gene Stanford and Marie Smith.

REPRODUCTION PAGE 113

AVOIDING INAPPROPRIATE INFORMAL LANGUAGE

INSTRUCTIONS: For each of the following expressions, write a usage that is more appropriate for formal writing.

1. snuck
2. all shook up
3. I could care less
4. kid
5. guy
6. phony
7. ripped off
8. rap
9. they fell out
10. had a fit
11. told her off
12. had a ball
13. out of this world
14. broke up
15. he's crazy
16. took the rap
17. a jerk
18. laid it on the line
19. guts
20. nuts
21. screwball
22. he bugged me
23. knock it off
24. get lost
25. they took off
26. it was neat
27. it was real good
28. out of his mind
29. up against it
30. she was carrying on
31. to have a fun time
32. cops
33. he faked it
34. she knocked their eyes out
35. he hit the skids
36. I dig him

Copyright © 1982 by Allyn and Bacon, Inc. Reproduction of this material is restricted to use with *A Guidebook for Teaching Composition,* 2nd Edition, by Gene Stanford and Marie Smith.

REPRODUCTION PAGE 114

PARAGRAPHS TO REVISE

INSTRUCTIONS: Change the pretentious language in paragraph A and the informal, nonstandard language in paragraph B to more appropriate words.

A. Her erudite asseverations are highly enigmatic. It certainly would behoove her to recapitulate and revise. Her rhetorical style, which is esoteric and hyperbolic, is an impediment to lucid communication. Her diction is neologistic and arbitrary. I am incredulous as to the discrepancy between her content and style.

B. Her smart ideas are confusing. It certainly would have been good if she thought it over and changed stuff. Her writing style, which nobody understands, is blown up and wrecks understanding. Her picking of words is new and made up. I don't get the difference in what she feels and wants to say and what she really says.

Copyright © 1982 by Allyn and Bacon, Inc. Reproduction of this material is restricted to use with *A Guidebook for Teaching Composition*, 2nd Edition, by Gene Stanford and Marie Smith.

REPRODUCTION PAGE 115

IDENTIFYING AND REPLACING CLICHES

INSTRUCTIONS: Locate all trite expressions and clichés in the following paragraphs. Rewrite each paragraph, replacing the overused expressions with fresh and original language.

A. First and foremost, with your permission, I'd like to give you a rundown of facts and figures on George Johnson, our captain. He is a fine figure of a man, towering over most ordinary men at a height of 6'3". He is as strong as a bull and light on his feet as well, with bulging muscles and rugged features. Rough and ready and always spoiling for a fight, he never runs from trouble but, to be perfectly frank about it, runs after it fast and furious. It will come as no surprise to you, then, to learn that trouble is his middle name or that he often finds himself on the wrong side of the law. Nonetheless he has a gentle side to his nature as well and is considered far and wide—when all is said and done—to be a pillar of the community.

B. The next member of the team to claim our attention is none other than Bob Jones, the pride and joy of the fans and a mountain of a man with a heart of gold. He is a tiger during games, but off the field he is as meek as a lamb, a paragon of manly virtues admired by young and old alike. He is generous to a fault and always ready to lend a helping hand to those less fortunate than himself. A cool customer when the game is

Copyright © 1982 by Allyn and Bacon, Inc. Reproduction of this material is restricted to use with *A Guidebook for Teaching Composition,* 2nd Edition, by Gene Stanford and Marie Smith.

REPRODUCTION PAGE 116

CHART ON STYLE

INSTRUCTIONS: Take turns reading your paragraphs aloud slowly. As other group members read their paragraphs aloud, fill in the chart below. You may need to ask them to read their paragraphs twice. Or your teacher may ask you to pass your paragraphs around so each of you may read each paragraph.

Name of student				
What words were used to describe the person in the picture?				
Would you describe the person's choice of words as simple, poetic, straightforward, or fancy?				
Did this writer choose to put any feelings into the writing?				
What did the writer emphasize about the picture?				
What did the writer choose to leave out?				

Which do you think the writer was trying to do?
    describe clearly
    be dramatic
    be poetic and creative				

What words would you use to describe the style of this paper (clear, imaginative, complex, or lively, for example)?				

Copyright © 1982 by Allyn and Bacon, Inc. Reproduction of this material is restricted to use with *A Guidebook for Teaching Composition*, 2nd Edition, by Gene Stanford and Marie Smith.

APPENDIX D

Feedback Form

Your comments about this book will be very helpful to us in planning other books in the Guidebook for Teaching Series and in making revisions in *A Guidebook for Teaching Composition*. Please tear out the form that appears on the following page and use it to let us know your reactions to *A Guidebook for Teaching Composition*. The authors promise a personal reply. Mail the form to:

Dr. Gene Stanford and Mrs. Marie Smith
c/o Longwood Division
Allyn and Bacon, Inc.
470 Atlantic Avenue
Boston, Massachusetts 02210

Your school: _____
Address: _____
City and state: _____
Date: _____

Dr. Gene Stanford and
Mrs. Marie Smith
c/o Longwood Division
Allyn and Bacon, Inc.
470 Atlantic Avenue
Boston, Massachusetts 02210

Dear Gene and Marie:

My name is _____ and I want to tell you what I think of your book *A Guidebook for Teaching Composition*. I like certain things about the book, including:

I do, however, feel that the book could be improved in the following ways:

There are some other things I wish the book had included, such as:

Here is something that happened in my class when I used an idea from your book:

Sincerely yours,

_____

284